SHAKESPEARE

"The critic . . . will, indeed, require, as the spirit and substance of a work, something true in human nature itself, and independent of all circumstances; but in the mode of applying it he will estimate genius and judgment according to the felicity with which the imperishable soul of intellect shall have adapted itself to the age, the place, and the existing manners."—*Coleridge*.

MASTER SPIRITS OF LITERATURE

SHAKESPEARE

BY
RAYMOND MACDONALD ALDEN

AMS PRESS
NEW YORK

Reprinted from the edition of 1922, New York
First AMS EDITION published 1971.
Manufactured in the United States of America

International Standard Book Number: 0-404-00307-9

Library of Congress Number:73-113539

AMS PRESS
NEW YORK, N. Y. 10003

PR
2894
.A4
1971

CONTENTS

CHAPTER	PAGE

PREFACE i

CHAPTER I. THE AGE.—Shakespeare's setting in Elizabethan England. The significance of the Renaissance in his literary environment. Classical and Italian influences. The new interest in poetry, and in art prose. The neo-platonic doctrines of love. Ideas of villainy. The Reformation in England; its relation to the Renaissance. The Elizabethan Londoners; the brilliancy and zest of their mental atmosphere. The blend of feudalism and nationalism; democratic influences. The blend of refinement and barbarism. Moral standards. Political theories. Superstitions. Elizabethan psychology. The popular stage; the early theatres and their dramatists. Types and ideals of Elizabethan drama. The characteristic blend of story and poetry. 3

CHAPTER II. LIFE AND WORKS.—Fact and fiction in Shakespeare biography. Birth, probable education, and marriage. Traditions of the migration to London. Shakespeare's reading. His early acquaintance with the theatre. The Greene and Chettle pamphlets. His début as poet: *Venus and Adonis* and *Lucrece*. Shakespeare as actor. The Lord Chamberlain's company. Established position and prosperity; the coat-of-arms; real estate. Meres's tribute. The Globe Theatre; Shakespeare's income. *The Passionate Pilgrim* and the sonnets on the friend and the "dark lady." Theatrical controversies and difficulties. Shakespeare in London and at Stratford. His friendships, known and guessed. His last years, death, and burial. Contemporary opinion of him, as poet and man. The publication of his poems and plays; quartos and folio. The Shakespeare canon. The order of composition; the assumed four periods. 56

CHAPTER III. THE POEMS.—Relation of Shakespeare's early poems to Ovid and the Italian Renaissance. *Venus and Adonis;* decorative sensualism. *The Rape of Lucrece;* greater earnestness. Style and imagery of the poems. *The Passionate Pilgrim, The Phoenix and the Turtle, A Lover's Complaint.* The Sonnets of 1609; uncertainty as to date and circumstances of composition. The Renaissance "conceit." Conventional and personal elements in sonnets of the Petrarchan school. The question of continuity in Shakespeare's. Influence of Sidney and of Daniel. Metrical form of the Shakespeare sonnets. The more trivial and conventional, and the more serious and individual, themes

vii

viii CONTENTS

and conceits. Sonnets on beauty, love, time, poetry, absence, death, estrangement; the "triangle" sonnets. Varying estimates of the Sonnets. Their maturity, in contrast with the narrative poems. 105

CHAPTER IV. THE CHRONICLE-HISTORIES.—The vogue of national drama in Shakespeare's period. Characteristics of the type; frequently primitive, naïve, undramatic. Marlowe's development of it. The group of plays on the reign of Henry the Sixth: the lost play on the wars in France, *The Contention,* and *The True Tragedy.* Relation of Shakespeare's *Henry the Sixth* to these. *Richard the Third;* its Marlovian character. Primitive elements of the tragedy of villainy; Shakespeare's development of the hero. *The Life and Death of King John;* a rewriting of an older play. Slight Shakespearean elements. The series on the house of Lancaster. *Richard the Second:* a chronicle-play becoming a tragedy of character. Primitive conventional elements mingled with Shakespearean characterization. *Henry the Fourth;* new problems in the dramatization of incident and personality. The comic elements; origin and development of Falstaff. The changes in these elements in the Second Part; difficulties raised by "the rejection scene." *Henry the Fifth;* a still different type of chronicle-history; its epic or pageant-like structure. The use of the prologue or chorus. Evolution of the comic elements surviving from the preceding plays. Brilliancy and yet inadequacy of the characterization of the King. Reversion to chronicle-history in the late patchwork play of *Henry the Eighth.* 147

CHAPTER V. THE COMEDIES.—Condition of English comedy at the opening of Shakespeare's career: the popular and classical traditions. Types of comedy in general: farcical and "high." Divergent moods: satiric and romantic. Shakespeare's experimentation in all these; his final emphasis on the comedy of romance. *Love's Labor's Lost* of uncertain origin and history. Satire of contemporary affectations. Slight elements of characterization. *The Comedy of Errors* based on a farce by Plautus; Shakespeare's contribution of certain more serious elements. *Two Gentlemen of Verona* the herald of his romantic comedy. Influence of Greene on this type. Shakespeare's daring use of improbabilities. The *Midsummer Night's Dream* a type by itself; a romantic farce, apparently occasional in origin. Its brilliantly complex structure. Combination, in the clownish characters, of farce comedy and realistic characterization. The first great poetic achievement among the comedies. *The Merchant of Venice* primarily a romance; improbabilities again daringly accumulated. Plausibility notwithstanding, attained chiefly by characterization. The

CONTENTS

problem of the Shylock story and its seeming approximation to a tragic mood. *The Taming of the Shrew* a revision of an earlier play; some blend of characterization with farcical action. *The Merry Wives of Windsor* another farce comedy; Falstaff and other familiar characters revived in a plot of domestic intrigue. *Much Ado about Nothing* notable for its multiple plotting; conventional romance and relatively original character comedy developed side by side. Beatrice marks the growing importance of women in Shakespeare's drama. *As You Like It* a blend of love and adventure, based on an earlier novel. Rosalind as the incarnation of Shakespeare's union of the spirit of comedy and that of romance. Brilliant technique marred by a somewhat negligent conclusion. *Twelfth Night* revives the elements of success in many earlier comedies; another notable case of multiple plotting. Queries as to the comic appropriateness of the Malvolio under-plot. The acme of Shakespeare's happier studies of love; some progress observable from the notion of love as "fancy" to its more serious aspects. 190

CHAPTER VI. THE TRAGEDIES.—The pleasurableness of tragedy, considered with reference to Elizabethan taste. Tragic types in general; the analogy with those of comedy. Senecan influence on Elizabethan tragedy. *Titus Andronicus*, of disputed or partial Shakespeare authorship, in the Senecan style. Significant use of madness, with mixed comic and tragic effect. Marlowe's influence; intense, villainous personality. *Romeo and Juliet* a tragedy of romance. The theme of fate or Fortune; emphasized particularly by Shakespeare's catastrophe. The total effect lyrical or musical rather than poignantly tragic. Mingled elements of poetic rhetoric and dramatic realism in Shakespeare's style. *Julius Caesar* analogous to the tragic chronicle-histories; drawn from Plutarch's studies in philosophic biography. A tragedy with two heroes; Shakespeare changes Plutarch's emphasis. Want of emotional intensity, coupled with almost perfect craftsmanship. *Hamlet* paradoxical in its union of sensational and intellectual interests. Sources of the story; Shakespeare's development of the plot obscured by the loss of his immediate original. Imperfect linking of the action and the hero's personality; various explanations of this. Hamlet's character presented by the soliloquy, an Elizabethan convention. Remarkable combination of comic elements with tragic seriousness. *Othello* a more unified and consistent drama; extraordinarily painful in presenting innocence suffering and evil dominant. The characters derived from the Italian source, but developed by Shakespeare with extraordinary creative power. Masterly tragic style of this period. *King Lear* even more painful than its predecessor, and marked by stormy and confused action. Material from the chronicle made tragic by a newly invented catastrophe; doubtful effect of this, and of the unusual double plotting. Another notable specimen of the mingling of comic and tragic matter. *Macbeth* a chronicle-history in origin; its plot and characters explained by the source. In type analogous to *Richard the Third;* its special quality due to the sympathetic treatment of the villain-hero. Varying interpretations of Macbeth's moral responsibility. Reasons for the supreme success of this play among the tragedies. *Antony and Cleopatra* another study from Plutarch. Historic tragedy now turned to tragedy of personal passion. Shakespeare's following of Plutarch in the principal presentation of Cleopatra; his departure from Plutarch at the close. The remarkable double catastrophe. Supremacy of the dramatic-poetic style. *Coriolanus* Shakespeare's final tragedy. Ironically stern in mood. Again following Plutarch, Shakespeare is now equally impartial with his source; the problem of the sympathies left open to divergent interpretations. The final step in the evolution of the Shakespearean tragic hero. 232

CHAPTER VII. THE TRAGI-COMEDIES.—Difficulty of classifying a number of the Shakespeare plays. Meanings of the term tragi-comedy: a matter of either plot or mood. *Troilus and Cressida* especially defiant of classification by type. Two plots, neither fully worked out. The mood equally baffling; an emotional hodge-podge. Some remarkable poetry, of a peculiar intellectual vein. *Measure for Measure* a firmly wrought story, yet inferior in characterization and of unsatisfying moral effect. The folly and vileness of human nature, especially in sex relations, emphasized in this period. *All's Well that Ends Well* marked by an adventurous romantic plot, but again by disagreeable elements and tragi-comic mood. Various possible explanations for this group of unhappy plays with ''happy endings.'' *Timon of Athens,* apparently the product of collaboration, classified as a tragedy. Dominated, however, by satiric if not comic spirit. *Pericles* again shows composite authorship. A dramatization of an elaborate ancient romance, strikingly undramatic in form. The fourth act, centered in the character of Marina, a kind of condensed drama by itself. *Cymbeline* shows more mature experimentation with similar romantic material. A romantic tragi-comedy, in a framework of chronicle-history, developed sensationally and with extraordinary technique. Characterization again confined largely to the heroine. The style typical of the final period of Shakespeare's verse; often cumbrous, difficult, overweighted with thought. *The*

CONTENTS   xi

Winter's Tale dramatized from a romance of Greene's. Further advance in the technical handling of a crowded romantic plot; in structure a tragedy plus a romantic comedy. Stage sensationalism again emphasized, and characterization undeveloped though charming. *The Tempest* apparently made for a festal occasion; a masque-like dramatic romance, perhaps shortened from a more conventional original. The tale of adventure now unified in perfect dramatic form. Supernatural elements characterized by high seriousness and a suggestion of symbolism. The tempting suspicion of an allegory of the author's own dramatic career. Emphasis on reconciliation, as in all the later plays. Different explanations of Shakespeare's interest in this new type. Alleged influence of Beaumont and Fletcher. The tendency toward drama of reconciliation natural in a matured dramatic artist.   290

CHAPTER VIII. SHAKESPEARE.—First of all an Elizabethan and a child of the Renaissance. As dramatist unoriginal in both material and method. His comedy characterized chiefly by the union of the comic and romantic spirits. His tragedy Elizabethan in form, but akin to Sophocles in its sombre irony and profound sympathy. His dramatic interest primarily in personality; his characters normally created for a given story. The fallacy of viewing them as existing independently of their setting, due to their vivid individualization. This vitality sometimes apparently the cause of a distortion of the author's dramatic purpose. In the realm of ideas Shakespeare also unoriginal. The opposite impression due chiefly to the vitality and intensity with which his ideas grow to expression. His view of moral evil and individual responsibility, of the tragic fault and poetic justice; both sides recognized. His moral effects characteristically sound. Emphasis on courage, serenity, faithful friendship, readiness, kindness. His view of society representative rather than personal, and so impartial as to be debatable; neither democrat nor feudalist. His treatment of love touched by Renaissance platonism, but realistic rather than mystical; plain-spoken, but idealistic. The permanence of true love especially emphasized. No system of philosophy to be inferred from his works. The greater tragedies in a sense both pessimistic and optimistic. Shakespeare's religion not definable theologically; his attitude predominantly reverent but not other-worldly. His personality but slightly revealed in detail. A humanist, more concerned with men and things than with his art. Combined wit and poetry, high seriousness and the comic spirit, objective keensightedness and subjective sympathy. His greatness due chiefly to his comprehensive thinking in terms of personality and conduct, and to his supremely poetic interpretation of action.   325

PREFACE

I HOPE it may not be judged an incompetent plea, in defense of the act of writing another book on Shakespeare, that the author had not meditated such a deed when it was proposed to him by the editor of the present series. On reflection, however, it seemed that there might be some justification of so agreeable an imprudence, even on the part of one who had no Shakespearean theories to propose, —or perhaps for that very reason. In the first place, some need has been felt for a compendium of the known facts respecting Shakespeare, and of the prevailing critical judgments of modern scholarship, sufficiently untechnical for the purposes of the general reader, and at the same time uncolored by any desire to prove a case. In the second place, the history of Shakespeare criticism has perhaps reached a point where one may profitably attempt some restatement of the main issues involved in the effort to adjust our view of a world-genius, whose values are absolute and timeless, to the special relationship which his work bore to his immediate audience and age.

The latter point deserves some further comment. The course of Shakespeare criticism, which began in anything like a formal way with the age of Dryden, may be roughly divided into three periods. In the late seventeenth and the eighteenth century Shakespeare's work was greatly admired, but it was observed to violate the rules of dramatic composition which prevailed in the neo-classical era;

hence the common assumption was that he was a kind of inspired irregular barbarian, who through ignorance of the laws of his art failed to attain the perfection which his genius in itself would have led one to hope for. In the early nineteenth century, on the other hand, the progress of romanticism led to wholly different views of the nature of genius: it was now held that genius makes or realizes its own laws, and that any great artist must be a source for the knowledge of the rules of his art, instead of being subject to testing by rules already laid down. This doctrine (which in its milder form no modern critic would dispute) was exaggerated to the point of viewing a poet of Shakespeare's greatness as an inspired, even an infallible, artist. "He never introduces a word or a thought in vain or out of place," said Coleridge. "If we do not understand him, it is our fault or the fault of copyists. . . . He never wrote at random, or hit upon points of character and conduct by chance; and the smallest fragment of his mind not unfrequently gives a clue to a most perfect, regular, and consistent whole." And De Quincey closed one of his essays with this apostrophe: "O mighty poet! Thy works are not as those of other men, simply and merely great works of art, but are also like the phenomena of nature, like the sun and the sea, the stars and the flowers, like frost and dew, hail-storm and thunder, which are to be studied with entire submission of our own faculties, and in the perfect faith that in them there can be no too much or too little, nothing useless or inert." Against this passionate orthodoxy of the earlier nineteenth century, the scientific and historical criticism of the later Victorians and their successors of the twentieth century naturally reacted. Shakespeare's inerrancy, like that of the Scriptures, was suspected because of the application of newer methods of study; he came to be viewed increasingly as a man of his age, whose works are to be explained primarily by the intellectual, the theatrical, and even the economic conditions of the time. The notion that he was possessed of super-normal, if not positively supernatural, knowledge of the workings of the human mind and heart was now replaced by the assumption that, being an Elizabethan, he must have been limited by Elizabethan psychology. The conception of him as striking out his great creations by aid of the inner light gave way, in some quarters, to that of a business-like person who studied the theatrical market with all the keenness of a modern manager, and wrote precisely what would sell. Some keen and learned critics have gone so far in this prosaically historical method of interpretation that the sympathetic reader of Shakespeare actually trembles before their disillusioning strokes, or, when they occasionally admit some extraordinary beauty or power in Shakespeare's workmanship, feels a thrill of gratitude for the condescension, as with Biblical critics of the corresponding school. The scene of the bibulous porter in *Macbeth*, following close upon the murder, was so revolting to Coleridge that he would have none of it. Since it was not good, it could not be Shakespeare's; he therefore denounced it as "an interpolation of the actors." To De Quincey, on the other hand, the scene was tragically effective despite its grotesqueness, and he wrote his essay "On the Knocking at the Gate" to show how it exemplified Shakespeare's subtle and unerring psychology. The modern critic, irreverently thrusting aside these romantic guesses, points out that the scene is explained by two elementary facts; first, that the Elizabethan audience expected and demanded at least one clownish scene in every tragedy, and secondly, that at the point in question there was a convenient opportunity for such an interlude, since the spectator must be made to perceive some lapse of time while Macbeth was washing the blood from his hands. Such is the contrast between absolutism and relativity!

It may now appear somewhat more clearly what was meant in saying that the time is opportune for the reconstruction of Shakespearean orthodoxy, with a view to avoiding the excesses of both the absolute and the historical positions. Coleridge himself, though he stood near one extreme in his doctrine of the poet's infallibility, was not wanting in grasp of the historical method, and in the sentence which I have taken as epigraph for this book he set forth the undoubtedly sound principle for using that method without abusing it. Another of his sentences, much like the one just referred to, again suggests the right point of departure: "As a living poet must surely write not for the ages past, but for that in which he lives and those which are to follow, it is on the one hand natural that he should not violate, and on the other necessary that he should not depend on, the mere manners and modes of his day." The present book is written from that point of view, aiming always to distinguish those elements in Shakespeare's work which are characteristically "of an age" from those which prove intrinsically valid "for all time." It is assumed that he based his writings upon the dramatic practice, the ethics, and the psychology of his own people, and that he neither professed to be, nor was suspected by his contemporaries of being, an innovator or a prophet; but that at the same time, since he was a very great poet, he might transcend the common practice at any point, in ways which, when we once observe them, it is highly profitable to study. The corollary is that one need never be ashamed to admit either a blemish or a superlative beauty, when evidence of it actually appears. Of course there is abundant room for difference of judgment; the way is not made clear when the right principles are accepted, and so long as Shakespeare is a vital element in the life of the English-speaking world, there can be no hardened unanimity in Shakespeare criticism. The test of these chapters must be whether they hold the balance reasonably true, representing with substantial fidelity the tendencies of the best judgment of our own time, and whether the writer has avoided the sin of dogmatizing about uncertainties in the interest of any pet theory of his own. The fact is, he envies those who take arms on behalf of such theories; to do so makes for much more of eloquence and wit than the humbler task of trying to follow the *via media* between so many interesting by-ways.

One aspect of the historical side of the subject has been frankly neglected: namely, that concerned with the more distinctively theatrical conditions, and the dramatic technique, of Shakespeare's age and his art. These matters have been so abundantly discussed in recent years, and so effectively treated for the general reader in the works of Professors George P. Baker, A. H. Thorndike, and Brander Matthews, that they may be slighted with the better grace, in order to give space for those phases of Shakespeare which more especially concern his position among the Master Spirits of Literature.

Plagiarism of many kinds may be frankly admitted, in a survey so condensed as this. During the past fifty years there have been few original thoughts respecting Shakespeare's writings, and nine-tenths of them are obviously wrong. Any one of us is fortunate if he seems to find himself with a fresh and happy interpretation once in a year or two, and still more fortunate if he does not presently realize that it was suggested to him by such and such a predecessor. I gladly affirm that most of the substantial ideas in this book are inherited. Despairing, in the space allowed me, of distinguishing their sources even in the instances where I was aware of them, I have abandoned all effort to give bibliographical references in the text. Any who wish them will find in the appendix, in connection with the brief general bibliography, references to those recent critical discussions of disputed matters which I have chiefly used or believe to be most worth while. But I wish more specifically here to acknowledge two or three cases of obligation. First, to Professors Felix Schelling and Barrett Wendell, who some twenty-five years ago, in their respective universities, introduced me to sound methods of interpreting Elizabethan drama in general and Shakespeare in particular, and whose books have since done the same for many a student. Then, to the unpretentious but valuable editorial material in Dr. W. A. Neilson's Cambridge edition of Shakespeare, and to Professor A. C. Bradley's monumental work on *Shakespearean Tragedy*, which—however one may find himself differing with details—has interpenetrated the texture of the thinking

PREFACE

of all students of the subject during the past fifteen years. Finally, I am under many obligations to my colleagues, Professors William Dinsmore Briggs and Henry David Gray, and to Professor Joseph Quincy Adams of Cornell University, who have graciously read portions of my manuscript and made a number of valuable suggestions.

R. M. A.

Stanford University, California
August, 1921.

SHAKESPEARE

CHAPTER I

THE AGE

IN 1564, when Shakespeare was born, Elizabeth had been on the throne of England for five and a half years, and the reign which more than any other still seems to represent the greatness of modern England was in full course. The Queen had already impressed her personality upon the government, and in a few more years was to make it felt throughout every corner of the land. After years of confused national feeling, and painful internal religious conflict, the beginnings of a stedfast political consciousness and of a fair degree of ecclesiastical unity were calming the hearts of the people, and making possible the great attainments of the early future in the fields of war, exploration, commerce, and the arts. When Shakespeare was six years old Elizabeth was excommunicated by the Pope; when he was eight, the court went into mourning in protest against the massacre of St. Bartholomew's Day; and by these events the popular strength of British Protestantism was confirmed. When he was thirteen, Francis Drake set out on his voyage to South America and around the world, returning to Plymouth in Shakespeare's seventeenth year. Seven years later, when the poet was probably a resident of London, Drake commanded the active division of the fleet which, in alliance with wind and ocean, defeated the Spanish Armada, and thereby made England definitively the leader of the Protestant powers. At the height of Shakespeare's dramatic career, in 1603, the reign of Elizabeth came to an end with her death and the accession of James; but the England which she had so long incarnated before the world is still called "Elizabethan" throughout the reign of her successor. The new régime, despite the many differences that marked the personality of the sovereign, was in most respects a continuation of the old, and the poets and playwrights who had made glorious the court of the Virgin Queen became servants and celebrators of His Majesty, just as the admirals and gentlemen adventurers continued the story of English achievements in the West. During the years when Shakespeare was bringing his active career as dramatist to a close, from 1607 to 1611, the colony in Virginia was being founded and struggling into permanent form; and in 1616, the year of his death, Raleigh was making preparations for his final ill-fated expedition to the Spanish Main. At about the same time the English separatists at Leyden were inaugurating plans for the migration which was to result in the settlement of New England. King James survived the greatest of his subjects by nine years, and saw, two years before his death, the publication of Shakespeare's collected plays. Twelve years earlier,—that is, five years before the death of Shakespeare,—had appeared the Authorized Version of the Bible. Thus it happened to be granted to James, and not to Elizabeth, that his reign should be made forever memorable by the appearance in close succession of the two books which are the chief glories of the English race.

If we now look at the same period from another standpoint, that of European culture rather than British history, we note first of all that it represents the culmination of the indefinable but pervasive moment which we call the Renaissance. Reaching Great Britain comparatively late, the influences covered by the word were only at the point, in early sixteenth-century England, which had long since been passed in Italy and only a little less long in France. The founding of John Colet's Grammar School in 1510, the first regular Greek lectureship at Oxford in 1520, and the appearance of Coxe's *Rhetorick* in 1524, are convenient landmarks for the impact of the new culture upon England. The Princess Elizabeth, as we know, received a sound and effective classical training (her tutor, Roger Ascham, himself a pupil of John Cheke at Cambridge, boasted that he had had the best master and the best scholar of his time), and could, at need, when Queen, harangue a displeasing ambassador in extempore Latin. By the time Shakespeare was a school-boy, there were "grammar schools" in most of the corporate towns of the kingdom, with curricula which seem commonly to have included Terence, Cicero, Virgil, Sallust, Horace and Ovid, so that the ordinary boy who was able to go through the local school had submitted himself to a decidedly more intensive classical discipline than the average American college graduate of to-day. He had, of course, heard nothing of economics, sociology, biology, or psychology, and knew rather more of the ancient world than he did of his own; knew, too, more of the legends of classical mythology than of the actualities of history,—more of Adonis and Phaëton than of the rise and progress of the English nation.

To us this is likely to seem so irrational that we must make a distinct effort to discover what it was of significance and value that was poured into the mind of the sixteenth century from the stream of classical humanism. The question is far too wide for hasty analysis; but, for the present purpose, one may answer briefly that a principal part of the endowment of Renaissance education was a sense of the beauty and richness of the realm of the imagination, combined with a denationalized or universalized method of exploring it. The imagination, of course, may be cultivated by materials of any kind,—by enriching the actual experiences of one's own dooryard, or the legends which lurk in the woods and hills immediately adjacent. And no people is without the means, in its own language, of satisfying the desire for such enrichment. A special quality, however, of pleasure and of fruitful stimulus lies in the sense that there is a great primal storehouse of imaginative material, common to the minds in every place and race that have learned the way to it,—a land of beauty and wonder into which all may pass, through the narrow gateway of a single discipline. The same thing appears in the realm of religion; for example, in the specific value, apprehended by Catholics of every land, of their common attitude of looking up to Rome, and back to the ancient life of the Church of Rome, as the center and source of their faith, and of finding this symbolized in such details as the use of the Latin tongue in their liturgy. From this special point of view (no matter what the more important merits of Protestantism), how inadequate seems the merely individual or local devotion of some modern sect, building its religious life directly, as needed, from the materials of daily experience, and perhaps expressing them in colloquial vernacular! What Rome is, then, to the Catholic, in the field of faith, Rome and Athens were to the cultivated man of the Renaissance in the field of the imagination,—and also, for that matter, in the field of thought, for the substance of their intellectual as well as their imaginative life had the same source. The richness and unity of this common experience, enjoyed by those trained in the narrow but extraordinary fruitful system of education thus developed, are values for which we of the twentieth century have found no comparable substitute, though we have sought it carefully and with tears. It may be added that the imaginative materials of Renaissance culture combined what we nowadays try to distinguish (in two of the most troublesome cant phrases of criticism ever invented) as the classical and the romantic elements of literary pleasure. Ancient story provided riches, beyond the dreams of avarice, of that compound of beauty, wonder, and emotional stimulus that we call romance; at the same time it was "classic" in its authoritative, established form, and its sense of "joy in widest commonalty spread" as distinguished from merely individual thrills.

All this, it may be said, is true enough of the more learned writers of the Renaissance, but has little bearing on the aspects of the sixteenth century which are pertinent to the study of Shakespeare. Let us see. In the most popular of Shakespeare's comedies there is a little love scene, set in a garden by moonlight, between a very ordinary young Venetian gentleman and a pretty Jewess. Here are a few lines of their talk:

Lorenzo. In such a night
Stood Dido with a willow in her hand
Upon the wild sea banks, and waft her love
To come again to Carthage.

Jessica. In such a night
Medea gathered the enchanted herbs
That did renew old Æson.

That is enough, in itself, to exemplify what has been said about the union of classic and romantic elements of pleasure. For the special atmosphere of moonlight and young love which Shakespeare desired to create, he drew upon the materials of ancient story akin to his purpose, and trusted to their familiarity, and the consequently instantaneous reaction of his hearers, to accomplish his end. The whole course of Renaissance culture was back of him, and he knew it, even if as linguist he boasted "small Latin and less Greek." Even on the linguistic side, it is worth recalling that he could be assured that a good part of any of his popular audiences would be able to follow bits of Latin phrasing occasionally introduced into the plays. And, apart from all knowledge of the original language, there were the materials of culture which began to be naturalized in the English tongue, to meet the demands of the age. Of these, two exemplars are of supreme importance, for what they contributed to Elizabethan wealth in the respective fields of ancient story and ancient history: Ovid's *Metamorphoses*, englished by Arthur Golding in Shakespeare's infancy in a form which became one of the most popular books of the age, and Plutarch's *Lives*, translated by Sir Thomas North from a French version in 1579, an English classic even to the present day.

But Renaissance culture meant, of course, something more than the transmission of the materials of Greek and Roman art and learning. In particular, for England, it meant a strong infusion of whatever Italy had to contribute to the age. For sculpture and painting, which we think of first in connection with sixteenth-century Italy, the influence in England was comparatively slight; for the lesser arts, such as those of dress and social manners, it was very great. Here one remembers Della Casa's *Galateo*, englished in 1576 with the sub-title "A treatise of the manners and behaviours it behooveth a man to use and eschew in his familiar conversation"; or, if it be a question of manners in a deeper sense and for higher walks of life, Castiglione's immortal work on *The Courtier* (*Il Cortegiano*), translated in 1561 by Thomas Hoby, by whom it was most justly declared to be "very necessary and profitable for young gentlemen and gentlewomen abiding in court, palace, or place." In literature the Italian material meant so much that for whole segments of poetry and imaginative prose of the sixteenth century one might almost say the language used is a superficial accident: Italian, French, or English, Italy is the home of its soul. These, perhaps, may be thought the chief landmarks: Sannazaro's pastoral romance of *Arcadia*, which appeared in 1504; Baptista Mantuan's satiric pastorals, or eclogues, from about the same time; Ariosto's romantic epic, the *Orlando*, from 1516; Bandello's *novelli*, from 1554; Giraldo Cinthio's *Hundred Tales* (*Hecatommithi*), 1565; Tasso's pastoral masque, the *Aminta*, 1573, and his *Jeru-*

salem Delivered, 1581. All these were both translated (wholly or partially) and imitated by the Elizabethans, becoming not merely importations but actual grafts into the stock of the native literature. Aside from English versions of outstanding works like these, we should remember William Painter's great collection of Italian stories called *The Palace of Pleasure,* published in 1566 and in many later editions, to which the plots of more than forty Elizabethan plays are traceable, and the numerous volumes of madrigals and other lyrics from the Italian, beginning with Yonge's *Musica Transalpina in* 1588, by means of which the stream of continental lyric flowed the more readily into that of Britain. Nor can we separate—as has already been hinted—the French stream from the Italian. The Petrarchans of France, notably Marot, Ronsard, Du Bellay, and Desportes, whose poetic collections all appeared between 1539 and 1573, transmitted to England many of the forms and methods of Italian lyric, particularly the sonnet, with results indistinguishable from those coming from Italy more directly.

The poets of both tongues had been studied on their own soil by Sir Thomas Wyatt, diplomatist and humanist of the court of Henry the Eighth, and his imitations of their work were promptly recognized by his countrymen as a new force in the refinement of English letters according to Renaissance standards. Now it happened that Wyatt's verse, though he died in 1542, remained unpublished until, seven years before Shakespeare's birth, the publisher Tottel brought out a good part of it in his far-famed collection of *Songs and Sonnets,* together with poems by Wyatt's follower the Earl of Surrey. From this date, 1557, and this anthology,—unappealing as a great part of it now appears,—we commonly date the flowering of Renaissance lyric in England, and the growing sense that the English tongue was capable of such beauties as only the continental poets had thus far achieved. Thus George Puttenham, twenty-two years later, wrote in a well-known passage: "In the latter end of [Henry the Eighth's] reign sprang up a new company of courtly makers, of whom Sir Thomas Wyatt the elder and Henry Earl of Surrey were the two chieftains, who, having traveled into Italy, and there tasted the sweet and stately measures and style of the Italian poesy, as novices newly crept out of the schools of Dante, Ariosto, and Petrarch, they greatly polished our rude and homely manner of vulgar poesy from that it had been before, and for that cause may justly be said the first reformers of our English metre and style."[1] In Shakespeare's boyhood Wyatt's and Surrey's poems, with the others in Tottel's *Miscellany*, were still being reprinted in numerous editions; and it is not improbable that the familiar volume is that to which Master Slender pays tribute, in the first scene of the *Merry Wives of Windsor*: "I had rather than forty shillings I had my book of Songs and Sonnets here." It was among these poems of Wyatt's and Surrey's that the sonnet first appeared in English poetry. For more than twenty years after it was thus made familiar, the form nevertheless languished with little or no growth on British soil; then, beginning with the posthumous publication of Sidney's sonnets in 1591, it burst into sudden and splendid bloom. During the last decade of the century every English poet,

[1] *The Art of English Poesy*, 1589, Arber Reprint, p. 74.

great and small, appears to have become a sonneteer, studying now the Italian models, now the French, now the beautiful exemplars of Sidney himself. And in the same era there began to appear treatises on the making of verse, giving rules for the exotic forms, specimens of experimentation in new metres, and stimulus for both scholars and gentlemen to further the expanding glory of English poetry. It was at this time that Philip Sidney was arguing, in his *Apology for Poetry*, that "for the uttering sweetly and properly the conceits of the mind, which is the end of speech," the English tongue "hath it equally with any other tongue in the world."

Art prose always lags behind poetry in development, but that too now had its chance. Here the Spanish Renaissance contributed more than in the field of verse, and such works as Guevara's *Golden Epistles*, translated in 1574, joined with the influence of *The Courtier* and other Italian classics to show that the same loving care which the poets lavished on their art might be bestowed upon even such relatively humble forms of composition as letter and dialogue. In the same year in which Spenser stimulated the practice of pastoral verse with his *Shepherd's Calendar*, 1579, John Lyly made the first notable experiment in artistic prose, in *Euphuës, the Anatomy of Wit*, and gave the word "euphuism" to the language. Sad, indeed, is the fate which has made a Euphuist—who ought, by authority of both etymology and Matthew Arnold, to be a wholly well-fashioned man, one "who tends toward sweetness and light"—to mean instead a person whose language is characterized by over-elaborateness and affectation; all because Lyly, in presenting his ideal Euphuës to England, sought to beautify his native prose by devices akin to the most daring and dangerous verbal conceits of the poets. In the stricter sense, this euphuistic style was a game of skill in phrasing which had a happily brief though important vogue (for a time, Edward Blount the publisher tells us, "that beauty in court which could not parley euphuism was as little regarded as she which now there speaks not French"); in its larger significance, it meant the new possibilities of an elegant prose which, in saner and more liberal form, appeared in Sidney's *Arcadia*, in Lodge's *Rosalind*, and, best of all, in the lightly scattered, flashing jewels of dialogue in *Much Ado* and *As You Like It*.

Not only the modes and manners of the continental Renaissance were brought to bear upon English literature at this time, but—as was inevitable—something also of its ideas. Its critical principles, for signs of which one would naturally look first, drifted in, of course, with all the other materials of the new culture; but their actual fruitage in English criticism was slight. English men of letters in almost every period have been far more interested in creating than in explaining how and why, and this was doubly true of the Elizabethans. Only Sidney's *Defence of Poetry* remains as a single flawless specimen of Renaissance criticism in Britain. The ideas which underlay the romance and the poetry of the Italians excited more interest; they were likely, however, to be treated with imperfect seriousness,—to be played with, utilized for romantic color, even satirized and condemned, rather than adopted into English thought. Of such ideas those concerned with the doctrine of love are perhaps most important. The probblem of love, as a phenomenon both of the sensuous and of the supersensuous life, is one which every generation meets afresh, and attempts to solve in its own way. In the medieval period the code of chivalry had furnished one influential means of interpreting the problem, setting up an artificial relationship between man and woman which at its best was spiritually ennobling, but which might, in ignoble hands, become a finely tapestried veil for sensuality. Something similar was true of certain forms of neo-platonism which were developed among the sixteenth-century Italians, and which came to England, at their best, in Hoby's version of *The Courtier*. Based on the genuinely platonic doctrine that the phenomena of the physical world are but shadows or types of eternal original realities, and that the love of physical beauty is an effort to draw near to the divine beauty, this theory became an elaborate means to the mystical interpretation of passion. On the one hand, it provided natures of a spiritual sort with a means of transition from earthly to heavenly love, in accordance with the view that the proper evolution of the affections is in that direction, the earthly object of passion gradually giving way to the celestial beauty for which it originally stood. On the other hand, it furnished more mundane natures with a romantically transcendental means of explaining very ordinary erotic experiences. In England, as has been said, there was not much disposition to take the doctrine seriously. Sir Philip Sidney, who well knew its baffling charms, refers to it more than once in his sonnets to Stella, but playfully renounces it for himself: Stella is too real and human for any such spiritualizing process! Spenser did take it seriously, at least for a time, and gives, in his *Hymns in Honor of Love and Beauty,* the classic expression of it for English poetry:

> Such is the power of that sweet passion,
> That it all sordid baseness doth expel,
> And the refined mind doth newly fashion
> Unto a fairer form, which now doth dwell
> In his high thought, that would itself excel,
> Which he, beholding still with constant sight,
> Admires the mirror of so heavenly light.
> (*Hymn in Honor of Love,* lines 190-96.)

But later, reproaching himself (or professing to do so) for undue emphasis on earthly love, he "retracted" the earlier Hymns in favor of those on Heavenly Love and Heavenly Beauty, distinctively Christian in content. All this neo-platonic talk, however, even if not fully naturalized in England, had its influence on the conventional interpretation of love; and the Elizabethan courtiers, poets, and dramatists were often engaged in the game of playing with passion in half-chivalric, half-spiritual terms. It was not always love between the sexes which concerned them: for one of the aspects of the Italian teaching was that love between man and man might be as passionate, as faithful, and more ennobling because free from fleshly ties. Hence the distinction between love and friendship, so heavily stressed in modern thought and literature, often had little, or a wholly different, meaning for the Elizabethans.

Not only love but villainy was a theme of extraordinary interest in the Italy of the sixteenth century, and thereafter in Elizabethan England. Romance and passion have always been linked with crime on their darker side, and never more so than in the era that looked back only a little way, with shuddering fascination, to the deeds of the Borgias. Tales of the papal and ducal courts united, especially in Protestant lands, to confirm the teachings of religion that man, unhindered by divine grace, was depraved in desires, and might easily become a monster of evil. Lust cruelty, avarice, revenge, were viewed not—as often in our more cheerful philosophy—as mild aberrations of character, unfortunate distortions of purposes good at bottom, but as the direct manifestation of pure evil, often deliberate and self-conscious in its ill designs. A curious and influential application of this view is found in the remarkable development of the traditional character of Machiavelli, the Florentine statesman who died in 1527. Already, before Shakespeare had begun to write for the stage, there was a Machiavellian myth which treated its hero as the very incarnation of evil. Modern students have traced this, in good part, to attacks upon Machiavelli's reputation by French Huguenots, notably one Gentillet, who in 1576 published a translation, with commentary, of portions of Machiavelli's great work, *The Prince,* tracing to its cynical doctrines many of the evils which had cursed the age, and including, as a particularly horrid example, the recent massacre of St. Bartholomew's Day. The book was promptly translated into English, and was widely circulated under the popular name of the *Anti-Machiavel.* Of the resulting popular belief the most interesting illustration is the Prologue to Marlowe's *Jew of Malta,* produced about 1590, in which Machiavelli appears as speaker, telling the audience that his soul had been incarnate in the French Duke of Guise, but since the Duke's death had crossed the channel to "frolic with his friends" in England. The villainous Jew whose story is to be told had filled his money-bags, says Machiavelli, not "without my means." Notwithstanding this, the villain proves to be not of England but of Malta, and the Elizabethan stories of crime were for the most part represented as having their place in Mediterranean lands. There, as in Byron's time, hot-blooded passion and villainy could have free course and be glorified, in the same romantic background which added to the fascination of beauty and love. For this reason, as well as because of the always different standards of realism and romance, one must be careful not to infer the actual moral conditions of Elizabethan society from the drama and other fiction of the period.

So much for matters which connect the Elizabethans with the continental Renaissance. But the sixteenth century was the age when the Reformation, as well as the Renaissance, had its full effect in England; and it has often been observed that we of the English race have special cause for gratitude that the two great forces, moving westward, arrived almost together upon that happy island. Germany had the Reformation without the Renaissance; Italy the Renaissance without the Reformation; in England they were united, and some of the finest elements in the following age are the product of that union. This, like all simple and attractive concepts, is a little too simple to tell the whole story, but there is enough of truth in it to serve useful ends. We dare not forget that the Reformation, so far as its actual external consummation is concerned, was not, in England, a great spiritual movement but a political *coup*, and a rather sordid one at that. A good part of the people must still have been essentially Catholic in religious feeling, the main question seeming, for the time, to be whether the headship of their Catholicism was at Rome or London. Hence it is typical that a good part of the literature of the age, including the plays of Shakespeare, while thoroughly Protestant on the political side, is neutral on that of personal religion, moving freely in the field of both Catholic and evangelical thought. On the other hand, it is also true that the Reformers, especially John Calvin, had come into full control of large elements of English life, including, for a considerable period, the dominant personalities in the Anglican Church. For very many Englishmen, then, the Reformation was a vital religious reality, and the visible center of their religion was neither at Rome nor London, but at Geneva. Calvin died in the year when Shakespeare was born. Four years earlier, in 1560, the Geneva version of the English Bible was issued,—a version destined to run through some two hundred editions in fifty years, and to become the household Scripture of the common people of England. In the year following the publication of the Geneva Bible, Calvin's *Institutes* appeared in their English form. Two years later came Foxe's *Acts and Monuments,* commonly called the *Book of Martyrs,* which for Protestants of a century to come was what the Saints' Legends were for medieval Christians. When Shakespeare was three or four years old, the term "Puritan" was first applied to evangelicals who proved particularly zealous to distinguish their religious practices from those of Rome. Later the word came to suggest not so much an ecclesiastical as a moral attitude, and its history is wrapped up with that characteristic middle-class British morality which, even to the present hour, we recognize as combining a spirit of intolerance, of hostility to beauty and pleasure, with a sturdy sense of personal responsibility to God and to man which has wrought strength and high-mindedness into the fibres of the whole race.

It is hard indeed, if not impossible, to sum up with any accuracy the meaning, for the spirit of Elizabethan England, of the combined action of all these forces which we have been calling to mind. In literature the Renaissance was certainly dominant. It had thrown off the shackles of spiritual authority which in the Middle Age made art so largely the mere servant of faith, and was developing, with the zest of a youth running away from a monastic school, the joyous possibilities of realizing for its own sake the life of this present world. The Reformation even aided this process, so far as concerns freedom from authority; at first thought one would say that it had little else to do with the arts. But a moment's reflection not only brings to mind certain poets, notably Spenser, in whom we see the deliberate and fairly successful attempt to fuse the beauties of the Renaissance with the moral seriousness of the Reformation, but assures us that even in the more worldly literature, such as the drama of Shakespeare's generation, we can feel the underlying substance of that same moral seriousness. In other words, though the players and the playwrights lost no opportunity to pay their debt of scorn to the Puritans, and the Puritans did all they could to make life a burden to the players, there was something which they had in common and which differentiated them from the men of Renaissance Italy. If proof be needed, consider (though the Elizabethans were not given to squeamishness, and dared to enjoy poems and plays which we promptly expurgate) how impossible it would have been that a work marked by the moral cynicism of Boccaccio's *Decameron* should become a representative classic of England, or that the moral sincerity characteristic, on the whole, of Elizabethan comedy, should have dominated the Italian stage. It must not be assumed that the element in English character which is here emphasized was the specific product of the Reformation: it doubtless appears, one way or another, in the more characteristically racial products of every previous era. For good or ill, the Anglo-Saxon has always been disposed to take life seriously on the moral side. The influences of sixteenth-century Protestantism were simply the special formative forces for the old spirit in the new age. In the seventeenth century they were to rise, for a time, to the point of dominating the chief literary products of the age; in the age of Shakespeare they were undercurrents, helping to determine, no doubt, the main course of the stream, while allowing its surface to bear freely hither and thither the bright airy elements of worldly pleasure. Thus but two Elizabethan poets of first-rate importance, Spenser and Donne, were important as interpreters of spiritual things, and in this aspect of their work they were children of the Middle Age rather than of the Renaissance. For the greater number God and the other world were no doubt realities, but, like Falstaff's hostess, they hoped there was no need to trouble themselves with such thoughts yet, while the things of this world were so many and precious.

What, then, were the people like among whom Shakespeare lived and for whom he wrote? From one point of view the question is a most foolish one, which we persist in asking of past ages in spite of knowing better. That is, we know very well that in every age there have been all kinds of people, as there are in ours, yet we insist, for other centuries as for other countries, in trying to make of them a composite photograph and to view it as the real man of his time. We also know, if we have studied the past to much advantage, that the people in it were much more like ourselves than any attempt to characterize them is likely to assume. If, for example, we should consult the preachers, satirists, and pamphleteers of the Elizabethan age, we should learn such things as these; that the economic tendencies of the time were causing the rich to grow richer and the poor poorer; that there was an alarming movement from country to city, with a corresponding decline of wholesome primitive simplicity of manners; that the young were forsaking the ways of their fathers for frivolity of dress and conduct, and ceasing to reverence the aged and the wise; that religious faith was giving way to atheism imported from the Continent; that the love of money and pleasure was corrupting the whole texture of English life. In a sense all these things were true,—as they have been alleged to be, and perhaps have been, in almost every age. Yet we know that we must not go to either preachers or satirists for well-balanced judgments of contemporary life. Certainly the second half of the sixteenth century was a time when economic conditions were rapidly changing the more primitive organization of society, increasing the wealth of the bourgeois or trading class, and making city life a more complex and brilliant affair than in any earlier period. London became the capital, at this time, in a more intensive and inclusive sense than hitherto; and the splendor of the court formed an appropriate center for the hurrying, dazzling scene. All this, of course, is relative; if we compare them with later instead of earlier ages, both the court and the London of Elizabeth were poor enough in wealth, numbers, and splendor. But the point is that the spirit of the time is dependent upon its own standards, not on those of later historians; if an age or a city is brilliant *for itself*, the psychological effect is absolute. If youth feels itself to be facing limitless new joys and opportunities, what age may say of them does not (thank heaven!) take the color out of youth's face and heart.

We are, then, in a sense justified in seeking to describe to ourselves the men of any former time, and also in taking their own word for what they were. And if we confine ourselves to London, to the men and women whom Shakespeare knew and who fixed the character of the atmosphere in which he worked,—admitting that there were whole masses of people who do not come into the picture at all, —there is a certain intelligible unity of impression which we bring away from any study of the records. In part this has already been suggested in what we have seen of Reformation and Renaissance, of the days of discovery and of increased centralization of national power and pride. A sense of youth—of intensity, freedom, opportunity, eagerness, color, and strength—pervades the impression first of all. If we should bring together a company of young men of college age, of whom a part purposed to be scholars, a part poets, and a part explorers, each of them deeply interested not only in the possibilities of his own career but in those of his fellows, yet not too maturely concerned therein to lose the exuberance of fun, of bodily pleasure, and of romance, proper to his age; and if we should have the privilege of overhearing their talk, now in rollicking, now in more sober or ambitious moods, the effect produced on us would be somewhat the same as that of the mass of Elizabethan writings of the imaginative sort. The Elizabethans were not all interesting, of course. Not only must there have been many dull ones whom kindly oblivion has kept from view, but a sufficient number left writings which have been preserved to show us that wit was no more certainly granted to those who found their way into print in those days than in our own. Yet the chance for some individuality of experience or expressiveness seems to have been pretty high. Sir Sidney Lee has calculated, on the basis of the names in the excellent dictionary of biography which he edited, that three times as many Englishmen of the sixteenth century gained individual distinction as of the fifteenth. The reasoning is doubtless erroneous, since the age of printing enormously increased, for any individual, his chances of being remembered by posterity; but we need not doubt that the chances of being interesting, or doing something interesting, were also largely increased by the conditions of the age.

The color of Elizabethan life was affected by the circumstance that the period was one of transition from the feudal age to that of modern social organization. In the London of Shakespeare it must have been possible to feel the pressure of both types of loyalty, for the time being in fairly harmonious equilibrium rather than in opposition. The attitude toward the Queen was strictly and almost universally of the old feudal sort, and so for the most part was that toward the nobility. The pageant-like beauties and emotional satisfactions of the age of chivalry had not wholly vanished, either from visible life or from the mood of both patriotism and poetry. Take, for example, an incident of the year 1581, when an embassy from the French court arrived to discuss a marriage treaty with the Queen. Among the entertainments provided for the visitors was one devised by four young noblemen, two of whom were among the most promising men of letters of the time: Sir Philip Sidney, Sir Fulke Greville, Lord Windsor, and the Earl of Arundel. Assuming the title of "the Four Foster Children of Desire," they engaged in a tournament-like siege of the Fortress of Perfect Beauty,—a structure erected in the tilt-yard at Whitehall. Some twenty-eight young gentlemen, on the other side, undertook to defend the fortress, which was understood symbolically to be that of the Virgin Queen. The conflict began on the 15th of May, and was concluded on the following day by the capitulation of the assailants,—the event, of course, being not unforeseen from the beginning. In this pageant Sidney appeared with a train of four spare horses on which rode four pages clad "in cloth of silver, laid with gold lace," and thirty gentlemen and yeomen, with four trumpeters, all "in yellow velvet laid with silver lace," Sir Philip himself wearing sumptuous engraved armor of blue and gold. One remembers, too, the equally brilliant pictures of the festivities at the Queen's "progresses" to provincial seats, at the head of all which stands the entertainment provided, in 1575, by Leicester at Kenilworth, whither many of his biographers would fain take the boy Shakespeare, since it was in Warwickshire within easy distance of his home. Such were some of the surviving glories of the feudal age. And over against them we must set the more sombre activities of the tradesmen and money-changers of the City,— themselves ambassadors of Britain in foreign parts quite as truly as the emissaries of the court,—whose growing class consciousness was destined soon to play a great part in English history. One can feel that the patriotism of the time is centered, now in the court and the Queen's person, now in that more prosaic Britannia that carried her Majesty's commerce into the seven seas. And the dramatists celebrated with equal enthusiasm English knights and noblemen defying the enemies of Britain at the gates of foreign cities, and English grocers' apprentices making their fortunes in the near East, rejecting the passionate advances of Moslem princesses, and returning home to become heads of their companies or Lord Mayors of London.

All this means, among other things, that, in spite of its being very far from democracy in either the theory or practice of government, there were certain aspects of Elizabethan life which may well be called democratic. The commingling of the interests of all classes in the results of foreign exploration and trade would seem to be one such aspect. Community of national feeling, so greatly heightened by the conflict with Spain, is another. On the lighter side of life the blend of many classes in the street life and the recreations of an increasingly metropolitan capital, is still more largely reflected in literature. Strongly as distinctions of class were felt, they disappeared for the moment at a bear-baiting or a play; for sport always tends toward democracy, and so, for the same reason, do many forms of art. Some of the art of the Elizabethans was essentially for a class; the sonnet, for example, their most memorable type of lyric, has in every age been a medium of expression for the cultivated few. But the song, in which they also excelled, may be the property of all; indeed a good song is perhaps more completely a unifier of all sorts and conditions of men than anything else in the world. This element of unity the progress of civilization, sadly enough, has fast tended to destroy, and already, in the sixteenth century, English lyric was breaking up conspicuously into the sophisticated literary and the popular song types. But enough was left of primitive conditions to make song still a fairly democratic element of the age; and music, instrumental as well as vocal, was far more nearly a universal possession than with us. What was true of lyric was also true of the drama: court play and popular play, literary and spoken play, were destined to go further and further apart, but in the most typical dramas of the Elizabethans the merits of both appear in unison. Of Shakespeare it is impossible to say whether the aristocratic or the popular element in his audience enjoyed him the more.

Nationalism of spirit, combined with internationalism of experience, always brings clashes of race temperament at the very moment when alien races are learning from one another. Hence, characteristically enough, we find the Elizabethans at the same time importing Italian clothes, fencing-masters, oaths, poetry, philosophy, and crime, and reviling all these Italian ways at the top of their voices. Sometimes it is different individuals who do the copying and the reviling; sometimes the same persons easily accomplish both. Roger Ascham, whose whole system of education rested on the Italian Renaissance, wrote thus in 1570: "If some yet do not well understand what is an Englishman Italianated, I will plainly tell him. He that, by living and traveling in Italy, bringeth home into England out of Italy the religion, the learning, the policy, the experience, the manners of Italy. That is to say, for religion, papistry or worse; for learning, less commonly than they carried out with them; for policy, a factious heart, a discoursing head, a mind to meddle in all men's matters; for experience, plenty of new mischiefs never known in England before; for manners, variety of vanities, and change of filthy living."[2] Turn now to an anti-foreign exhibit of the more popular and concrete sort. On a February evening in 1584, Messer Giordano Bruno, virtuoso in philosophy human and divine, being on a visit to England whereby he might confute all the doctors of that kingdom, set out by invitation for the house of Sir Fulke Greville, and lost his way in the dark and muddy streets near a Thames landing where some boatmen put him ashore. His own account of his adventure runs in part as follows: "The artisans and shopfolk, who know you to be in some fashion a foreigner, snicker and laugh and grin and mouth at you, and call you in their own tongue dog, traitor, and stranger, which with them is a most injurious name, qualifying its object to receive every

[2] *The Schoolmaster*, Arber Reprint, p. 78.

wrong in the world, be he young or old, in citizen dress or armed, noble or gentle. And now, if by evil chance you take occasion to touch one of them, or lay hand to your arms, lo, in a moment you will see yourself, for the whole street's length, in the midst of a host that has sprung up quicker than the men-at-arms, in the fiction of the poets, sprang from the teeth sown by Jason. They seem to come out of the earth, but in truth they issue from the shops, and give you a most lordly and noble view of a forest of sticks, long poles, halberds, partisans, and rusty pitchforks; and these things, though the sovereign has given them for the best of uses, they have ever ready for this and like occasions. So you will see them come upon you with a peasant fury, without looking where, how, or why, or upon whom, and none of them thinking of any other; every one discharging the natural despite he hath against the foreigner.'"[3]

This glimpse of a London mob and its manners reminds us that in many ways the sixteenth century presents an odd blend of culture and barbarism, of refinement and savagery. Not only the manners of the mob, but of the aristocracy, sometimes left much to be desired. We recall how the Queen could swear like a fishwife, and box the ears of an earl. The young gentlemen of Elizabethan London put whole fortunes into their dress, and studied the arts of life, as we have seen, in works written for their use; but one finds evidence that their table manners would not bear examination by modern standards. More serious than bad manners was the downright brutality which still

[3] Quoted by Elton, *Modern Studies*, p. 14 (essay on "Giordano Bruno in England").

prevailed in many departments of life. Bear-baiting and bull-baiting ministered to the most unlovely type of capacity for enjoyment, and appear to have awakened no serious protest. Insanity and idiocy were not merely neglected, or treated only with reference to the interests of others than the sufferers, but—what is peculiarly difficult for modern sensibility to tolerate—were often viewed as primarily comic, both in real life and on the stage. The attitude toward Jews was still almost wholly medieval, both the law and common opinion holding them outcasts from Christendom, "odious" (in the words of the great Chief Justice Coke) "both to God and man." Penology was brutal to an almost incredible degree. Dozens of relatively trifling offences were punished by death, accompanied by various legalized and extemporized means of torture; and one knows not whether to wonder more sadly at the prospect of a country boy hanged for stealing a sheep, or that of a Jesuit missionary executed for fidelity to his faith. "The greatest and most grievous punishment used in England," we read in William Harrison's *Description* (1577), "for such as offend against the state, is drawing from the prison to the place of execution upon an hurdle or sled, where they are hanged till they be half dead, and then taken down, and quartered alive; after that, their members and bowels are cut from their bodies, and thrown into a fire provided near at hand and within their own sight, even for the same purpose."[4] Strenuous training this, in stoicism and in loyalty. For both these qualities, indeed, the Englishman of Shakespeare's day was famed throughout the world, as ever since; if anything of good can be found in the rude school to

[4] New Shakespere Society ed., 1, 222.

which he went, it must be that. All through the seventeenth century we find French travelers and critics, in comment on what they had seen of England both in real life and on the stage, crediting its people with such indifference to death as could not be found elsewhere in Christendom.

As to the common morality of the people it is very difficult to speak with assurance. Literature does not always record moral conditions truthfully; at certain points it is silent concerning ugly facts, at others it makes more of them than life does. Certainly the Elizabethans themselves, as we have seen, believed that their morality had been unfavorably affected by the strong continental influences of the age (it is to be feared that Englishmen have always shown a tendency to attribute their vices to importations from Italy or France); and we need not doubt that, as a result of such influences, there was some laxity of both imagination and conduct. There was much talk of poison, of the stiletto, and other means of assassination, but it is doubtful whether Italian types of crime counted for much outside of books. Concerning sex morality there was much looseness of speech, but no more, it would seem, than in the days of Chaucer or of Dryden; and the characteristically Anglo-Saxon standards of monogamous love were treated, on the whole, with little cynicism and much respect. The chief social scandal of the period was the matter of liaisons between bourgeois wives and seductive gentlemen, a theme which made the current joke respecting the "horns" of citizens as stale as certain much-worn allusions on our vaudeville stage. This, so far as it was based on actual conditions, may be traced in part to the extraordinarily early marriages which were still in vogue among all classes of society. The theatre, of course, developed its own special taste for unclean speech, and we must doubtless admit that the discrepancy between the standards of decency on the stage and in real life was less than we have reason to hope it is in our own time. That is, the Elizabethans made more of the sensual aspects of sex, in their common life and talk, than has been admissible since the time of Addison. But in all these matters their sins impress us as those of youth, relatively innocent because due to youth's momentary fulness of life on the side of the senses, and the undeveloped realization of the seriousness of that with which it jests so lightly; they are not the sins of cynical, vice-worn maturity, which we find in the age of the Restoration.

All these things tempt us to try to ask still more penetrating questions as to the Elizabethan point of view concerning such matters as liberty and authority, reason and superstition, motives and standards of conduct, or what we should now call their social and political theory, their working philosophy, their psychology and ethics. It would be a bold man who should undertake to answer these questions comprehensively. The most that can be done is to call to mind certain impressions likely to be made upon students of the period, which, though inaccurate as such generalizations are bound to be, assist us in the understanding of its literature.

The Elizabethans, as we have seen, had developed a strong spirit of nationalism, and at the same time retained something of the feudal attitude toward the throne and the nobility. Hence obedience to constituted authority was their normal political morality, and there was little disposition to view this authority as arising from the people themselves. The word "liberty" was often on the lips of Shakespeare and his contemporaries, but it usually stood, not for any abstract state in which men thought of themselves as entitled to live, but for the simple objective fact of being out of prison and unrestrained by one's superiors from doing what one desired. Those who occasionally rebelled against the lawful sovereign did so, not on grounds of "political justice" or "the rights of men," but on the theory of the lawful sovereignty of some one else. The same thing, of course, was generally true in the region of religious thought: those who refused adherence to one authority rarely set up their own souls in its stead, but professed obedience to an outside authority of another sort. Whole areas of political and religious consciousness, then, which became observable in the seventeenth century, conspicuous in the eighteenth, and dominant in the nineteenth, are almost totally wanting in the recorded thought of the Elizabethans. Of course there were exceptions. Fulke Greville, for instance, whom we have seen inviting the heretic Bruno to an evening of discussion at his house, could write a chorus for priests whose opening and closing stanzas startle us with the spirit of rationalism which we may have thought of as wholly modern:

> O wearisome condition of humanity!
> Born under one law, to another bound;
> Vainly begot, and yet forbidden vanity;
> Created sick, commanded to be sound;
> What meaneth Nature by these diverse laws?
> Passion and Reason self-division cause.
> * * * * * *

> We that are bound by vows, and by promotion,
> With pomp of holy sacrifice and rites,
> To preach belief in God and stir devotion,
> To preach of heaven's wonders and delights,
> Yet when each of us in his own heart looks,
> He finds the God there far unlike his books.
> (*Mustapha*, Works, ed. Grosart, iii, 416-17.)

We remember, too, the rationalism, not to say atheism, commonly attributed to those who had drunk too deeply of Italian life or literature, and the more harmless skepticism of Montaigne, whom many Elizabethans evidently knew well and sympathetically. It was, indeed, in the field of religion, more than in that of politics, that the question of authority was rationalized in this age; and it was the problem of the authority of the church which gave rise to the one outstanding work on the subject,—Richard Hooker's *Ecclesiastical Polity*. This great book, the first part of which was issued in 1594, though undertaken apparently only for the purpose of justifying the Elizabethan organization of the Anglican Church, nevertheless dug deep, for its foundation, into the whole basis of the social order, and set forth doctrines which, had they not seemed to be a part of so lawful a design, might have aroused the wrath of much more important persons than the Puritan Dissenters. As is well known, Hooker defended what later came to be known as the theory of the Social Contract, stating that mankind had given "their common consent all to be ordered by some whom they should agree upon, without which consent there were no reason that one man should take upon him to be lord or judge over another,"[5] and

---
[5] *Works,* ed. Keble, 1, 175.

interpreted the power of kings in a sentence to which some have even traced the language of the American Declaration of Independence: "By the natural law whereunto God hath made all subject, the lawful power of making laws to command whole politic societies of men belongeth so properly unto the same entire societies, that for any prince or potentate of what kind soever upon earth to exercise the same of himself, and not either by express commission immediately and personally received from God, or else by authority derived at the first from their consent upon whose persons they impose the laws, it is no better than mere tyranny."[6] This, we must again remember, is not the average or the orthodox Elizabethan doctrine; but it gives us a glimpse of the more liberal thought of the age,— thought which, despite ecclesiastical differences, was also echoed in the doctrines of the Calvinists and other founders of the free churches, in those of the American colonists of the same period, and, some will have it, in the utterances of the more far-sighted poets, including Shakespeare himself. Apart from such exceptional persons, it also prevents us from thinking of the age as wholly naïve and docile in its attitude toward the question of authority, as we are often tempted to assume.

The fact is, every generation regards itself as distinctively rational, and earlier generations as naive, credulous, and childlike. It is much as if mankind were forever passing down a long street, and occasionally, turning back, were interested to discover that the people a mile away lived in much smaller houses than those where the observer stood. For pretty obvious reasons, our own age is pecu-

[6] *Ibid.*, 176-77.

liarly liable to this misinterpretation of perspective. It behooves us, then, to remember that the Elizabethans, like ourselves, lived in days of discovery and of vigorous intellectual activity, and in consequence supposed themselves (as we do) to be comparatively free from inherited errors. We should recall this when we hear them charged with credulity and superstition. This, again, is a perpetual impression which the present has of the past; for the superstition of one age is the accepted belief of an earlier age;—one might almost add the converse, that the irrationality of the past becomes the reasonable certainty of the present. From the ordinary standpoint of our own time, then, the Elizabethans were no doubt superstitious. But we should not assume that this implies a different kind of mental capacity or attitude: it may be merely a question of the evidence available to us and to them. They believed universally, it would seem, in ghosts and other apparitions, but we must not judge them too hastily for that, since mankind has never come to agreement on the subject, and at this moment seems further from it than ever. It is a more serious thing that they believed in demonology and witchcraft, and that many poor creatures suffered the intolerant penalties of church and state, when either malice or piety had opportunity to persecute those suspected of dealings with the Prince of Darkness. But we must also recall that England produced, when Shakespeare was twenty years of age, a notable protest against this group of superstitions, in the liberal and humane Reginald Scott's *Discovery of Witchcraft,*—a work which was honored by being attacked for its heresies by King James the First. The belief in fairies was still commonly extant, occasionally adding a touch of terror to life's mysteries, but on the whole contributing more of charm than sadness. In the case of some of these credulities it is difficult, as always, to determine to what extent they were still a real part of the mind of the age, and to what extent only an imaginative inheritance which floated lightly through common talk and fancy. For instance, the astrological tradition; certainly among the Elizabethans some relationship between the stars and human fate was a living element of daily speech, but how far a reality of belief one is less certain. All myths pass by indefinable gradations from the sense of fact to the sense of fiction, and the student of imaginative literature need hardly trouble himself with the distinction; for the life of the imagination has its uses for ghosts and fairies, apart from any question of what we fumblingly call their objective reality, and this is understood by all poets as by all children.

Of the mythic figures which, in the sixteenth century, hovered near the border between imagination and belief, there is one of no small interest, never mentioned in connection with the familiar superstitions of the age: this is the figure of Fortune. She came down to the Elizabethans through the Middle Age, and for centuries had stood, in the language of the educated classes, for much the same mystery that she had personified as Fortuna at Rome,— the mystery of human vicissitudes which seemed too capricious, too lacking in moral significance, to be attributed to the divine will. It is impossible to put one's finger on any age or place in which she was held to be an actual supernatural person; certainly, in the fairly orthodox Christian days which we are contemplating, no Englishman would have admitted to setting up an altar to Fortune either in house or heart. Men believed in divine Providence, all-powerful and somehow all-just. Yet the reader of the literature of the time—as of Chaucer's time—soon becomes aware, once his attention is directed to the matter, that the Fortune of the poets is something more than a passing figure of speech; she is a concept, more or less vital, now treated playfully in popular song ("Fortune, my foe, why dost thou frown on me?"), now more seriously represented, like the Necessity of the ancients, as symbolic of a force or order less reverend but no less formidable than God Himself.

Of psychology, as we understand it, the Elizabethans knew very little. Even physiology was still in large part a theoretical or deductive science, and the spiritual part of human nature was of course even freer from inductive examination. The prevailing views of both body and mind were largely medieval in form. On the physical side, the chief theory is that of the four elements, encountered so often in Elizabethan literature: air, water, fire, and earth, supposed to have their counterpart in the four great constituent "humors" of the body, blood, phlegm, yellow bile or "choler", and black bile or "melancholy." Mixed in ideal proportions, these make possible a perfect organism and an equable and happy temperament; but commonly one will dominate the rest, producing a temperament either sanguine, phlegmatic, choleric, or melancholy,—adjectives which still curiously preserve for us this primitive science. It was a natural sequel that a quality which distorted the symmetry of a personality by extravagance or excess should come to be called a "humor"; that is, as Ben Jonson defined it,

> when some one peculiar quality
> Doth so possess a man that it doth draw
> All his affects, his spirits, and his powers
> In their confluctions all to run one way.
> (*Every Man Out of His Humor*, Induction.)

And since comedy is often concerned with those extravagances of character which make personality laughable and awaken satire by affecting the equilibrium of society, the "comedy of humors," in which Jonson was interested, remains an important type on the stage and in fiction.

In the deeper analysis of human nature, where it transcends the physical, the main question was of the soul; though there was also the doctrine of the vital spirit or spirits, running through both arteries and nerves,—a substance more tenuous and ethereal than blood, fit to serve as means of communication between body and soul. As for the supreme soul, who could say with certainty what it truly is?

> One thinks the soul is air, another, fire,
> Another, blood, diffused about the heart;
> Another saith, The elements conspire,
> And to her essence each doth give a part.
>
> Musicians think our souls are harmonies;
> Physicians hold that they complexions be;
> Epicures[7] make them swarms of atomies,
> Which do by chance into our bodies flee.

[7] That is, the Epicureans.

> Some think one general soul fills every brain,
> As the bright sun sheds light in every star;
> And others think the name of soul is vain,
> And that we only well-mixt bodies are.

So wrote Sir John Davies, in 1599, in a preliminary survey of the vagaries of the human intellect, before setting forth the truth in no uncertain terms. That truth, in few words, was this:

> The soul a substance and a spirit is,
> Which God Himself doth in the body make;
> Which makes the man, for every man from this
> The nature of a man, and name, doth take.
>
> And though this spirit be to the body knit,
> As an apt means her powers to exercise,
> Which are life, motion, sense, and will, and wit,
> Yet she survives although the body dies.
> (*Works*, ed. Grosart, i, 26-29.)

If we should go further into this orthodox doctrine, we should discover that the soul has three aspects, distinguished (in John Donne's words, for example) as "a soul of vegetation and of growth," "a soul of motion and of sense," and "a soul of reason and understanding, an immortal soul." We might learn also that of the "vegetable soul" *appetite* is the quality which most powerfully affects the higher part of one's nature; that of the sensible soul the chief functions are reason, imagination, and memory; and that of the highest or reasonable soul the supreme powers are understanding (or *wit*) and will. Further details will easily be spared; but it must not be supposed that all these speculations were remote from the living thought of the age, as expressed in literature. On the contrary, the poetry of the Elizabethans often can be only imperfectly understood without some recollection of the terms of their psychology. And it is not merely a matter of incidental terms, but of the fundamental understanding of the relationship of sensation, desire, judgment, and volition. All through the literature of the sixteenth and seventeenth centuries we find matter which depends on the concept of the senses ministering to appetite, of appetite referred to the reason for judgment, and of the will as determining the resultant action. To go back once more to Castiglione and his account of love, we learn that the cause of love's "havoc in men's minds is chiefly sense, which is very potent in youth, because the vigour of flesh and blood at that period gives to it as much strength as it takes away from reason, and hence easily leads the soul to follow appetite."[8] Sometimes, then, the soul, being forced to beg her "first notions" of things from the senses, "believes them and bows before them." At other times, especially in mature life, she exercises her sovereign powers according to true reason. Davies sums it all up in more of his pregnant quatrains:

> And as this Wit should goodness truly know,
>   We have a Will, which that true good should choose;
> Though Will do oft (when Wit false forms doth show)
>   Take ill for good, and good for ill refuse. . . .
>
> Wit is the mind's chief judge, which doth control
>   Of Fancy's court the judgments false and vain;
> Will holds the royal sceptre in the soul,
>   And on the passions of the heart doth reign.
>   (*Ibid.*, pp. 78-79.)

[8] *The Courtier,* Opdycke trans., pp. 290-91.

Here, one might say, is the essence of drama; and Elizabethan drama is often only the outworking of such lines as these.

In the last place, we have to recall, very briefly but with such distinctness as we may, this drama of the Elizabethans. We have already noticed it as one of the chief unifying forces for the period, because of its appeal to both aristocracy and commonalty, and its union of the elements of art and popular recreation. And we know that it is one of the most remarkable instances in all history of Nature's effective adaptation of the times to the man, that Shakespeare should have come to maturity at precisely the moment when the English theatre was ready both to give to and receive from his individual genius. The main facts are readily recalled. When Elizabeth came to the throne there was no theatre in London, and no popular drama in England save what survived from the Middle Age, in such forms as miracle-play, morality, interlude, and local "mummers' plays" like those on St. George. Looking back, we can now see that certain influences of the Renaissance were preparing the way for a more regular vernacular drama, in stimulating the imitation, at school and college, of the comedies of Plautus and Terence and the tragedies of Seneca; while at the same time the growing population of London was developing the importance of simple popular drama in the hands of strolling troupes of players. Two years before Shakespeare's birth the play of *Gorboduc*, written by young gentlemen of the Inns of Court and performed before the Queen, shows the union of Senecan tragedy with the materials of British history, in a manner highly significant for the future; but it was some years before experiments of this kind affected the work of writers for the common people. Again, two years after Shakespeare's birth George Gascoigne was making the first English version of a Renaissance Italian comedy, in his *Supposes;* and once more the modern student, looking back upon the incident, perceives its significance for the popular comedy to come,—dependent, as it was so largely, upon the streams of Italian story.

Meantime the popular players were performing, largely in the roomy courts of London inns, dramas whose names and texts have for the most part been lost to view. They were doing so with the increasing opposition of the respectable—and in good part Puritan—bourgeois of the City, who disliked the noisy crowds which gathered at the plays (especially on Sundays), feared the danger to public health which such crowds intensified, especially in times of plague, and at bottom had grave doubts respecting the morality of drama under any circumstances. When Shakespeare was ten years old, in 1574, the Corporation of London passed a famous ordinance banishing the plays from the city limits, except under extraordinary restrictions, because of the "sundry great disorders and inconveniences" which "have been found to ensue to this city by the inordinate haunting of great multitudes of people, specially youths, to plays, interludes, and shows." But the city fathers found themselves, in such efforts, between the upper and nether millstones of the court and the populace, and their will never really reached fulfillment. Not only the aristocracy but the Queen herself was deeply interested in the performances of the players, and sometimes gave them royal license in direct opposition to the wishes of the city authorities.

As a happy compromise between remaining within the liberties of London and forsaking his metropolitan audiences, James Burbage, manager of the troupe of players whose patron was the Earl of Leicester, in 1576 built a playhouse, in the open ground between Finnsbury Field and Shoreditch, to the north of the city, which proved to be an important center of dramatic activity for more than twenty years. When Shakespeare came to London he found plays being performed not only at this house, called "The Theatre," but also at "The Curtain," which had been built close at hand in the following year. At the same time he found a popular theatre in operation on the Bankside, across the Thames, at Newington-Butts; while, for audiences of higher rank, the boys of St. Paul's Cathedral choir, under the direction of their master Thomas Giles and his assistant John Lyly, were performing, under the special patronage of Her Majesty, both at court and in their own building near the cathedral. Shortly after Shakespeare's coming, Philip Henslowe built on the Bankside the first really adequate theatre, "The Rose," in 1587; and the following decade saw the erection of the great trio of Elizabethan playhouses, "The Swan," "The Globe," and "The Fortune." Meantime the office of the Revels at court was developed with increasing importance and brilliancy, its master, Edmund Tilney, outlasting the reign of Elizabeth and serving her successor in the same capacity until 1610. To entertain both court and populace was the ambition of all the dramatists and players. The choir-boy actors, whether of the Chapel Royal or St. Paul's, had a right to exist as players only for the Queen's pleasure, but they (or their masters) were glad to turn an honest penny, when allowed, by giving public performances for gentlemen, at higher entrance fees than the regular theatres. On the other hand, the professional players, though they actually gave most of their time to audiences of the meaner sort, found it needful to seek protection under the ægis of some noble patron, were eager to be summoned to court to repeat their plays, and often found opportunity to play within the city limits on the convenient pretext that they were "rehearsing" in Her Majesty's interest. Naturally enough, the plays which came to be written under these circumstances were most desirable when of a character to please both courtier and common citizen,—to be good for a performance at Whitehall, at the Curtain, or in an inn courtyard. Yet certain of them, of course, were suited only to the one purpose or the other. The modern reader is likely to forget this distinction of clientèle, until reminded of it by some detail of one or another Elizabethan play, clearly existing for the sake of a courtly or a popular audience. It may be only that the elements of scenic display—perhaps rising to the elaborateness of a masque—are such as to suggest the prodigal outlay which the Master of the Revels would permit out of compliment to royal eyes, but which could not be undertaken on the simple stage of the playhouse. Or, mayhap, the story of the play itself—the wondrous fortunes of an apprentice of the Strand or a fair maid of Cheapside—brings up at once the vision of the crowded pit of the Theatre or the Rose, with the upturned faces of eager citizens whose thoughts deck out the heroes strutting on the big bare stage. But three-fourths of the plays that we first think of as representing the age were equally welcome at court and among the people.

As for the dramatists: by 1585, when Shakespeare came of age, only Lyly and Peele had distinguished themselves, among those whose names we now remember,—both of them in dramas for the court. An unknown dramatist had begun, about 1580, the long line of popular chronicle-plays dealing with English sovereigns, in *The Famous Victories of Henry the Fifth,* but it was nearly a decade before this type developed in an important way. Then, about 1586 or 1587, came a great outburst of brilliant dramatic experiment, among the results of which we chiefly remember Thomas Kyd's enormously popular *Spanish Tragedy* and Christopher Marlowe's epoch-making *Tamburlaine.* The four writers whose names have been recalled continued to write plays into the last decade of the century, and in the same period Greene and Nash, both of short-lived dramatic career, did their work. Of those who appeared after Shakespeare had begun to write for the stage, but still before the end of the century, the chief are Heywood, Chapman, Jonson, Dekker, and Marston, all of whom long outlived him. In the following decade Middleton, Webster, Beaumont, and Fletcher began careers which, with the exception of Beaumont, also reached far beyond Shakespeare's into the new century. It is interesting to remember that in the year 1611, when Shakespeare was bringing his active period to a close, there appeared on the stage *The White Devil,* the first of two great tragedies by John Webster, the only dramatist of the age worthy to be mentioned beside his master in respect of tragic power, and the tragi-comedy *A King and No King,* by Beaumont and

Fletcher, who were destined to be Shakespeare's chief rivals for popularity on the stage throughout the century. Those were the days of the dying glories of Elizabethan drama, though we still commonly call "Elizabethan" the comedies of Massinger and the tragedies of Ford, which belong to a later generation.

The forms of drama to which these men devoted themselves are conveniently summarized in the license granted to Shakespeare's company in 1603, which gave the members thereof permission "to use and exercise the art and faculty of playing comedies, tragedies, histories, interludes, morals, pastorals, stage plays, and such other like." Here we note first the three dominant types, with the survival of two older forms (interlude and morality) already comparatively rare, the minor and hardly distinct form of pastoral, and the concluding omnibus category of "stage-play," doubtless designed to cover whatever might otherwise escape classification. Another type which we might look for, the masque, was primarily a matter for performance at court, and by persons of rank rather than professionals. It is clear, in any case, that the accurate discrimination of types is of much more interest to the historians of Elizabethan drama than it was to the Elizabethans themselves. For an age so rich in drama, this one was singularly lacking in dramatic criticism, and we may count it none the less happy that its playwrights worked out their art free from the restraint of those doctrines of composition which loomed so large on the Continent. The classical distinction between tragedy and comedy was, on the whole, accepted by both authors and public; but they admitted to equal honor their own characteristically native form of chronicle-drama or "history." Some evidences of a regard for tradition appear where we should scarcely look for it, and where the dramatist must sometimes have felt hampered by its claims, —notably in the practice of dividing every play into five acts, according to the Latin practice, no matter what the story itself suggested.

As for the "unities of time and place," which so vexed the souls of Italian and French students of the drama, and of some of the English at a later time, the Elizabethans lost no sleep over the matter, but for the most part followed in the line of their old popular drama in passing freely from one region and one generation to another,— not to mention the minor liberties of changing from room to room and from day to day. Sir Philip Sidney, to be sure, held to his masters of the continental Renaissance, and lamented the plays "where you shall have Asia of the one side, and Africa of the other, and so many other under-kingdoms that the player, when he cometh in, must ever begin with telling where he is." And as for time: "Ordinary it is that two young princes fall in love. After many traverses, she is got with child, delivered of a fair boy, he is lost, groweth a man, falls in love, and is ready to get another child, and all this in two hours' space. Which how absurd it is in sense, even sense may imagine, and art hath taught."[9] This was written about 1580, before any of the great dramatists of the next age had begun their work. But they did not heed the warning; and in 1616 Ben Jonson, arch-classicist of all the Elizabethans, could write of his *Sejanus*: "If it be objected that what I publish is no true poem, in the strict laws of time, I con-

[9] *Apology for Poetry*, Smith's *Elizabethan Critical Essays*, i, 197.

fess it...... Nor is it needful, or almost possible, to observe the old state and splendor of dramatic poems, with preservation of any popular delight.'' The typical Elizabethan drama, then, refuses to give the pleasure of concentration, produced by the *Œdipus* of the ancients or the *Ghosts* of our own time, but depends instead upon the pleasurableness of multiplicity and freedom of movement, to a degree which with us is associated with the photoplay rather than with the regular drama. Of course the practice of Shakespeare's time was closely connected with the conditions of his stage. Without elaborate and changeable scenery, the imagination of the audience freely followed the actors' placing of themselves in time and space. As Sidney just told us, the player "must begin with telling where he is"; and he goes on to say that "by and by we hear news of shipwreck in the same place, and then we are to blame if we accept it not for a rock." In other words, the actor and his action made the time and place. Sometimes they made it definitely, sometimes indefinitely; for there are many scenes in Elizabethan plays, laboriously located by the modern editors as occurring in such and such a house or street or room, which, in the view of the original audience, were not precisely located at all. They happened, that was all, between the action that preceded and the action that followed; if you wanted to know just where and when, so much the worse for you. But the moment a realistic or "picture" stage is undertaken, together with a corresponding conception of a clear division of the action into certain hours or days, this loosely roving imaginative method becomes impossible. It is therefore more than a coincidence that it was in the days of the elaborate development of stage mechanics that an interest in the "unities" came to the front in English criticism.

Rather more serious, however, is the unity of plot or action; and here also the Elizabethans were heretical to a shocking degree. In one sense, to be sure, this problem takes care of itself, for a really effective play is bound to be based on some essential unity of interest. But tastes differ very widely respecting the effect of introducing other interests than the dominant one. What we may call the classical spirit seeks to throw them into the background, or altogether to exclude them; what we may call the vaudeville spirit seeks to multiply them and magnify them, until we even become uncertain which interest is chief. And this is not merely a matter of plot or story, but of mood. The diverse interests may be—are likely to be—of different emotional colors; and the vaudeville spirit is glad to have these colors clash in conspicuous dissonance,—to follow a death scene with a laugh, or an acrobatic feat with a bit of lyric sentiment. Now the traditional spirit of British drama was of the vaudeville type; the popular players had always found it worth while to blend their stories and mix their moods. Even the old sacred drama had done it daringly, the classic examples being the mystery-play of the Flood in which Noah's wife and her drunken cronies haggle and balk over entering the ark, and the mystery of the Nativity in which a comic under-plot of a thieving shepherd is entwined with the sacred scenes at Bethlehem. At the height of Elizabethan drama this tendency, of course, was refined and regulated, but by no means abandoned. Why should a play contain but one good story, especially when it is expected to be in five acts, and that measure provides room for two or three plots? Why should it be wholly serious or wholly comic, when the world is full of both sorts of things, and they press inseparably upon our emotions, perhaps thrilling us by the very combination of pleasure and pain? This seems to have been the reasoning of Shakespeare's contemporaries, though they nowhere discuss the subject. Later critics discussed it abundantly: they argued, for example, on the one side, that since real life mixes the serious and the comic, dramatic art may properly do the same; and on the other side, that it is the very business of art to give us more unity of experience than life provides. There is a good case either way. In these days, then, we may freely admit both the pleasure of singleness of experience and singleness of mood, and the pleasure of mixed experiences and mixed moods. For the former we go, first in all the literature of the world, to the drama of the Greeks; for the latter first of all to the drama of the Elizabethans.

What, then, can we say was the dominant idea, in this age, of a good play? The chief point (as for any people at any time, unless natural taste is distorted by some sophistication) was that it should tell at least one good story, —and the more the better. This story would commonly be announced as either comedy, tragedy, or history. If comedy, the outcome would be foreseen to be happy, and the course of the action would move in regions—as more than one author and manager advertised it—"full of mirth and delight"; perhaps, too, full of buffoonery and horseplay, so far as occasion allowed. The characters would be in good part from the common walks of life, but might either represent familiar scenes and social types (especially contemporary foibles and follies), or rise into the greater beauty and seriousness of the persons of romance. With two or more stories at the dramatist's command, both these possibilities might be fulfilled together. There was, of course, likely to be a complication threatening grave difficulties to the principal characters, but avoided in the dénouement by the happy coalition of Fortune, virtue, and dramatic skill. Such a complication might even be due to positive villainy, almost as black and ominous as that depicted in tragedy, but with the difference that the evil would be found in persons of minor importance, and that its defeat would be readily foreseen.

If tragedy, the story would be of the most stormy and passionate kind, with high personages for its principals, and a growing sense of a great, inevitable crash at the close. It would revel in deeds of darkness, in views of families broken by lust and shadowed by revenge, in the appearance of ghosts warning of evil hitherto undiscovered and counseling still unthought-of violence; and when the last word was said, the stage was likely to be strewn with bodies of the slain,—corpses which, for want of a falling curtain, must be borne off in a dead march wherein the solemn and the grotesque must often have mingled strangely. But the tragedy was not forbidden its humbler persons and its lighter scenes. Not to speak of clowns and bumpkins, one remembers Dr. Faustus the Protestant scholar, represented as invisible to all but the audience and Mephistopheles, hilariously boxing the ears of the Pope, in a drama whose theme is the damnation of his own soul. In the hands of the more serious playwrights, to be sure, a tragedy would have more of unity, both of action and mood, than a comedy of corresponding grade; but when wrought by cruder or more time-serving workmen, its tragic and comic elements might so divide the honors that at the close one could scarcely say to which the final word should be given.

If history, the story would normally deal with the reign of an English king, and combine something of patriotic feeling with the interest of its action. That action would be likely to prove partly military in character, presenting, in the naïvely simple manner of the Elizabethan stage, the alarms and excursions, the single combats and major battles, the sieges, surrenders, and treaties, which the national chronicles recorded. A genuine plot would not be demanded, since the mere succession of pertinent events was the sufficient matter of such a play; but in the hands of the more skillful dramatist something like a plot might be developed, and this, in the reigns of unhappy kings, might well take on so tragic a cast that the drama would be called a tragedy as well as a history. Comic matter was not so readily found in the important actions of warriors and kings, but, as in the case of scriptural play and tragedy, the writer did not hesitate to supply it with the aid of suggestions of familiar life from which even the lives of princes are not entirely free.

Whether for comedy, tragedy, history, or a blend of types in the daring method of the time, the qualities of richness, vitality, and intensity of story interest were as much the first demand of the Elizabethans, in the greatest days of English drama, as of a Broadway "movie" audience to-day. But to satisfy this demand, the playwrights made little effort to invent new stories for themselves; instead they ransacked the storehouses of national tradition, the recent accumulation of gossip on current events, and the wealth of foreign matter which the Renaissance had furnished for their use. All which can hardly be better told than in the words of Thomas Heywood, one of the most resourceful of his profession, as found in the famous prologue to his play of *The Royal King and the Loyal Subject*:

> To give content to this most curious age,
> The gods themselves we have brought down to the stage,
> And figured them in planets; made even hell
> Deliver up the Furies, by no spell
> Saving the Muses' rapture. Further we
> Have trafficked by their help; no history
> We have left unrifled; our pens have been dipped
> As well in opening each hid manuscript
> As tracts more vulgar, whether read or sung
> In our domestic or more foreign tongue.
> Of fairy elves, nymphs of the sea and land,
> The lawns and groves, no number can be scanned
> Which we have not given feet to; nay, 'tis known
> That when our chronicles have barren grown
> Of story, we have all invention stretched,
> Dived low as to the centre, and then reached
> Unto the *primum mobile* above
> (Nor scaped things intermediate) for your love.

All this might, however, have been true, and the English drama would still not have been ripe for Shakespeare. Though for the audience the element of story was the chief thing, another element, as we now look back, we see to have been of even greater importance for the special achievement of the age,—namely, that of poetry. For the sixteenth century, drama was a form of poetry, a fact whose significance we are tempted by various modern conditions not to apprehend. It meant that the dramatist felt himself to be in the tradition of the great poets of all the past, as one who newly created and newly interpreted human individuals and interests on a high level of imaginative experience. It meant, further, that his persons spoke a different language from that of common life, one which transfigured their utterances in accordance with the old mysterious powers of rhythm and the style which rhythm generates. No passion could be too intense, no aspiration too daring, no experience could transcend too far the limits of common sobriety and mediocrity, to exceed the capacity of this language to bring it to birth. The Elizabethans inherited this view of poetry as the normal dramatic form, from their predecessors of both native and classical tradition, and they developed it to the highest point which had been attained since the days of Euripides. They were, of course, not uninterested in the development of prose; and Lyly, in particular, taught them the art of finished prose dialogue in a way which may be thought to have influenced the whole generation. But that proved a trifling contribution to the drama, in comparison with what Marlowe taught in the sonorous harmonies of the blank verse of *Tamburlaine*. In the utterances of his heroes, dramatic personality poured itself out in a streaming lyric fervor which for the first time showed Englishmen what could be accomplished by the union of poetry with stagecraft. There was in his style, however, a certain admitted want of realism,—of the quality of actual human speech in the making. It was reserved for Marlowe's successors to learn the art of adding this element also, and to produce a dramatic style which is at once true speech and true poetry. This, as we find it at the great moments of Elizabethan drama, may be considered to be the highest attainment of our race in respect to language. Of late we have been led to emphasize, more than the readers of the past century or two, the methods and achievements of the age of Shakespeare in the field of dramatic technique, and this may have been a wholesome tendency, requiring us to study the drama of that period with constant reference to the theatrical conditions which produced it. Yet after all, the most characteristic contribution which the Elizabethans made to literature and to the drama was not technique, as it was not a system of thought: it was the spirit of poetry. The rich stream of life, as it moved by them, freighted with the spiritual treasures of antiquity and of the new lands and seas of the modern world, they turned, in large measure, into the alembic of the poetic imagination, and for these fortunate alchemists there came out gold.

One might say, then, that it was precisely the combination of the new materials for the satisfaction of the ever-present human love of story, with the new sense of the powers and processes of poetry, which made the Elizabethan drama the chief glory of that age.

CHAPTER II

LIFE AND WORKS

EVERY outline of the life of Shakespeare consists of two parts, that which is known to be true, and that which might, could, or should be true; and the second is commonly much the larger half. The modern world, with all its facilities for prying into the past, has refused to be convinced that it cannot gain an intimate view of the deeds and personality of one of the greatest of the sons of men, especially since he is tantalizingly near in time, and of an age when much writing and printing gave opportunity for abundant memorabilia. Hence conjecture has rushed in to take the place of evidence, and Shakespeare's biography has been freely played with by that myth-making faculty which civilization tries in vain to extinguish among mankind. The fact is, we know quite as much of him, in the externals of his life, as we have any right to expect to know of one who was not a subject of public record, like a king, a general, or a pope; the only exceptional circumstance is that he was a writer, and in the case of writers we always have hope that they will record themselves—the facts of their mental and spiritual life—in works both directly and indirectly autobiographic. That Shakespeare failed to do this, to an extent unparalleled by any poet since Homer, is the unforgettable grievance. Hence, in connecting the known facts of his existence as an objective person with the creations of his art, the unknown quantity of his emotional and intellectual development is supplied by the less conscientious biographers as if it had been revealed to them by some supernatural process, and by the more conscientious with such cautions as "we may safely assume," "it has been credibly inferred," and "no sensitive reader can doubt." Even in the field of purely objective fact, literary biography often follows the same method as village gossip, aware that an admittedly unverified rumor, repeated often enough, will soon seem to have the charm and certainty of truth. It is quite likely that in the present chapter these familiar methods will be discoverable; at any rate the reader has been warned of their nature. What we have to do is to bring to mind, in the first place, the story of Shakespeare's life as verified by the records, together with traditions whose origin seems to make them worthy of more cautious remembrance, and inferences which may be naturally drawn from his writings as to any of his experiences not otherwise known. Inferences of another character, respecting his opinions, moral and spiritual traits, and point of view as an artist, will be reserved until we have given consideration to his works.

In the middle of the sixteenth century Stratford, on the pleasant river Avon in Warwickshire, was a thriving town, probably of some two thousand persons, known both as the center of an agricultural district and as the seat of considerable manufacture of wool. The Church of the Holy Trinity, a fine structure dating in part from the twelfth century, overtops a wooded bend of the river and forms the central feature of a prospect which is now familiar to the mind's eye of the whole English-speaking world. In this church was baptized, on April 26, 1564, William Shakespeare, son of John and Mary Arden Shakespeare, of Stratford. The father was a well-known merchant of the town,—seemingly a glover or tanner, and dealer in skins and wool,—who at various times won local honors in the offices of burgess, constable, chamberlain, alderman, and bailiff. Perhaps for us moderns the most interesting incident of his career is found in the duty he performed in 1568 or 1569, when, as bailiff of Stratford, he welcomed to the Guildhall two visiting companies of players, the Queen's and the Earl of Worcester's. It is not to be presumed that his son William enjoyed the privilege of attending these performances; but there were numerous others in later years,—for example, in 1573, when the boy was nine, and again in 1577, when he was thirteen, came visits from the Earl of Leicester's company, with important members of which he was afterwards associated.

Stratford possessed one of the free grammar schools of which mention was made in the preceding chapter, and there William Shakespeare no doubt obtained the rudiments of a classical education. Bits of Lily's Latin Grammar, the standard for the time, are echoed in the schoolboy scene of *The Merry Wives,* and reminiscences of the authors on the conventional program of readings, Ovid above all, are found in many another play and poem. How long Shakespeare attended the school, or what point his formal education reached, we have no means of knowing. There is a tradition that he was withdrawn when comparatively young, because of his father's impaired financial condition, and this is supported, in some small way, by evidence that, about 1577 and in the years following, John Shakespeare was in pecuniary difficulties.

Meantime, on November 28, 1582, in his nineteenth year, William Shakespeare was licensed to marry Anne Hathaway of Shottery, a hamlet adjourning Stratford. The circumstances of the marriage seem to have been unpropitious: the bride was older than her husband by some eight years; the banns for the wedding were not cried in the local church, according to the common form, but instead a special license was obtained from the Bishop of Worcester, with certain farmers of Shottery as guarantors; and no part in the proceedings was taken, so far as we know, by the parents of the bridegroom,—although, since he was a minor, they must have given their consent. These things, taken together with the fact that the first child of the union was born in the following May, tend naturally to the supposition that the marriage was of a more or less hurried sort, made desirable by the fact that marital relations had been permitted (as was not uncommon in the period) during betrothal. Many words have been spent on the subject, both on the part of those who are not displeased to view the poet as treading early the primrose path of dalliance, and of those who feel it important to represent him as of "a pure unstained prime." But we are totally without evidence to warrant us in inferring either the details of the marriage or the emotions of those who had part in it. As to the special license, it was by no means so uncommon an arrangement as was formerly supposed; whether Mistress Anne's Shottery neighbors applied for it as grim defenders of her honor, or as good-natured abettors of a romance which John and Mary Shakespeare very naturally disapproved, one cannot say. The same thing is true of the question respecting the married life of the poet. The facts are few enough: no children were born to his wife after 1585; he seems to have resided in London during the great part of his active life, while his family remained at Stratford, and to have returned to spend his closing years with them. There is no reason to suppose that Anne Shakespeare could have been a woman whose education or development fitted her to mingle happily with her husband's friends in the capital, or to share intimately the life of the imagination which must have been so large a part of his existence. At best, one would say, the marriage was one of those, not uncommon for great men, which fill only one portion of life, as distinguished from those that penetrate every fibre of it. On the other hand, there is not a shred of actual evidence of unhappiness. It is no more reasonable to quote the words of the Duke in *Twelfth Night*,—"Let still the woman take an elder than herself," —as of special significance for Shakespeare's own experience, than to cite the poet's declaration that love "is an ever-fixed star" as proof that he was never unfaithful. If conjecture must be indulged to human weakness, the circumstance that he chose to come home to live, at the close of a long and brilliant career at the capital, is at least as pertinent as anything which has been urged of less favorable omen.

The seven years following the birth of Shakespeare's youngest children (the twins Hammet and Judith), in February 1585, are a sad blank in the extant records. It is commonly assumed that within a year of his coming of age he went up to London, and began the apprenticeship of which some actual knowledge would be so precious. One and another tradition has undertaken to fill the gap. Most persistent, because most picturesque, is the story that Shakespeare was given to poaching on the neighboring estate of Sir Thomas Lucy of Charlecote, who (in the words of Davies, an untrustworthy clerical gossip of the end of the seventeenth century) "had him oft whipt, and sometimes imprisoned, and at last made him fly his native county." Another tale, picked up at Stratford about the same time, relates that the young man was apprenticed to a butcher, but broke his indentures to run away to the capital, where he was received into the play-house as a "servitor." John Aubrey, gossip and antiquary of the same century, had heard that Shakespeare was for a time a country schoolmaster, a supposition wholly unverified, but for which, of course, there is ample room in the years of which we know so little. Once in London, the favorite story (deviously traced to Sir William Davenant, a reputed godson of Shakespeare's) represents him as making his way by caring for the horses of gentlemen who rode out to the Theatre or the Curtain; another legend, as we have seen, makes him a "servitor" of the theatre itself; another a call-boy under the manager or prompter. In themselves all these versions remain unauthenticated and open to doubt; they are especially to be suspected as implying rather more of youth and less of education than William Shakespeare probably possessed on reaching London; yet the view that he early attached himself to the theatre, in one capacity or another, scarcely admits of doubt. There, sometime before 1592, he had made good progress in learning his trade.

Our curiosity respecting the externals of Shakespeare's youth may perhaps be only half legitimate,—a mere ill that flesh is heir to; but the desire to know more of his reading, his intellectual and imaginative development, is surely one of which we need not be ashamed. And since here also we must depend on inference, let us make of such inference all that with right reason we may. Aside from the school-books of the current system of education, what may Shakespeare have read before leaving home? First of all, the Bible, the Book of Common Prayer, and the Catechism; all these we know of, both from antecedent probability and the evidence provided by his writings. Biblical and ecclesiastical matter was not "elective," in days marked, as those were, by the authority of church, state, and home; and the ears of the young Shakespeare must certainly have been wide open to the verbal harmonies and the imaginative vividness of both Prayerbook and Scripture, however he reacted to their content. Recent scholarship has tried in vain to prove his special familiarity with one of the three English Bibles which were naturally within reach in his youth,—the "Great" and the "Bishops'" Bible of the Established Church, and the "Geneva" version of the dissenters,—but without success: apparently he knew them all. At the opposite pole of secularity, there were current versions of old romances and ballads,—those of Guy of Warwick, Bevis of Hampton, Robin Hood, and the rest; and, more than possibly, accessible copies of Chaucer's poems. and Gower's, and Caxton's ever popular Book of Troy. It is unlikely that reading folk at Stratford would have failed to make the acquaintance of Tottel's great miscellany, the *Songs and Sonnets* of 1557, whose significance we saw in the preceding chapter, or of the popular collection of moralized and versified historic tales called *The Mirror for Magistrates* (published 1559 and 1563), or, again, of the storehouse of continental romance in Painter's *Palace of Pleasure* of 1566. And the schoolmaster, at least, might well have had, for the use of himself and his more promising scholars, Golding's version of Ovid, and one or another of the versions of the Senecan tragedies which had been made in the two decades following 1559. We may also suspect familiarity with both Stow's and Holinshed's chronicles of English history, and with North's great rendering of Plutarch's *Lives*. It is not so certain that Stratford would be concerned with Lyly's romances concerning Euphuës, or those of Barnabe Rich and George Whetstone (wherein are to be found the plots of *Twelfth Night* and *Measure for Measure,* with many another Italian story), though there was ample time for them to reach the provinces before Shakespeare's twentieth year. These, then, are among the possibilities respecting his reading in the adolescent period; — more than possibilities, if we extend our inquiry to the time of his London apprenticeship, for it is reasonably certain that he read every work that has here been recalled, the only question being when. The point is that before his migration to the city there may have been opened up to him some of the chief treasures of the ancient world, in both Latin and English forms, together with some of the riches of Italian romance, and the new experiments on the means of glorifying both the prose and verse of his own tongue.

And in London! One conceives him prowling about the bookstalls that haunted the churchyard of St. Paul's, or borrowing new publications from his friend Richard Field of Stratford, who was just completing his apprenticeship as printer and stationer in the city. Of the works that appeared in the years just preceding Shakespeare's own emergence as author, there is a rich array whose interest for him we may in some cases be sure of, in others suspect. Thus in 1588 and 1589 appeared the romances of the brilliant young scapegrace Robert Greene, the *Pandosto* and *Menaphon;* in the latter year, also, Thomas Lodge's Ovidian poem on Glaucus and Scilla; and in 1590 Lodge's romance of *Rosalynde*, destined to be made immortal through Shakespeare's rewriting it a decade later. About the same time came the first edition of Hakluyt's work on the *Principal Navigations, Voyages, and Discoveries of the English Nation*, the Elizabethan Bible of the spirit of Westward Ho. Then the first three books of the *Faery Queene*, and both the *Arcadia* and the *Astrophel and Stella* of Sidney — well known before his death to those of his own circle, but now made the property of the general reader,—and the sonnets of Daniel, with a multitude of others in their train, and the pastorals of Drayton and his followers, and lyrical miscellanies like the *Bower of Delights* and the *Phoenix' Nest*. But we have now reached the point, about 1593, when the spirit of Elizabethan poetry had burst forth in all its glory, and when Shakespeare was making his own first contribution to the display.

When we turn to the drama, we imagine him not among the bookstalls but in Shoreditch, earning or otherwise finding his way to a performance at the Theatre or the Curtain,

—or, it may be, attaining the more luxurious pleasure of a play of the Paul's Boys at their choir-house. At the latter place he would see one of the allegorical comedies of Lyly, from whom, as is commonly thought, he learned something of the art of dramatic dialogue in prose. But some broader comedy, or brave ranting tragedy of the Senecan order, on one of the more popular stages, would more often be at his command. And it is impossible (though we admittedly tread the thorny and pathless regions of conjecture) to forbear some effort to conceive the emotions with which he first apprehended what we have seen to be the characteristic achievement of that moment, the union of the glories of the new poetry with the popular dramatic art. Within a few months of his coming to the capital, he may have seen an early performance of Kyd's *Spanish Tragedy*,—have thrilled to the sonorous ghostly prologue,

> When this eternal substance of my soul
> Did live imprison'd in my wanton flesh,—

or have heard the same voice sum up, at the close of the play, the "blood and sorrow" of the action:

> Horatio murdered in his father's bower;
> Vile Serberine by Pedringano slain;
> False Pedringano hang'd by quaint device;
> Fair Isabella by herself misdone;
> Prince Balthazar by Bel-imperia stabb'd;
> The Duke of Castile and his wicked son
> Both done to death by old Hieronimo;
> My Bel-imperia fall'n as Dido fell,
> And good Hieronimo slain by himself:
> Ay, these were spectacles to please my soul!

At about the same time he was likely to see the domestic tragedy of *Arden of Feversham,* containing the finest effort at criminal characterization which the English stage had thus far produced, and the tragic chronicle-play of *Locrine,* in which the materials of legendary British history were treated in a series of stormy scenes in the Senecan manner, interspersed with broad vernacular comedy in the manner dear to the English heart. Or, it may be, Kyd's play of *Hamlet* haunted him with the shadowy revelation of a personality which was to linger brooding in his mind for fifteen years to come. We may be even more certain that he was among the youthful admirers of the youthful Marlowe, when that poet's dramatic star suddenly rose into the heavens;—that he was present when Edward Alleyn (another young god of this Elizabethan Olympus) made his early fame in *Tamburlaine,* and that the listener's pulse throbbed, almost with pleasurable pain, to the new melody of the mighty lines that thrilled the theatre:

> Now clear the triple region of the air,
> And let the majesty of heaven behold
> Their scourge and terror tread on emperors.
> Smile, stars, that reign'd at my nativity,
> And dim the brightness of their neighbour lamps!
> Disdain to borrow light of Cynthia!
> For I, the chiefest lamp in all the earth,
> First rising in the East with mild aspect,
> But fixed now in the meridian line,
> Will send up fire to your turning spheres,
> And cause the sun to borrow light of you!

In allowing ourselves to contemplate for the moment Shakespeare's dawning ambition to be a poet, we are anticipating the proper course of biography, which is bound to assume that he was first an actor, and only secondly a dramatist. Yet the two activities apparently became so early intertwined that the first glimpse which we seem to have of his emergence into public notice already combines them. This is in a famous little pamphlet written by Robert Greene, a young Oxford man, who, after a brief brilliant career as novelist, satirist, and dramatist, died in poverty and gloom early in September 1592. The quarrels in which he had engaged during his life were perpetuated after his death; and his friend Henry Chettle presently published, "at his dying request," the tract called *Greene's Groatsworth of Wit, bought with a Million of Repentance*. Here occurs an address to certain of his friends "that spend their wits in making plays" (probably Marlowe, Nash, and Peele), warning them against the actors who take advantage of those that furnish them the means for their trade,—"those puppets, I mean, that speak from our mouths, those antics garnished in our colours." In particular "there is an upstart crow, beautified with our feathers, that with his *tiger's heart wrapt in a player's hide* supposes he is as well able to bombast out a blank verse as the best of you; and, being an absolute *Johannes factotum*, is in his own conceit the only Shake-scene in a country." That this upstart crow is Shakespeare, students of the passage are pretty well agreed, though the precise situation which gave rise to Greene's indignation is not so clear. The italicised phrase about the "tiger's heart" is a quotation from the play called *The True Tragedy of Richard, Duke of York* (probably written, at least in good part, by Marlowe); and Shakespeare, when he rewrote the play in the form known to us as the **Third Part** of *Henry the Sixth,* kept the line unchanged. Now an old play called *Henry the Sixth* (probably the work of Peele or Greene, or both of them) had been presented by Shakespeare's company as early as March 1592, and had won remarkable popularity in the dramatic season of that spring and summer. The most natural interpretation of Greene's words, then, is that Shakespeare had not only won profit as actor in this popular play, but was now known to be rewriting, or to have rewritten, Marlowe's plays in the same field, and would be claiming at the same time the profit and glory of both author and actor. However this may be as to the saucy passage in question, the combination of employments seemingly alleged of Shakespeare is precisely that which we know was his during many years to come; and it is very likely, as we have seen, that in the group of chronicle-histories dealing with the reign of Henry the Sixth he found his first notable chance under this double star of his fortune. The unpleasant taste of his character which Greene's malicious words leave with us need give us no concern, for not only are they sufficiently explained by the tone and circumstances of the whole pamphlet, but they seem to have been explicitly withdrawn a little later by the editor. In December of the same year Chettle issued a pamphlet of his own, called *Kind-Heart's Dream,* in the preface of which he expressed regret that he had not cut out from Greene's work passages which had offended "one or two" of the persons referred to. "With neither of them," he proceeded, "that take offence was I acquainted, and with one of them I care not if I never be. The other, whom at that time I did not so much spare as

since I wish I had;...... that I did not, I am as sorry
as if the original fault had been my fault, because myself
have seen his demeanour no less civil than he excellent in
the quality [i.e., profession] he professes. Besides, divers
of worship [i.e., persons of honour] have reported his up-
rightness of dealing, which argues his honesty, and his
facetious grace in writing, that approves his art." Posterity, tempted by the appropriateness of the words to a
certainty which we must admit cannot be vouched for,
has agreed that this acquaintance to whom Chettle made
such handsome amends can be none other than Shakespeare.
If so, we have another glimpse of him as both actor and
author, viewed now through friendly eyes.

Early in the following year Shakespeare made his début
in the field of non-dramatic poetry, publishing *Venus and
Adonis* at the press of Richard Field, a stationer—as has
already been noticed—of Stratford origin. The poem
would seem to have been an instant success, and was followed later by *The Rape of Lucrece*. Other editions of
both works came out at intervals, and there can be no
doubt that from this time Shakespeare was known as poet
in circles which would never have applied that honorable
word to a mere writer for the stage. In the Dedication to
Venus and Adonis he spoke of the work as "the first heir
of my invention," which some would take as evidence that
he had written it before attempting any original work in
the drama. That this was the case may well be, but the
words themselves certainly do not prove it, having to do
only with formal published literature. Both the poems
were dedicated, according to common custom, to a nobleman, the young Earl of Southampton, who came of age

in 1594, the year of *Lucrece*. The earlier dedication is marked by appropriate formality and dignity of tone: "Right Honourable, I know not how I shall offend in dedicating my unpolished lines to your Lordship,"—with no suggestion of personal acquaintance, much less intimacy. The second, preceding *Lucrece,* is of bolder and warmer tone: "The love I dedicate to your Lordship is without end...... What I have done is yours; what I have to do is yours; being part in all I have, devoted yours." The natural inference is that my lord had received the former offering with approbation, and given the poet signal evidence of willingness to be his patron; but those who are acquainted with the language of Elizabethan dedications, and who have no special plea to prosecute, will not infer that the relations of Southampton and Shakespeare had grown to be those of bosom friends. Of the later story of their relations we know nothing. Shakespeare never dedicated another book, and the frankly worldly reasons which he doubtless had for introducing himself to a noble patron soon disappeared, with his growing success in another sphere of art. Tradition, however, with many a modern devotee of conjecture, has continued to couple their names; and the batch of Shakespeare gossip which is traced to Sir William Davenant includes an item to the effect that Southampton once made his protégé the munificent gift of a thousand pounds.

The period of *Lucrece* and of the Southampton patronage was the moment in which the art of sonneteering was rising on a full tide of fashion, and it is quite likely that Shakespeare's bark rode gaily into port with the rest. Like some other poets, however, he did not care to publish any of his sonnets, and, as we shall see in the next chapter, we are singularly helpless in trying to date them with any certainty. In the absence of contrary evidence, to suppose that many of them were written in the period of the two poems and of contemporary sonnets is surely natural; nor can we complain of the same natural tendency to associate a portion of them with the name of Southampton, if only the effort be made to preserve the distinction between what is known and what is guessed. The 26th Sonnet, dedicatory in tone, is admittedly an interesting poetic parallel to the prose of the dedication of *Lucrece:*

> Lord of my love, to whom in vassalage
> Thy merit hath my duty strongly knit,
> To thee I send this written ambassage,
> To witness duty, not to show my wit;
> Duty so great, which wit so poor as mine
> May make seem bare, in wanting words to show it,
> But that I hope some good conceit of thine
> In thy soul's thought, all naked, will bestow it;
> Till whatsoever star that guides my moving
> Points on me graciously with fair aspect,
> And puts apparel on my tattered loving,
> To show me worthy of thy sweet respect:
> > Then may I dare to boast how I do love thee;
> > Till then, not show my head where thou mayst prove me.

On the other hand, to claim that this *must* have been written at the same time and to the same person as the dedication is absurd. A similar view may be taken of the sonnets which stand at the opening of Shakespeare's collection,— a group in which a beautiful young gentleman is fancifully urged to perpetuate his beauty by founding a family. This was, it would seem, a highly appropriate compliment to pay to a nobleman like Southampton, who remained unmarried to the age of twenty-five; and no sufficient reason has been shown why the verses may not have been sent to him with the compliments of the author of *Lucrece*. Of how many others of the sonnets the same thing may plausibly be conjectured, is a mooted and dangerous question not lightly to be brought in here.

We must now return to Shakespeare the actor. Whatever the time of his entering the theatre, it is commonly assumed that he found his opportunity in connection with the group of players headed by James Burbage, the leading manager of the age and father of the chief tragic actor of the younger generation, though there is no real evidence for Shakespeare's association with them for some three years after he is supposed to have opened his career as dramatist. Burbage and his associates, at some time within a few years of Shakespeare's coming to London, appear to have joined with the company of players called Lord Strange's men, afterward the Earl of Derby's, and in 1594 organized a new company which was known as the Lord Chamberlain's until 1603. In 1592 they were occupying the Rose Theatre, on the Bankside, where the old play of *Henry the Sixth* won such fame; in 1594 the new company began a brilliant career at the old Theatre playhouse. It happens that at the end of this year the records give us the first definite mention both of Shakespeare as actor and of the performance of one of his undoubted plays. On December 26 and 28 his name appears, together with those of the chief tragedian and the chief comedian of the company (Richard

Burbage and William Kemp), as performing two "comedies or interludes" before the Queen at Greenwich Palace, for a total fee of twenty pounds; and on the same day as the second of these performances, the *Comedy of Errors* was presented before the benchers and students of Gray's Inn. This, of course, does not mean that we find at this time the beginning of Shakespeare's original dramatic authorship. Aside from what has already appeared of *Henry the Sixth*, the *Comedy of Errors* may well have been a familiar play when performed at Gray's Inn, and other evidence makes it probable that two other comedies, two other chronicle plays, and at least one tragedy of Shakespeare's had been produced by the end of 1594.

It is clear that we now approach the period of Shakespeare's established position and prosperity. An incidental sign may be found in the fact that in 1596 his father, John Shakespeare, made application to the College of Heralds for the right to display a coat-of-arms as a gentleman, on such grounds as that he had been bailiff of Stratford, that his grandfather had been rewarded for service to King Henry the Seventh, and that he had married into the "worshipful" family of Arden. Since no final patent for the issue of the coat-of-arms is extant, and there is a debatable problem respecting the relation of this application to one of 1599 (when John Shakespeare wished to impale the arms of the Ardens with his own), the whole matter is shrouded in uncertainty; but there is little doubt that it was favorably determined,—probably at the time of the original application in 1596. Whether William Shakespeare or his father was the more interested in the matter, it is impossible to say. There is no reason to doubt that the poet would be honestly pleased with the opportunity, in a highly undemocratic age, to obtain for his family and himself the right to be counted among the gentry, at the same time that he might have laughed, among friends, at their slender grounds for the claim, just as a modern author may accept an honorary academic degree with some formal pride in its associations and also with a laugh in his sleeve at its essential unimportance. At any rate, we now occasionally find "William Shakespeare, Gentleman" among the records; and the arms, as drawn up by the Heralds, were eventually displayed on the monument above his grave.

Tokens of prosperity multiply in the succeeding years. In May 1597, Shakespeare bought New Place, one of the largest houses in his native town. From 1598 letters are extant, written by Stratford citizens, showing hopes of his aid in pecuniary difficulties. The same year happens to have left us a number of interesting memorials of his professional life in the capital. It was at this time that Ben Jonson's notable comedy, *Every Man in His Humor,* was produced by Shakespeare's company, with Shakespeare as one of the "principal comedians." According to a tradition recorded by Rowe, from an uncertain source, "Jonson, who was at that time altogether unknown to the world, had offered one of his plays to the players, in order to have it acted; and the persons into whose hands it was put, after having turned it carelessly and superciliously over [how like the adventures of some young modern playwright!], were just upon returning it to him with an ill-natured answer that it would be of no service to their company, when Shakespeare luckily cast his eye upon it, and found something so well in it as to engage him first to read it through, and afterward to recommend Mr. Jonson and his writings to the public." In the same year, again, Shakespeare's name first appeared on the title-page of copies of his own plays, the publishers of earlier quartos of the same character not having troubled themselves to give the author's name. What is most interesting of all, it was in 1598 that Francis Meres, a pedantic and euphuistic Master of Arts, earned the eternal gratitude of the modern world by issuing his singular literary tract called *Palladis Tamia*, containing "a comparative discourse of our English poets with the Greek, Latin, and Italian poets." In no less than nine paragraphs of this discourse Meres introduced the name of Shakespeare, who had quite evidently become one of his idols, and thereby provided us not only with the most useful single clue to the chronology of the poet's plays but with an exceedingly significant view of his contemporary reputation. These are the more important of the passages:

As the Greek tongue is made famous and eloquent by Homer, Hesiod, Euripides, Æschylus, Sophocles, Pindarus, Phocylides, and Aristophanes; and the Latin tongue by Virgil, Ovid, Horace, Silius Italicus, Lucanus, Lucretius, Ausonius, and Claudianus: so the English tongue is mightily enriched and gorgeously invested in rare ornaments and resplendent habiliments by Sir Philip Sidney, Spenser, Daniel, Drayton, Warner, Shakespeare, Marlowe, and Chapman.

As the soul of Euphorbus was thought to live in Pythagoras: so the sweet witty soul of Ovid lives in mellifluous and honey-tongued Shakespeare; witness his *Venus and Adonis*, his *Lucrece*, his sugared *Sonnets* among his private friends, &c.

As Plautus and Seneca are accounted the best for comedy and tragedy among the Latins: so Shakespeare among the English is the most excellent in both kinds for the stage. For comedy, witness his *Gentlemen of Verona*, his *Errors*, his *Love's Labours Lost*, his *Love's Labours Won*, his *Midsummer Night's Dream*, and his *Merchant of Venice*; for tragedy, his *Richard the 2*, *Richard the 3*, *Henry the 4*, *King John*, *Titus Andronicus*, and his *Romeo and Juliet*.

As Epius Stolo said that the Muses would speak with Plautus' tongue if they would speak Latin: so I say that the Muses would speak with Shakespeare's fine-filed phrase if they would speak English.

(*Elizabethan Critical Essays*, ed. Smith, i, 315-18.)

In the following year the great event was the building of the new Globe playhouse, on the Bankside,—in good part out of the materials of the old Theatre,—and the formation of a stock company for the purpose of administering it, whereof Shakespeare was one of the chief partners or "housekeepers." The remainder of his career must be largely associated with this theatre, truly splendid for its time. It was for the Globe stage that the great plays from *Julius Caesar* to *Coriolanus* were probably written, as well as a number of Jonson's in which Shakespeare appeared. A considerable amount of evidence, incidental to suits at law involving Globe shareholders or their heirs, has survived to indicate the profitable character of this great theatrical enterprise. Shakespeare's income from his own holding of shares has been variously estimated to have been from seventy-five pounds a year to twice that amount; and in the later years of his life there was added a considerable sum from the profits of the Blackfriars Theatre, which his company opened for winter performances in 1610. Besides this source of income, he received other profits as actor-sharer in the company, and fees from the office of the Revels for performances at court,—his total gains as actor doubtless exceeding one hundred pounds annually. There were also his fees as author, which have been estimated to reach from thirty to fifty pounds annually during the later period. When we remember that the purchasing power of English money in his age was anywhere from four to seven times what it was at the end of the nineteenth century, it will be seen that Shakespeare accomplished a reconciliation between art and worldly substance of no contemptible sort.

Another event of 1599 introduces us to questions of a very different character,—the publication by William Jaggard, a more or less piratical stationer, of a little miscellany called *The Passionate Pilgrim,* under the name of William Shakespeare. This consisted of some twenty poems, of which four or five may be affirmed to be Shakespeare's, four or five may be ascribed with some definiteness to other authors, and the remainder are wholly open to conjecture. That Shakespeare had anything to do with the publication is out of the question, and we should hardly care to pause over it were it not for the two opening poems, sonnets which later appeared—with slightly different text —in the whole collection of Shakespeare's sonnets as brought out a decade later, and which suggest a personal significance. The first of them (No. 138 in the standard arrangement) is a cynical account of the lies which the poet and his "false-speaking" mistress tell one another regarding their fidelity and their age. The second (No. 144) runs as follows:

> Two loves I have, of comfort and despair,
> That like two spirits do suggest[1] me still;
> My better angel is a man right fair,
> My worser spirit a woman colour'd ill.
> To win me soon to hell, my female evil
> Tempteth my better angel from my side,
> And would corrupt my saint to be a devil,
> Wooing his purity with her fair[2] pride.
> But whether that my angel be turn'd fiend,
> Suspect I may, yet not directly tell;
> For being both to me, both to each friend,
> I guess one angel in another's hell.
>   The truth I shall not know, but live in doubt,
>   Till my bad angel fire my good one out.

This picture of the two friends, "the better angel" and "the worser spirit," appears to be sketched again in certain other sonnets, presumably of similar date and origin; while a few (especially those numbered 131, 137, and 147 in the collection of 1609) etch with still more acid touch the portrait of the false woman, dark in both complexion and character. Most interesting, in connection with the sonnet just quoted, are five (numbered 40, 41, 42, 133, and 134) which apparently represent again the incident of a mistress stolen from him, for a time, by the poet's dearest friend. The effort has been made, from one and another point of view, to avoid the natural impression of actuality which these poems make upon the unsophisticated reader,

---

[1] I.e., tempt.
[2] The later text reads "foul pride," which is obviously preferable.

—to explain them as dramatic fictions, literary exercises on the familiar Renaissance theme of a conflict between love and friendship, and the like; but it cannot be said that this effort has met with success. The sonnets on the friend and the mistress bear no marks of Shakespeare's familiar art of fictional composition; they have every appearance of being fragments that survive some experience in which the poet was playing at the same time with passion and the art of sonnetizing it, and occasionally realizing that he had been playing with fire. One may naturally assume, then, that in the period preceding the issue of *The Passionate Pilgrim* Shakespeare had taken a half sincere, half cynical part in the triangle which he depicted with those few memorable strokes, and that his friends could have told us (if they had foreseen, and cared to comply with, the insatiable peering scrutiny of his editors and biographers) the names of the dark woman and the forgiven friend. But this is not at all to imply that the incident was of profound or long-lasting significance for the poet's life: for such a view there is no shred of proof. In the same connection we may recall the story of another triangle in which a bit of contemporary floating scandal linked Shakespeare's name with that of one who was certainly among his most intimate friends. John Manningham, a law student of the Middle Temple in 1602, recorded in his diary, on the authority of his room-mate, that Shakespeare had lately overheard his colleague Burbage, at a performance of *Richard the Third,* making an appointment with a lady "citizen" in the audience, and had later anticipated him at her house. When Burbage arrived and knocked at the door, he heard his friend's voice reminding him that "William the Conqueror was before Richard the Third."

The years 1600 and 1601 were times of strife, and of some diminished prosperity, for the Lord Chamberlain's men. For one thing, they were involved in a complicated professional controversy in which the other leading combatants were the dramatists Jonson, Marston, and Dekker, and the children's companies of St. Paul's and the Chapel Royal. Into this subject we cannot enter, since Shakespeare's personal connection with it is extremely uncertain. An anonymous college playwright, in a skit called *The Return from Parnassus*, credited him with having given that "pestilent fellow" Ben Jonson "a purge;" and some have found this medicine in a supposed burlesquing of Jonson as Ajax in Shakespeare's *Troilus and Cressida*. It is quite as likely, however, that the allusion is explained by the conduct of his company rather than by anything in his own work, which, in general, even during the period of the quarrel, is singularly free from suspicion of personal controversy. The only unmistakable part which he took in the proceedings was to make an exception to his usual practice and introduce into the second act of *Hamlet* a purely "topical" reference to the children's companies. Rosencrantz, it will be remembered, relates that the tragedians of the city seem to be less favored than formerly, not because of any deterioration of their art, but because of popular excitement over the "aery of children" that are being "tyrannically clapped" for their part in the satiric warfare. "There has been much throwing about of brains," says Guildenstern. But Shakespeare admits that "the boys carry it away," even to the point of running off with "Hercules and his load,"—that is to say, the sign of the Globe Theatre, in which Hercules bore the world on his back. This light-hearted and good-natured banter would seem to be characteristic of Shakespeare's attitude toward the whole affair.

More serious were conflicts with the civil authorities. At this period the Lord Mayor and the corporation of London renewed their hostility to the theatres, being especially excited by the new enterprise of the Fortune playhouse, and the Privy Council made some pretense of abetting them by imposing (in June 1600) certain new restrictions upon the companies; the ordinance, however, can hardly have been intended seriously, and was not enforced. In the following winter the Lord Chamberlain's men ran risks of a more capital character. They were employed by some of those concerned in the Essex conspiracy to present Shakespeare's "play of the deposing and murder of King Richard the Second" at the Globe on the day (February 7, 1601) preceding the attempted uprising against the Queen. Indeed it was later charged that a number of performances of the same drama had been given about this time, in streets and inn-yards as well as on the regular stage, with a view to converting the public to the righteousness of deposing a tyrant. A clumsy psychology, this, one would say, since the last act of *Richard the Second* develops the wrong and pity of the murder to a point fit to satisfy any sovereign's heart. At any rate, the London populace refused to be roused to sedition, and the conspiracy, as we know, came to a prompt and tragic end. Essex was executed, and Lord Southampton imprisoned indefinitely. It is wholly uncertain whether the presenting of his play for an unlawful end was done with Shakespeare's personal approval; but the incident, coupled with the fact that he had gone out of his way to compliment Essex in one of the prologues in *Henry the Fifth,* and the fact that one of the Essex conspirators was his old patron Southampton, has led to the suspicion that he sympathized with the rebel cause. His company, however, was not proceeded against by the government, and continued to enjoy the favor of the Queen.

Just two years after the ill-omened performance of *Richard the Second* the Lord Chamberlain's men gave their last play before her Majesty. In a few more weeks she was dead,—having lived long enough, one is glad to believe, to see the greatest play of the greatest of her subjects; for *Hamlet* had probably been produced during the preceding year. It has been widely conjectured that Shakespeare referred to her death in his 107th Sonnet (as the "eclipse" of "the mortal Moon"), and welcomed King James in the statement that under his auspices "peace proclaims olives of endless age." This interpretation is very hazardous; but if Southampton was still Shakespeare's friend, the poet had cause for rejoicing in the earl's release from prison on the accession of James, and certainly his own professional fortunes were favored by the same event. The king, who while still in Scotland had shown his love of the stage by forbidding the sessions of the Kirk to interfere with its interests, had been in London but a few weeks when he elevated the Lord Chamberlain's men to be "His Majesty's players," and during his whole reign he continued to give them proofs of his favor. In March 1604, when the royal procession through the City of London was about to take place, Shakespeare's name headed a list of nine actors who, as Grooms of the Chamber, were each granted four and a half yards of scarlet cloth by the master of the wardrobe, to make them festal suits. How long Shakespeare continued to appear in performances before the sovereign it is impossible to say; no doubt, we may suppose, for some time after he had withdrawn from the regular stage. It happens that the first presentation of Jonson's *Sejanus,* in 1603, is the latest mention we have of his name as a public actor, and that in similar lists for 1605 and 1610 he does not appear with his colleagues; the inference is natural that he gave up acting while still busy as a dramatist. In the latter capacity the accession of James of course found him at the apex of his career. During the five years since the publication of Meres's list of his works, he had produced, it would seem, about two new plays each year. During the eight years to come he was to average one a year.

When we attempt to review Shakespeare's career in what, strictly speaking, was his profession, we find very little, after all, to enable us to conceive it vividly. No contemporary allusion remains respecting his achievements on the stage, save the doubtful one in Chettle's statement as to one who was excellent in his "quality," and a line in some verses by John Davies of Hereford, to the effect that Shakespeare acted "some kingly parts." Two vague fragments of tradition have floated down, the one that he played the ghost in *Hamlet,* the other that he took the part of Adam the old serving-man in *As You Like It,*—tales which in themselves would suggest either that he was not distinguished among his colleagues or that he had the habit of taking minor parts in which he happened to be interested. In the folio edition of his plays his name heads the list of the "principal actors," but whether it would have done so if he had been only an actor one cannot say. As to his attitude toward his profession, we seem to see it, from one standpoint, in that of prince Hamlet, who calls the actors "the abstract and brief chronicles of the time," and gives them sound advice respecting their delivery. And on the other side, it seems to many readers that in his 111th Sonnet we find Shakespeare, in a mood of gloom or disillusion, referring to some fault or blunder that he had committed as due to a professional training "which public manners breeds," and stains his nature with the hue of "what it works in, like the dyer's hand." The evidence is too slight to enable us to be dogmatic, and the larger part of it certainly implies a vigorous, cheerful, and well-rewarded devotion to the actor's art. The attitude taken by Elizabethan society to the actor cannot be said to have differed greatly from that of our own time. That is, in the large, his profession was viewed as on the borders of respectability; but when he attained distinction and success, society made its usual compromises. Certainly Shakespeare's was by no means an unique instance of a man of the theatre achieving wealth, social position, and fame.

Meantime, in 1601 John Shakespeare had died, and the poet had become head of the family. In the following year he bought a considerable addition to the Stratford property, 107 acres of land adjoining the town, as well as a cottage and garden in Chapel Lane; and a few years later (1605) we find him making a further investment of over four hundred pounds in the funding of the Stratford tithes. It is clear that during this period he was in a very real sense a resident of both his home town and the capital, though it is impossible to say what proportions of his time he gave to the two. Lawsuits at Stratford, in which he sought to recover on loans, appear in the records at various intervals (for example, in 1604, 1608, 1609), but it is quite uncertain how far these were under Shakespeare's immediate observation, how far mere formalities carried on by his local agent. Curiously enough, a London lawsuit of 1612, in which he was not principal but witness, has revealed the whereabouts of his residence in the city during 1604 and for some uncertain length of time previous. This was in the house of one Christopher Mountjoy, a Huguenot merchant, at the corner of Silver and Muggle (now Monkwell) Streets, Cripplegate, a little to the northwest of the present General Post Office. It was a substantial neighborhood, within a few minutes—as we happen to know—of the homes of both Hemings and Condell, Shakespeare's associates and first editors; and the walk was an easy one across Cheapside to the Thames, where boatmen would take the pedestrian to the Bankside and the environs of the Globe. It happened that Shakespeare, their lodger, assisted the Mountjoys in arranging the terms of marriage between their daughter and their apprentice Stephen Bellott, who were wedded in November 1604. A later quarrel —which we can hardly be blamed for counting fortunate— respecting the dowry forced the poet to recall the circumstances, and to leave for us, in his deposition, a fugitive intimate glimpse of his personal relations in London during the year in which he was probably writing *Othello*. In

1608 we have another glimpse of him back in Stratford, after the death of his mother, serving as godfather to the infant son of a neighbor. Two years earlier, if tradition be trusted, he had stood godfather to William Davenant, whose parents kept the Crown Inn at Oxford, Shakespeare's usual stopping-place on his journeys between London and Warwickshire. At any rate late seventeenth-century gossip—furthered, it would seem, by the loose-tongued Sir William himself—made much of the poet's intimacy with the family of the innkeeper, and even hinted that he had been over-fond of Mistress Davenant, "a very beautiful woman of a good wit and conversation." It will surprise no one familiar with the methods of those moderns who construct Shakespeare's biography by divination, to learn that recent writers have announced that the fair hostess may unhesitatingly be identified with the dark woman of the sonnet episode.

Aside from such banalities, and from the real though admittedly unimportant incident of the Mountjoys, can we say anything of Shakespeare's friendships? Those of his theatre come first and with most certainty: Richard Burbage, the chief interpreter of his plays, and Hemings and Condell, sharers in all his professional fortunes, who eventually collected the plays "to keep the memory of so worthy a friend and fellow alive as was our Shakespeare." On the higher level of letters, there would seem to be little doubt of Ben Jonson's paramount claim. It would be hard to find contemporaries of more opposite tempers than Jonson and Shakespeare, and it is impossible that both their opinions and interests should not have clashed. Thus we have some evidence, and more rumor, of hostility between them both in "the war of the theatres" and elsewhere; but it is extremely slight in comparison with the evidence of their cooperation and friendship. Shakespeare, as we have seen, took part in some of Jonson's principal plays, and his company did what it could for a dramatist bound by his nature to be unpopular. No doubt he rallied his friend for the saturnine and superfluous learning with which Jonson weighted his dramatic fortunes, as Jonson certainly reproached him for the swift, unrestrained flow of words and wit that dazzled every faculty save the stern judgment of the scholar. All this was summed up by the younger dramatist in his memorable note in *Timber,* running: "I remember the players have often mentioned it as an honor to Shakespeare, that in his writing, whatsoever happened, he never blotted out a line. My answer hath been, 'Would he had blotted a thousand,' which they [and, we may interpolate, some unintelligent modern readers] thought a malevolent speech. I had not told posterity this but for their ignorance who chose that circumstance to commend their friend by, wherein he most faulted; and to justify mine own candor [i.e., kindliness], for I loved the man, and do honor his memory on this side of idolatry as much as any."[3] With such passages in mind, it is not difficult to credit the well-known picture drawn by Thomas Fuller, though it was not (as the words by themselves might imply) based on personal experience: "Many were the wit-combats betwixt [Shakespeare] and Ben Jonson; which two I behold like a Spanish great galleon and an English man-of-war; Master Jonson, like the former, was built far higher in learning; solid,

[3] Schelling ed., p. 23.

but slow, in his performances. Shakespeare, with the English man-of-war, lesser in bulk, but lighter in sailing, could turn with all tides, tack about, and take advantage of all winds, by the quickness of his wit and invention."[4] That such combats as these took place at the famed Mermaid Tavern—situate in Bread Street, on the natural route between the house of the Mountjoys and the River —the modern world has come firmly to believe. We know that Jonson frequented the place, and are unwilling to conceive Shakespeare absent from gatherings made vivid to us by Francis Beaumont's lines:

> What things have we seen
> Done at the Mermaid? heard words that have been
> So nimble, and so full of subtle flame,
> As if that every one from whence they came
> Had meant to put his whole wit in a jest,
> And had resolved to live a fool the rest
> Of his dull life.
>
> (*Letter to Ben Jonson.*)

Of relations between Shakespeare and other poets of the time, we know nothing definite. Spenser, easily the chief among them when Shakespeare's career was opening, has been thought to have complimented the author of *Venus* and *Lucrece* (and to have played on that author's name) in certain lines of the poem called *Colin Clout's Come Home Again,* wherein he referred to a "gentle shepherd" named Aetion,

> Whose muse, full of high thought's invention,
> Doth, *like himself, heroically sound;*

[4] *Worthies of England: Warwickshire.*

and Shakespeare may have returned the compliment in a passage in the *Midsummer Night's Dream*.[5] But no evidence of personal friendship has appeared. Spenser's disciple Drayton, who, unlike his master, did considerable work for the stage, was more probably a familiar figure in the group which included both Jonson and Shakespeare. He was an occasional visitor at the country-seat of Sir Henry Rainsford, not far from Stratford, and we are told that he was once cured of an illness by John Hall, the physician who in 1607 married Shakespeare's daughter Susanna. Not only so, but it was Drayton, according to a bit of gossip most uncertain in itself yet significant for the associations which would give rise to it, who joined Ben Jonson in "a merry meeting" at Shakespeare's house, to which the latter's death was in part attributed. The other poets with whom Shakespeare would have been most likely to enjoy intellectual comradeship were Samuel Daniel and George Chapman, but there is no evidence of his having been intimate with either. In the case of Chapman there has even been no little suspicion to the contrary,— namely, that he and Shakespeare felt themselves to be rivals, and engaged in occasional literary hostilities. In some half-dozen of his sonnets Shakespeare refers good-humoredly to another poet by whom he is in danger of being eclipsed in the favor of the person addressed, and whom he calls, either humbly or ironically, a "better spirit" than himself. Every endeavor has been made to identify the features of the man thus immortalized as rival to the greatest, without success, but with a tendency to

[5] V, 1, 52-3, commonly taken as an allusion to Spenser's poem *The Tears of the Muses*.

favor the name of Chapman. The identification, however, stands on very slippery ground; and even if it were admitted to be conclusive, it would imply only a temporary (and apparently, as we have seen, a good-natured) rivalry in the graces of some patron like Southampton, rather than anything in the nature of a long-standing quarrel. Still less evidence has been scraped together for the theory that Shakespeare was ridiculing Chapman in the pedant Holofernes of *Love's Labour's Lost,* or was making the story of Troilus and Cressida ridiculous in deliberate despite of Chapman's classical studies.

There must also have been among Shakespeare's friendships those of a wholly non-professional character, though the only certain instance is that of his neighbor John Combe, member of a wealthy Warwickshire family, who left the poet five pounds in his will. Among other names on which conjecture has lingered is that of John Selden, the great jurist and publicist, who lived in the Inner Temple, kept a "plentiful table," and entertained Jonson and Drayton, at least, among the poets. Another is Sir Dudley Digges, a diplomatist and member of the Council of the Virginia Company, whose brother Leonard wrote two poems in praise of Shakespeare. Still another is Sir Henry Rainsford, who we have seen was a country neighbor of the Stratford people; Shakespeare, no doubt, was as likely to visit Drayton at the Rainsford seat of Clifford Chambers, as Drayton to come across the fields to call at his friend's Stratford home. A still more interesting country neighbor (though also a more distant one, by a matter of some seven miles) was Sir Fulke Greville, youthful friend of Sidney and kinsman of Essex, himself no mean poet, as well as philosopher and statesman. After 1606 Greville was Recorder of the Borough of Stratford, and it is greatly to be hoped that his official visits to the town gave him excuse—if he needed it—for discovering the personality of the proprietor of New Place. All these are pleasant imaginings. For the bulk of mankind it has apparently been still more pleasant to conceive Shakespeare as personal friend of a peer of the realm,—either my Lord Southampton, on grounds which we have already seen, or Lord Pembroke, who, with his brother the Earl of Montgomery, was said by the editors of Shakespeare's plays to "have prosecuted both them and their author" with "much favor." But here we touch the difficult matter of the distinction between patronage and friendship, a matter which may perhaps have bothered Shakespeare as well as ourselves.

It seems evident that, as we approach the last five years of Shakespeare's life, we may conceive of his periods of residence in Stratford as tending to grow longer, and those in London to diminish correspondingly, until at length Stratford became again his principal home. A long tradition, at least, represents him as returning to Warwickshire for his closing years, and is contradicted by no known facts. We have a record of a performance of *The Winter's Tale* in May, 1611, and another of *The Tempest* in November of the same year; thereafter, as it has seemed to many, Shakespeare felt that his work in London was definitely done. But in the spring of 1613 we find him buying a house in the capital; and we imagine him as not absent from the great festivities, in that same season, celebrating the marriage of the Princess Elizabeth, when at least a half-dozen of his plays were revived at Whitehall Palace, like a pageant-memorial of his whole incomparable career. Presumably at the same time he made arrangements for the putting on by his company of the play of *Henry the Eighth,* in small part his but largely the work of John Fletcher, who was destined to be his chief successor in popular drama during the next generation. At any rate, on June 29th the play was being given, before a great audience (among whom, as he happens to have told us, was Ben Jonson), when the roof of the Globe took fire from the wadding of cannon fired in salute on the stage entrance of King Henry, and within an hour the entire theatre was in ashes. Whether Shakespeare was present at this thrilling dénouement, we cannot say. However he learned of the destruction of the great playhouse with which his career had been so intimately associated, one can fancy him musing on the appropriateness of the coincidence of its end with the end of that career. He was prompt to join with his associates in plans for a new Globe, which was opened in the following year; but there is nothing to indicate that he wrote a line of new drama for its stage.

For the interval between the burning of the Globe and the end of our story, though nearly three years elapsed, we know almost no details of Shakespeare's life. During 1614 and 1615 a troublesome municipal contest was raging at Stratford, due to an effort on the part of two citizens to enclose certain of the common lands of the town, and Shakespeare, because of related property interests, was incidentally involved. He did not live to see the settlement. In February 1616, his younger daughter Judith was married to Thomas Quiney, the son of a former neighbor and friend of the poet's, and Shakespeare and his wife were left, so far as the immediate family was concerned, to live alone; their only son Hamnet had died in 1596. In March, Shakespeare executed his will, leaving the bulk of his property to his elder daughter, Susanna Hall; and on April 23rd, almost if not exactly at the end of his fifty-second year, he died. He was buried, on April 25th, in the chancel of the Church of the Holy Trinity, where his grave has remained untouched to this day, guarded by the doggerel inscription which, according to tradition, the poet wrote to deter such light-hearted sextons as he had portrayed in *Hamlet* from disturbing his dust:

> Good friend, for Jesus' sake forbear
> To dig the dust enclosed here;
> Blest be the man that spares these stones,
> And curst be he that moves my bones.

At an uncertain date within the next few years, and under auspices of which we have no record, there was erected a sculptured monument, with portrait bust, on the north wall of the chancel overlooking the grave, bearing the inscription:

> *Judicio Pylium, genio Socratem, arte Maronem,*
> *Terra tegit, populus maeret, Olympus habet.*[*]
>
> Stay, passenger, why goest thou by so fast?
> Read, if thou canst, whom envious death hath plac'd
> Within this monument; Shakespeare, with whom
> Quick Nature died; whose name doth deck his tomb
> Far more than cost; sith all that he hath writ
> Leaves living Art but page to serve his wit.

[*] That is: "One who was a Nestor in judgment, a Socrates in genius, a Virgil in art, the earth covers, the people mourns, heaven possesses."

It is well known that one may not safely trust to the language of epitaphs for the honest judgment of their contemporaries upon the persons therein described; but Shakespeare was so happy as to hear of himself, while yet alive, appreciative words which equal any penned to commemorate him dead. Indeed there seems to have been no period, after he had once made his début as writer, in which he could have suffered from any want of favor on the part of those for whom he wrote, or have feared any criticism so much as that of his own perceptions, which sometimes led even him to covet "this man's art, or that man's scope." In the years following the publication of his early poems, it was they which called forth tributes to his success, in terms of which Richard Barnfield's verses (published 1598) are typical:

> And Shakespeare thou, whose honey-flowing vein,
> Pleasing the world, thy praises doth obtain;
> Whose Venus and whose Lucrece, sweet and chaste,
> Thy name in fame's immortal book have plac'd.

Meres's tribute to both poems and plays, from the same year, we have already seen. In the following decade, naturally enough, the fame of the dramas tended to obscure that of the poems. Yet in *The Return from Parnassus*, a college play brought out at Cambridge in 1601 or 1602, both groups of Shakespeare's works were discussed. In the first act the character Judicio expressed the wish that the poet would devote the sweetness of his verse to graver subjects than those of *Venus* and *Lucrece*. In the fourth act the most popular of Shakespeare's fellow-actors, Burbage and William Kemp, are represented as discussing contemptuously the dramas made by university wits, who "talk too much of Proserpina and Jupiter." "Why, here's our fellow Shakespeare," says Kemp, "puts them all down; aye, and Ben Johnson too." This is all ironic in tone; but we find a serious echo of the same comparison in the lines which Leonard Digges contributed to a collection of Shakespeare's poems made in 1640:

> So have I seen, when *Cæsar* would appear,
> And on the stage at half-sword parley were
> Brutus and Cassius: O how the audience
> Were ravish'd! with what wonder they went thence!
> When some new day they would not brook a line
> Of tedious (though well-labour'd) *Catiline.*
> *Sejanus* was too irksome: they priz'd more
> Honest Iago, or the jealous Moor.

Sometimes, he proceeds, even Jonson's comedies, *Volpone* and *The Alchemist,* have not paid the cost of heating the theatre and feeing the door-keepers; "when let but Falstaff come," with Hal, Poins, and the rest, or Benedick and Beatrice, or "that cross-garter'd gull" Malvolio, and

> The cock-pit, galleries, boxes, are all full.

Here may also be noted the tribute of Christopher Brooke, man of law and amateur of letters, who in his poem *The Ghost of Richard Third* (1614), represents the spirit of the king as thus eloquently associating his name with Shakespeare:

> To him that impt my fame with Clio's quill,
> Whose magic raised me from oblivion's den;
> That writ my story on the Muses' hill,
> And with my actions dignified his pen:

> He that from Helicon sends many a rill,
> Whose nectar'd veins are drunk by thirsty men:
>   Crown'd be his style with fame, his head with bays;
>   And none detract, but gratulate his praise.

When Spenser, chief poet of the earlier Elizabethans, had died in 1599, he was given burial in the "Poets' Corner" of Westminster Abbey, close to the grave of Chaucer; and a month before Shakespeare's death the brilliant young dramatist Francis Beaumont was laid at their side. Whether official consideration was given to the question of Shakespeare's burial in the same place, we do not know; presumably the matter was settled wholly at Stratford, in accordance with his known wishes. But William Basse, a minor poet of the day, gave utterance to his feeling on the subject in some lines which have proved a worthy memorial both to Shakespeare and himself:

> Renowned Spenser, lie a thought more nigh
> To learned Chaucer, and rare Beaumont, lie
> A little nearer Spenser, to make room
> For Shakespeare in your threefold, fourfold tomb.
> To lodge all four in one bed make a shift
> Until Doomsday; for hardly will a fifth
> Betwixt this day and that by Fate be slain,
> For whom your curtains may be drawn again.

Ben Jonson also meditated on Shakespeare's place of burial and his monument, and, when invited to contribute a memorial poem to the great first folio collection of the plays, found his opportunity, alluding to Basse's verses, to interpret the theme in the most important, if not the finest, tribute that one great poet has paid to another.

Only a few of the more significant lines must here represent the whole:

> My Shakespeare, rise! I will not lodge thee by
> Chaucer or Spenser, or bid Beaumont lie
> A little further, to make thee a room:
> Thou art a monument without a tomb,
> And art alive still, while thy book doth live,
> And we have wits to read, and praise to give.
> That I not mix thee so, my brain excuses,—
> I mean with great but disproportion'd Muses:
> For if I thought my judgment were of years,
> I should commit thee surely with thy peers,
> And tell how far thou didst our Lyly outshine,
> Or sporting Kyd, or Marlowe's mighty line.
> And though thou hadst small Latin, and less Greek,
> From thence to honor thee I would not seek
> For names, but call forth thund'ring Æschylus,
> Euripides, and Sophocles to us,
> Pacuvius, Accius, him of Cordova dead
> To life again, to hear thy buskin tread
> And shake a stage; or, when thy socks were on,
> Leave thee alone for the comparison
> Of all that insolent Greece or haughty Rome
> Sent forth, or since did from their ashes come.
> Triumph, my Britain! thou hast one to show,
> To whom all scenes of Europe homage owe:
> He was not of an age, but for all time!
> And all the Muses still were in their prime,
> When like Apollo he came forth to warm
> Our ears, or like a Mercury to charm.

All these tributes, naturally enough, concern primarily Shakespeare's greatness as artist, not his personal qualities as man. For their relationship to the latter, we can only say that not a word is extant, either from these friends or (if he had them) from his enemies, which opposes Chettle's early characterization of one who was honest, upright, and civil of demeanor, or Jonson's late pregnant words upon his friend: "He was indeed honest and of an open and free nature." There is ample evidence that the poet's self, as well as his work, was beloved. The rest we can only infer: on the one hand, from the solid structure of success which he built for himself in the world of men and affairs, of houses and lands, in his own generation, and on the other hand from that structure of thought, imagination, and feeling, which both reveals and conceals his personality from one generation to another.

In Shakespeare's lifetime there were published the two narrative poems which he seems to have issued under his own direction, two collections of poems (*The Passionate Pilgrim* and the *Sonnets*) doubtless issued without his consent, and at least thirty-eight cheap quarto editions of sixteen of the plays. (*Othello*, the seventeenth in order of printing, did not appear till 1622.) It has commonly been believed that these issues of the plays were wholly unauthorized; that their publication was in defiance of the interests and rights of the theatrical company which owned the copyrights and found it profitable to suppress publication, so far as possible, of plays still in their acting repertoire. That this is partly true there can be no doubt, and certain of the quartos give ample evidence of being printed from garbled versions obtained by one surreptitious means or another. Recent scholarship, however, tends toward a different view. It appears improbable that so large a number of the plays of the Lord Chamberlain's men should have been printed against their will at a time when the company was in the highest favor at court, and—even in the want of a protective law of copyright—should have had means at its command to prevent the outrage. A similar inference is drawn from the admirable character of the text used in a fair proportion of the quarto issues. One may suppose, then, that at certain seasons it was to the advantage of the company to publish one or another of its popular plays; and it is reasonably certain that some of the Shakespeare quartos, as we have them, were printed from the regular copies used in the theatre, if not from the manuscript of the author himself.

In 1623, seven years after Shakespeare's death, his friends and colleagues Hemings and Condell brought together the first folio collection of his plays, "according," as they said, "to the true original copies"; and inasmuch as they refer specifically to the author's manuscript ("What he thought, he uttered with that easiness that we have scarce received from him a blot in his papers"), it may again be true that portions of this volume were set up directly from Shakespeare's copy. All this is admittedly open to much doubt every way. What is certain is, that Hemings and Condell caused eight of the plays which had already been published to be printed from the quarto copies, and eight more of those already in print from we know not what copies of their own; the seventeenth, *Pericles,* they did not reprint at all. But their great service was in adding twenty plays which, so far as evidence has appeared, had not been published before, including such priceless works as *Macbeth, Antony and Cleopatra,* and *The Tempest.* It was these two good friends of Shakespeare's then, together with their publishers Jaggard and Blount, who were left to erect to his memory the one imperishable monument which, as a poetic contributor to the volume observed,

> When brass and marble fail, shall make [him] look
> Fresh to all ages.

This folio edition, we have seen, included thirty-six plays, omitting the *Pericles* and some half dozen others which had been claimed for Shakespeare by the publishers of unauthorized quartos. If we add *Pericles*, for whose partially Shakespearean origin there is some good evidence, we get the usual Shakespeare canon of thirty-seven plays, as commonly issued under his name. To this some would add *The Two Noble Kinsmen*, published in 1634 as by Fletcher and Shakespeare, and some, for the sake of certain disputed scenes, the early plays *Arden of Feversham* and *Edward the Third*, and the play of *Sir Thomas More*, which has come down in the players' manuscript copy, with two sheets in what has been alleged to be the handwriting of Shakespeare. On the other hand, it is generally admitted that some nine or ten of the thirty-seven plays in the standard collection show evidence of joint authorship, Shakespeare's portions perhaps varying from those cases where he contributed only a scene or two to those in which his work constitutes the main portion of the composition. These plays are the three parts of *Henry the Sixth, Titus Andronicus, The Taming of the Shrew, Troilus and Cressida, Timon of Athens, Pericles, Cymbeline,* and *Henry the Eighth*. There remain, then, twenty-seven dramas which we have little reason for viewing as other than Shakespeare's independent work.

For the order of composition of the plays, the order of publication gives us little aid,—none at all, indeed, except that the dates of the quartos sometimes indicate the latest possible dates of composition. For a long time this question of chronology aroused little curiosity among Shakespeare's editors, and there are still a few critics to whom it appears a matter of indifference whether *The Tempest* was written at the beginning or the end of its author's career; but these are anomalies, in an age when all life seems to find its meaning in the movement from one stage of being to another. Since the closing years of the eighteenth century all manner of scrutiny has been cast upon the plays, and upon contemporary documents, for evidence of dates of composition. Definite external evidence, after all is said, remains very slight; it gives us, perhaps, some indication of the dates of a bare dozen of the plays. Internal evidence, of one kind or another, is more abundant, but usually hazardous and vague: perhaps the only definite piece of it, on which criticism relies, is the reference in *Henry the Fifth* to the Essex expedition of 1599. Yet despite this incompleteness in details of proof, there has come about a pretty general agreement respecting the main outlines of Shakespeare chronology, and the qualities of style which seem to be characteristic of the different stages of the dramatist's career. The upshot is that, though we are not willing to set down particular dates, with any sense of certainty, for more than five or six of the plays, we feel reasonably certain as to which were early, which were late, and as to the order of time in which the greater number of them may be arranged. If a new play of Shakespeare's were suddenly discovered, with no external indication of the time of its production, we should even be likely to agree, within three or four years, on the date when it might be assumed to have been written. This is not the place to go into the reasonings by which the subject has been developed, though many of the details will come to light in the succeeding chapters. For the present we have only to note the general results. These may be summed up, in a word, in the agreement that Shakespeare's development as an artist was remarkably regular, normal, and representative; that he began, as a healthy young writer should do, by being primarily an imitator and assimilator of the art and the spirit of his age, and developed his more individual traits by way of experimentation and self-correction; that he did many things first with relative lack of skill, and thereafter with a visibly practiced hand; and that in the end, the curve of his workmanship was similar to the curve of development of Elizabethan drama in the period from its rise to its decline.

A corollary of this analysis of Shakespeare's development is the division of his work into four periods,—periods not marked by definite boundaries, and not to be supposed as clearly realized either by himself or his contemporaries, but characterized by the dominance of different dramatic types. In the first period the types vary, as it were experimentally, with a tendency to favor the chronicle-history; in the second, comedy is easily chief; in the third, tragedy; in the fourth, a type commonly described as tragi-comedy or romance. Much modern criticism, casting its eye rather over-intently upon the problem of the dramatist's personality, and too little upon his dramatic environment, has read these periods in terms of personality, with results which every one knows. But this is a process of very doubtful soundness. If our survey of Shakespeare's life, as given us through external sources, exhibited any biographic reasons why he should have written chiefly comedy in one period, and chiefly tragedy in another, it would no doubt be significant to find that he actually did so; but in the absence of such evidence, the passage from the types of his work to the facts of his personal life is one only for acrobats of the imagination. This, of course, is not to deny that the growth of an artist's mental and spiritual nature is normally reflected in changes in the depth and quality of his art. So, no doubt, was Shakespeare's. The point to remember is that there is no obvious and determinable relationship between objective and subjective conditions. We have no reason to suppose that Shakespeare found the writing of tragedy easiest when he was at odds with the world. He is quite as likely to have passed upstairs from a merry bout of words with Mistress Mountjoy, his landlady's daughter, to work out the agonies of Othello's temptation, as to the writing of a pastoral or a clownish scene. If this caution had only been considered, how many sheets of good white paper would have been spared from Shakespeare biography to some homelier use!

Yet criticism cannot fail to be interested in the grouping of the plays, admittedly inaccurate as it is, and the student of Shakespeare will eventually form for himself a working notion of the order which proves most plausible in view of all the evidence. For biographic purposes, the chronological list will intermingle all the types, as it did in the dramatist's career, and in that form it is set down below, without prejudice as to the precise dates of particular plays. For critical purposes, it may be well to re-group the plays according to type; and that plan will be the basis of the following chapters.

FROM 1590 *TO* 1594
Henry the Sixth (I, II, III)
Love's Labour's Lost
Comedy of Errors
Two Gentlemen of Verona
Richard the Third
King John
Titus Andronicus

FROM 1594 *TO* 1601
Midsummer Night's Dream
Romeo and Juliet
Richard the Second
Merchant of Venice
Taming of the Shrew
Henry the Fourth (I, II)
Merry Wives of Windsor
Henry the Fifth
Much Ado about Nothing
As You Like It
Julius Caesar
Twelfth Night

FROM 1601 *TO* 1608
Troilus and Cressida
Hamlet
Measure for Measure
All's Well that Ends Well
Othello
King Lear
Macbeth
Antony and Cleopatra
Timon of Athens

FROM 1608 *TO* 1613
Pericles
Coriolanus
Cymbeline
Winter's Tale
The Tempest
Henry the Eighth

CHAPTER III

THE POEMS

SHAKESPEARE'S earliest work in poetry represents him as wholly a child of the Italian and the English Renaissance. Recalling what was said in the first chapter of the poetic significance of this term, we are enabled to conceive him as fired with the ambition to give new and lovely expression to the old-time loveliness revealed in Latin and Italian art. Ovid, whom he knew both in the original and in translation, had presumably been the first to show him the possibilities of narrative poetry for this end; and *Venus and Adonis* was in the first place a study in rewriting certain of Ovid's lines. Here, in the *Metamorphoses* and other works of the same poet, was a type of narrative verse which appealed to the Renaissance more fruitfully than the greater type of the epic;—the latter was easier to praise than to imitate. The lesser form did not demand greatness of story or amplitude of structure, representative national feeling or moral dignity. It existed first for the sake of the incidents themselves,—striking, pretty, perhaps erotically suggestive,—and secondly for the sake of the beauty wherewith they might be embroidered. Let us linger lovingly (says the poet of this order) on the story of Phaëton, Pygmalion, or Philomela, not because of any significance which it has for our race, nor because I personally have been deeply stirred by it to the expression of intimate lyric feeling, but because it may touch us with emotion rich enough to satisfy the taste for sentiment yet not so poignant as to grip the heart with pain, and at the same time will enable us to indulge all the wealth of our fancy and the melodies of our verse in telling it once again. In such a field, then, there is admirable schooling for a poet eager for the resources of his art but still too young to have had deep experiences and too sincere to profess them.

Aside from the works of Ovid and Italian poems with which Shakespeare's acquaintance is only a possibility, there had been English experiments of the kind in question, coming to view at just the time of his apprenticeship. Of these the most important are Thomas Lodge's *Metamorphosis of Scylla* and Marlowe's *Hero and Leander.* The former poem treats of the Ovidian story of the sea-god Glaucus and the nymph Scylla, but alters its source by introducing a scene in which the nymph, smitten by Cupid's darts after a long period of coldness, herself woos the now disdainful god with hopeless passion. Incidentally it makes use of the device of the mocking echo which Shakespeare—and many another Elizabethan poet—adopted as an ingenious embellishment of his story. Lodge's poem had been published in 1589. *Hero and Leander,* on the other hand, remained unpublished (and unfinished) until 1598, but there is little doubt that Shakespeare shared in the considerable circulation it must have had in manuscript form. Almost at the opening of this tale is a description of Hero's dress, the sleeves embroidered

> with a grove
> Where Venus in her naked glory strove
> To please the careless and disdainful eyes
> Of proud Adonis that before her lies;

and a little later Adonis is called "rose-cheeked," the epithet which Shakespeare borrowed for his opening lines. These were not the only passages in contemporary poetry which he may have found suggestive for his treatment of the tale of Adonis. Robert Greene, for example, had introduced into his romance of *Perimedes* a song telling how

> In Cyprus sat fair Venus by a fount,
> Wanton Adonis toying on her knee,

and how the boy blushed at her kisses. Spenser, in his elegy of *Astrophel* commemorating the death of Sidney, had adapted the legend of Venus' weeping over the beautiful body of the dead youth, and the flower which sprang from the place where he lay. And it is quite possible that there was already in circulation a poem of Henry Constable's (not published, apparently, until some years after *Venus and Adonis*), so close to Shakespeare's that, whichever was earlier, we may be certain one borrowed from the other:

> Him her eyes still woo,
> Him her tongue still prays,
> He with blushing red
> Hangeth down the head;
>
> Not a kiss can he afford;
> His face is turned away,
> Silence said her nay;
> Still she wooed him for a word.

All this, then, and more which might be added, makes clear the frankly imitative character of "the first heir" of Shakespeare's "invention." Drawing thus, as he and his contemporaries were accustomed to do, from all accessible storehouses, he worked up the story of Venus' love for the beautiful boy to a narrative of nearly twelve hundred lines, in fluent and limpid verse, enriched with every device of decorative phrasing, in which the passion of the queen of passion is portrayed as dispassionately as one could conceive possible. There are lascivious touches, to be sure, characteristic both of the sensualism of youth and of Elizabethan taste; but they remind us of the weaving of such matters into carved friezes, or the tracery upon a silver bowl, having neither the vivid human reality of Marlowe's more earthly creatures in *Hero and Leander* nor that of many rich-blooded lovers whom Shakespeare was later to bring into being. Hence, as Coleridge observed, "though the very subject cannot but detract from the pleasure of a delicate mind, yet never was poem less dangerous on a moral account." Indeed, as we proceed with the encounter, we presently find Adonis breaking into a moral discourse very un-Ovidian and un-Italian, on the difference between love and lust:

>Love comforteth like sunshine after rain,
>But Lust's effect is tempest after sun;
>Love's gentle spring doth always fresh remain,
>Lust's winter comes ere summer half be done;
> Love surfeits not, Lust like a glutton dies;
> Love is all truth, Lust full of forged lies.

(Lines 799—804.)

Strange doctrine, this, for a poem primarily devoted to Venus! It is not introduced, we may be sure, for any consciously ethical end, but only because, in developing Adonis' opposition to Venus, the poet fell naturally into a strain of characteristically English quality; for English taste has always been easily moved, even on the esthetic side, by moral distinctions.

This quality of earnestness is far more noticeable in the second poem, *The Rape of Lucrece*. The story of Lucrece was also found in Ovid,—and, it may be noted, in a work (the *Fasti*) which had not yet been englished; Shakespeare seems also to have known it in the prose account given by Livy. It had been told in English by Chaucer and Gower, and lately by Painter in one of the novels of *The Palace of Pleasure*. It would seem, however, that the only work in his own tongue from which Shakespeare drew important suggestions for his *Lucrece* was Samuel Daniel's *Complaint of Rosamond*, a poem dealing with an entirely different story, that of the mistress of Henry the Second, but containing elements of style, mood, and dramatic psychology which he found happily applicable to the older tale. The subject of Tarquin's lust might easily have been treated in a manner intended to satisfy the baser instincts for which some Elizabethan poetry found ample room; it was handled very vilely, for example, in Heywood's play on the same subject. Not so with Shakespeare. He does not boggle vaguely with the narrative of the crime; on the contrary he presents it with daring vividness; but he interested himself chiefly, it is clear, in the theme of remorse and revenge as lust's followers. Indeed, if one considered only the point of view from which the poem was written, as distinguished from its style, it would be difficult to conceive it as the work of a man only a year older than the author of *Venus and Adonis*. Here we find the wholly serious out-working of that sketch of lust which Adonis had drawn hastily, in his mood of vexatious revolt against passion:

> And then with lank and lean discolour'd cheek,
> With heavy eye, knit brow, and strengthless pace,
> Feeble Desire, all recreant, poor, and meek,
> Like to a bankrupt beggar wails his case.
>
> (Lines 708—11.)

The soul of Tarquin, a defiled or "spotted" princess, is portrayed as the victim of a dreadful conspiracy of the senses, which have defaced her temple and conquered intelligence by brute *will* (here, as often, a synonym of evil desire):

> She says her subjects with foul insurrection
> Have batter'd down her consecrated wall,
> And by their mortal fault brought in subjection
> Her immortality, and made her thrall
> To living death and pain perpetual;
>   Which in her prescience she controlled still,
>   But her foresight could not forestall their will.
>
> (Lines 722—28.)

The soul of Lucrece, on the other hand, though itself undefiled, is so profoundly troubled by the ruin of the body which confines it, that only by escape therefrom can it be comforted; so that at length, when she sheathes a knife "in her harmless breast," it is to "unsheathe" her soul:

> That blow did bail it from the deep unrest
> Of that polluted prison where it breathed.
>
> (Lines 1725—26.)

All this, on the one hand, we may admit, is playing with words in the manner of Elizabethan poetic ingenuity; but it is at the same time a spiritual interpretation of the aftermath of crime.

For the rest, *Lucrece* is developed, like the earlier poem, by the accumulation of detail, valued frankly for its own sake. There is the same almost breathless fluency; one feels, indeed, that this story was written more rapidly than its predecessor; and because the details are less lovely, the more than eighteen hundred lines to which they attain are the more readily admitted to be far too many. In the *Venus* the details were primarily concrete, with an effect, from first to last, as of a long-drawn decorative frieze. In *Lucrece* they are often more abstract, consisting of reflective comment on sorrow, on woman, on opportunity, on the power of time; thus the narrative is weighted heavily, even if our respect for its serious content be increased. In the latter part of the poem Shakespeare introduced (taking a hint from a familiar passage in Virgil) the description of a great painting of the siege of Troy, daringly matching his handiwork with the great classic experiments in presenting one art in terms of another:

> A thousand lamentable objects there,
> In scorn of nature, art gave lifeless life:
> Many a dry drop seem'd a weeping tear,
> Shed for the slaughter'd husband by the wife;
> The red blood reek'd, to show the painter's strife;
>   And dying eyes gleam'd forth their ashy lights,
>   Like dying coals burnt out in tedious nights.
>   (Lines 1373—79.)

In another passage he similarly vied with a succession of poets who had celebrated, in many languages, the invincible ravages of time; and here, conventional as the thought and even the imagery may be, we seem to catch something of the deep Shakespearean harmony which we know from the work of later days:

> Time's glory is to calm contending kings,
> To unmask falsehood and bring truth to light,
> To stamp the seal of time in aged things,
> To wake the morn and sentinel the night,
> To wrong the wronger till he render right,
>   To ruinate proud buildings with thy hours,
>   And smear with dust their glittering golden towers;
>
> To fill with worm-holes stately monuments,
> To feed oblivion with decay of things,
> To blot old books and alter their contents,
> To pluck the quills from ancient ravens' wings.
>   (Lines 939—49.)

It will be seen that in both these poems we have far more of what is Elizabethan than of what is distinctly Shakespeare's. To any reader of them, on their appearance, familiar with earlier poems of the same type, they would have seemed distinctive only in the writer's relatively effective mastery of the verse and the vocabulary of his age; and so they won for him and his work such epithets as "honey-tongued" and "fine-filed phrase." To us, looking back, they show him studying what was to be his supreme art of re-making familiar materials by passing them through his visual and his spiritual imagination. Primarily, the stories of Adonis and of Lucrece present golden fragments of the lore of antiquity, such as the Renaissance was forever gathering up and resetting, like an antiquarian jeweler. But this is not quite all: sometimes Shakespeare introduces elements not from books, but from his own visual memory. It used to be said that Adonis' horse was a great example of this kind,—

> Round-hoof'd, short-jointed, fetlocks shag and long,
> Broad breast, full eye, small head, and nostril wide;
> (Lines 295 ff.)

so spoke Shakespeare the lad from Warwickshire, where horse-flesh was a familiar theme. The research of impertinent scholars, to be sure, has shown that even here the poet probably had his eye upon a book (such, for instance, as Blundevill's standard work on horsemanship). But when Adonis lifts his chin for an unwilling kiss

> Like a dive-dapper peering through a wave,
> Who, being look'd on, ducks as quickly in,
> (Lines 86—87.)

or tells his goddess that

> The owl, night's herald, shrieks; 'tis very late;-
> (Line 531.)

when we see the injured snail who "shrinks backward in his shelly cave with pain," or the spent dogs returning from the hunt,

> Clapping their proud tails to the ground below,
> Shaking their scratch'd ears, bleeding as they go,
> (Lines 923—24.)

we feel pretty certain that the imagery is from the poet's own boyish experience. Sometimes it hints at London scenes instead, as in the unexpected vivid comparison of the night echoes which answer Venus' cries to "shrill-tongu'd tapsters answering every call,"[1]—the same boys that are forever crying "Anon, anon!" in the tavern scenes of *Henry the Fourth*. Of really dramatic touches of this kind there are surprisingly few, for a poet whose chief method was soon to be dramatic. Yet those few show us that Shakespeare is really following the inner action of his characters, even in largely pictorial poetry. Thus Venus, after an outburst of fury against Death, when there comes a momentary hope that Adonis is still alive, makes a cringing apology to the "king of graves": she had but jested, she tells him:

> Now she unweaves the web that she hath wrought;
> Adonis lives, and Death is not to blame;
> It was not she that call'd him all to nought;
> Now she adds honours to his hateful name.
> (Lines 991—94.)

And Lucrece, catching sight of the traitor Sinon in the painting of Troy, tears at him with her nails, comparing him with Tarquin, till sane perception recovers itself; then

> At last she smilingly with this gives o'er;
> "Fool, fool!" quoth she; "his wounds will not be sore."
> (Lines 1567—68.)

[1] Line 849.

But the chief element which we recognize, first to last, as characteristic, is the fundamental one of a sense of the magic powers of *words*. The Elizabethans were all fascinated by the newly discovered art of phrasing; and youth, if characterized by literary taste at all, is always fascinated by the same art, often wholly refusing to perceive, what maturity tries to teach, that words are mere counters, empty of value unless they stand for substantial fact. The youthful Shakespeare, then, was in every way normal in giving himself over, again and again, to irrepressible joy in jugglery with the mere verbal materials of his art. We have seen it at the moment of tragic catastrophe:

> Even here she sheathed in her harmless breast
> A harmful knife, that thence her soul unsheathed.
> (*Lucrece*, 1723—24.)

Death is "king of graves and grave for kings."

> [Love] shall be fickle, false, and full of fraud,
> Bud and be blasted in a breathing while.
> (*V. & A.*, 1141—42.)

> The little birds that tune their morning's joy
> Make her moans mad with their sweet melody.
> (*Lucrece*, 1107—08.)

Yet even in these instances there is more than the mere words; there is identity of word and image, and identity of image with ultimate fact. When these identities are felt to be of more importance than the charm of the words themselves, we rise to the poetic method of maturity; in the *Venus* and *Lucrece* not often, but occasionally, this is anticipated. For instance:

> For sorrow, like a heavy-hanging bell,
> Once set on ringing, with his own weight goes;
> Then little strength rings out the doleful knell;
> *(ibid.,* 1493—95.)

or this:

> Let him have time to live a loathed slave,
> Let him have time a beggar's orts to crave,
> And time to see one that by alms doth live
> Disdain to him disdained scraps to give;
> *(ibid.,* 984—87.)

or—what seems most mature of all—the revelation of the power of monosyllabic intensity:

> Oh, that is gone for which I sought to live,
> And therefore now I need not fear to die.
> *(ibid.,* 1051—52.)

We cannot here consider in detail the minor poems which were attributed to Shakespeare in two or three publications of more of less doubtful authenticity. In the *Passionate Pilgrim* volume of 1599 there are found, besides the two sonnets discussed in the preceding chapter, three or four experimental sonnets on the Adonis theme, the little pastoral ditty beginning "Crabbed age and youth cannot live together," and two or three poems in the six-line stanza of *Venus and Adonis* for the Shakespearean authorship of which neither proof nor disproof can be offered. In 1601 an elegy on two dead lovers, called *The Phœnix and the*

THE POEMS

Turtle, appeared under Shakespeare's name in a little collection appended to Robert Chester's poem entitled *Love's Martyr*. The style of the elegy is unlike any known work of Shakespeare's, in its emphasis on both symmetry of form and metaphysical processes of thought, but again there is no convincing reason for rejecting it. Much more extensive is the poem called *A Lover's Complaint*, in forty-seven stanzas of the form used in *Lucrece*, which the publisher of Shakespeare's Sonnets included in the same volume with them in 1609. This is a minor example of the same type of narrative poetry which we have seen the Elizabethans found so attractive, but differs from those already noticed in not being founded on classic myth and in being set in a pastoral frame. A betrayed and deserted maiden, sitting by a river-side, tells an old herdsman the story of her love and sorrow, and sketches with some skill the character of the beautiful youth that broke her heart. Admittedly the tale is of no great value, and it is marked by some affectations of style—including a considerable number of odd or newly-coined words not found in Shakespeare's known work—which throw doubts on its authenticity. A clever critic, studying these peculiarities, has lately made out a temptingly plausible case for the authorship of George Chapman. On the other hand, the poem exhibits something of the fluency, the sense of values of word and phrase, and the blend of sensuous and psychologic representation of passion, which we have noticed in Shakespeare's early poems, and which no known contemporary (Chapman by no means excepted) could boast in the same degree.

We come now to the Sonnets of 1609. These too are

without authentication, and at certain points diverse authorship has been suspected; but the great number of the one hundred and fifty-four in the collection are universally accepted as Shakespeare's. Unfortunately we know nothing of their date, their order of composition, or to what persons they were originally addressed, so that the result is a kind of single equation with three or four unknown quantities, upon the solution of which conjecture has spent itself in vain. The stationer Thomas Thorpe in some way obtained manuscript copies of the sonnets, of which only two (as we have seen) had previously been published; and he dedicated them to a "Mr. W. H.," whom he called their "only begetter." This cryptic dedication has been almost more discussed than the text of the poems themselves, usually on the assumption that, if we could identify Mr. W. H., we should know what friend of Shakespeare's inspired the sonnets of friendship; though it is also held that the person so complimented may have been only the friend of Thorpe's who obtained the manuscript. The critics who have had cause to become excited on this subject are those who believe they can identify, on other grounds, the person to whom a great part of the sonnets were addressed, and who therefore find the dedication either confirming their theory or raising a difficulty to overcome. But simple honesty must confess that nothing worthy of the name of proof has ever been produced in connection with the whole matter; Thorpe and his dedication may as well, then, be allowed to rest in peace.

In like manner there have been many affirmations respecting the date when the sonnets must have been composed, but the only real grounds for reasoning in that field are the facts that two of them had been published in 1599, that Francis Meres was acquainted with a number of them in 1598, and that many of them show admitted resemblances to the style of Shakespeare's other writings at one or another period. As to these resemblances, opinions differ; but they have certainly been more often observed for the writings of the decade ending with 1600 than for those of the time when the sonnets chanced to be published. In the want, then, of definite evidence to the contrary, it is natural to assume that Shakespeare began to write sonnets at the time when everyone else was doing so,—that is, in the years following the publication of Sidney's and Daniel's in 1591 and 1592,—and continued to write them in diminishing numbers for an indefinite period. Clearly he never undertook to compose a formal sequence, for publication, in the manner of so many of his contemporaries.

This manner of his contemporaries we must make some effort to recall, both for the sake of the likeness to it, and of the divergence from it, which the sonnets of Shakespeare exhibit. In the hands of the Italians, and of their numerous imitators in France, the sonnet had become the typical formal lyric of love (both of man for woman and man for man) according to the conventions of the Renaissance. It combined in a singular way certain advantages more often found in opposition. Thus it was highly conventional and formal, yet recognized as intensely personal; it was lyrical in sweetness and depth of feeling, but often rigorously logical in intellectual structure; it was compact and concentrated, yet could be multiplied in sequences and so developed with much variety and complexity. For rhetorical embellishment, like other forms of Renaissance literature, it made very large use of what is known as the *conceit*. This is a term so important for our purposes that we must pause to give it a moment's separate examination.

A "conceit" used to mean a noticeably clever or pretty idea or turn of thought, and as such was an adornment to any style. But, like other adornments, it came to awaken suspicion through excess of use, and in modern criticism is commonly a term of reproach. If we try to avoid any implication either of merit or fault, we may say that the conceit, as used by Renaissance poets, is a figure of speech, or similar imaginative notion, so elaborated and emphasized as to attract attention to itself rather than to the experience which it represents. It tends, therefore, to substitute a process of *thought*, at least for the moment, for the naturally pure emotional or imaginative processes of poetry. The figure may be verbal in character, elaborating what to begin with is a mere pun or other word-play. It may be (and most commonly is) imaginative, elaborating something of the nature of metaphor or personification, to a point beyond the normal. Or it may be logical, based on some fanciful bit of reasoning, real or paradoxical, appropriate to the poetic theme. On the one hand it may be marked by originality, and bring reproach upon the poet because of the apparent effort to be ingenious; and on the other hand, having once come into fashion, it may be used conventionally to the point of triteness, and lay the lyrist open to the charge of being merely imitative. All these things are exemplified in the sonnets of the Petrarchans, whether in Italy, France, or England, as they wrought out decorative methods for the beautifying of their familiar theme. Love, it may be, was presented in the aspect of an exchange of hearts,— the lover's heart was found in the lady's bosom, and his in hers; or it might appear as a fire which, paradoxically enough, could inflame the heart of the lover while that of the beloved remained cold. Perhaps the chief of all the themes of such lyric conceits was the relation of love, beauty, and fame: beauty was bound to fade, but love, linked with the poetic art, could immortalize it in verse, so that coming generations might sadly realize what they had lost. When one poet had thus immortalized his lady, as Petrarch his Laura, it was open to one of a later day to boast that, though he did not possess the art of the master, yet he had a mistress so much lovelier that it might still be possible to surpass the master's verse. All such imaginings, it will be noticed, when first struck out had the quality of novelty; when repeated and conventionalized, they had primarily the quality of imitative art. This is the perpetual evolution of poetic fashion, as of all fashions, like—for example—that of dress: even the same generation will revel in both newness of form and conformity to that already in vogue.

Now it should be noticed that neither ingenuity nor conventionality is of necessity opposed to sincerity of feeling, as the language of critics often implies. One who feels deeply may seek to enrich his expression either by devoting his art to novelty of form, with all the wealth of invention which he can command, or, on the other hand, by pouring his feeling into molds of the most rigorously conventional sort. A bride of one mood may wish to be married in a motor-car or an airplane, in order to express the newness and greatness of her experience in the most startlingly fresh and daring way; another may wish for all the liturgy and pageantry which a cathedral service can provide, in order to link her experience with all that is best and most beautiful in the past of her race. The bride still otherwise minded, who prefers to be married in a traveling gown and with the simplest ceremony obtainable, because that seems to her most real, has no occasion to suspect either of the other two of less depth of feeling than her own. So also with poetry. For many a lover a sonnet is altogether too much an artifice to express his passion; for another, his passion will be glorified by whatever art can do for it. But the critics forget this, and make the fate of the Renaissance poets hard indeed; for they will now tell us that this sonneteer cannot have felt his passion truly, or he would not have sought out such an ingeniously original form for communicating it, and presently, that this other is equally convicted of insincerity, because his sonnets only say over what dozens of others had said before. Love, happily, laughs at such reasonings; and in the case of a number of the Petrarchan poets, both of Italy and of England, we happen to have evidence of the union of personal feeling and conventional art in their use of the sonnet form. On the other hand, it is quite true that the reader who has become familiar with their modes will be able to make interesting distinctions between the more formal and the more individual elements in their work, without which it might sometimes be very imperfectly understood.

The common form for the celebration of love or friendship, in the age of the sonneteers, was a sequence of many sonnets, not necessarily composed—or demanding to be read—with strict consecutiveness, but centering about the one personal theme, and, in the more artistic compositions, progressing from beginning to end according to some dominating plan. In France and England the sequences were practically all written in praise of ladies, and were entitled, most commonly, from an ideal name given to the object of the poet's affection: Stella, Delia, Diana, Idea, Fidessa,—successors to the Beatrice and Laura of the Italian masters of the art of love. Sidney's sequence, the first and most finished which England produced, was named for both lovers, "Astrophel and Stella"; Thomas Watson's was called, more abstractly, "Tears of Fancy," and Spenser's simply "Amoretti" or "Love-Lyrics"; otherwise the English sonnets, in general, appeared under the single feminine name.

But when we come to Shakespeare's we presently discover that they have not the appearance of a sequence at all. They were published simply as the Sonnets of Shakespeare. They celebrate no lady, or other single subject, under any literary name. They give some evidence of arrangement, but none of continuity from first to last, and exhibit many elements of miscellaneousness. The contents would seem to bear out what the publisher apparently professed, that the collection is made up of all Shakespeare's sonnets on which he could lay his hand. There is therefore no obvious reason for viewing them as having been composed at one time, addressed to one person, or arranged for publication by their author. Many a pretty theory, biographical and otherwise, would have perished at birth (or sooner), if these things had been observed. The arrangement, which we may assume to have been the publisher's, amounts to this: at the beginning of the collection are placed a number of sonnets addressed to a young man, and from that point through the 126th there is no sonnet which could not, conceivably, have been addressed to one of the same sex, though there are many which give no definite indication of that matter, and would doubtless be thought to be addressed to ladies if found elsewhere. At the close, beginning with the 127th, are a number of sonnets addressed to, or concerned with, a woman, together with some of a wholly miscellaneous character. The general process followed by the editor is sufficiently obvious, and the only problem which his work suggests is the question whether he obtained the greater number of the sonnets from a single source, and whether, on this account or for other reasons, he knew that that greater number (by which one means most of those numbered from 1 to 126) were originally written to the same person. On that matter we are not likely to have any great light.

As to continuity, there is none, as has been said, when the collection is viewed in the large, but plenty of evidence that certain of the sonnets are to be read in pairs, trios, and sometimes larger groups. There is also some positive evidence of discontinuity,—a brief sequence occasionally being interrupted by some casual disarrangement, or a recurrence appearing, after the lapse of many pages, of a theme or situation which implies that sonnets composed at the same time have been widely separated in the printed form. On the whole, our inference would be that the poems came into the editor's hands on many independent sheets of manuscript, but with a number of sonnets either grouped on single sheets fastened together for the purpose, —groupings which might originally have been despatched like letters, and have been preserved in the proper connection,—while for the most part he was left to his own resources in determining the order. This is all that a rationally agnostic attitude will permit us to say. On the other hand, it is true that there is a fascinating appearance of possibility, which many readers have chosen to emphasize, that all the sonnets from 1 to 126 (sometimes called "the First Series") came in a single disarranged manuscript from the hands of the man for whom they were written, and that most of the remainder came in another manuscript which had had an equally interesting history.

Clearly there is abundant room here for the conjectures of critics of the biographical school, and they have not failed to fill it. Equally clearly, the case of the sonnets is such as to leave the literary critic free to consider them first of all as poems, proper to be read in whatever order their contents make desirable, and to be interpreted with reference to what we may know of Shakespeare's lyric art rather than what we may guess of his life.

It is highly probable, as has already been hinted, that Shakespeare first studied the art of the English sonnet in the sequences of Sidney and Daniel. The former poet, we may suppose, interested him in the traditional uses of the conceit in sonnet form, and in the possibility of expressing personal feeling in melodies derived from those of Italian verse; at any rate, Sidney had done both these things in a manner rarely surpassed to this day. But Shakespeare found both the mood and the style of Daniel's sonnets rather more consonant with his own. The same seriousness of tone which he had apparently found suggestive in *The Complaint of Rosamond* for his treatment of the story of Lucrece, he also adopted in the sonnet. Sidney's most characteristic work in the *Astrophel and Stella* is playful,—profoundly playful, if one may say so, and with plenty of feeling underneath, but marked especially by the enormously clever use of charming dramatic conceits. Shakespeare never produced a sonnet of this type so good as the best of Sidney's, or, for that matter, so good as Drayton's famous "Since there's no help, come let us kiss and part." On the other hand he easily caught, and excelled, the expression of rich, gloomy moodiness, and of moral earnestness, as practiced by Daniel.

He also followed Daniel in adopting the "English" type of sonnet form, which had seemingly been invented by Surrey as a modification of the Italian type, and which most of the Elizabethans, despite Sidney's influence to the contrary, preferred. This form, consisting of three separately rimed quatrains, plus a final couplet, commonly produces a wholly different effect from that of the more intricately composed lines of the Petrarchans; it is rather more colloquial in tendency, more fluent, more suggestive of spontaneous utterance. On the other hand it rarely produces the exquisite sense of highly wrought perfection, as of an ivory carving, which the best specimens of the Italian type attain. It makes an impression of movement, of thought and feeling in evolution, as distinguished from that of thought and feeling recollected and made permanent "in tranquillity." At its best the three quatrains seem like incoming waves of imagery, each following upon its predecessor and rising a little higher; then there is a pause, when the couplet more quietly sums up or comments on the meaning of the three. Of this the unsurpassed example is Shakespeare's 73rd:

> That time of year thou mayst in me behold
> When yellow leaves, or none, or few, do hang
> Upon those boughs which shake against the cold,
> Bare ruin'd choirs where late the sweet birds sang.
> In me thou see'st the twilight of such day
> As after sunset fadeth in the west,
> Which by and by black night doth take away,
> Death's second self, that seals up all in rest.
> In me thou see'st the glowing of such fire
> As on the ashes of his youth doth lie,
> As the death-bed whereon it must expire,
> Consum'd with that which it was nourish'd by.
>   This thou perceiv'st, which makes thy love more strong,
>   To love that well which thou must leave ere long.

Sometimes, again, as in the equally well beloved 29th sonnet ("When in disgrace with Fortune and men's eyes"), the poet may be thought to combine the advantages of the Italian and the English types, adding to the quatrain structure the characteristic Italian stroke of a pause and change of thought at the end of the eighth line, whereby we pass into a second scene distinct from that of the octave. And many other variants of structure will be noted by the careful reader. Perhaps the weakness of this form of sonnet lies chiefly in the possibility that the three quatrains may sufficiently carry out the poet's thought, and leave the final couplet as a mere appendix or anti-climax. This tendency Shakespeare did not wholly escape; even so fine a sonnet as the 116th (quoted on pp. 138-139) may seem to many readers to be at its best with the closing pair of lines forgotten.

It has been hinted that Shakespeare's sonnets are unlike Sidney's in making relatively little use, of a characteristic sort, of the conceit. This does not mean that he avoided conceits of any of the conventional kinds; but it is not for them that we remember the poems. Many of Sidney's best sonnets are wholly animated by the conceits that gave rise to them: the poet's ingenious imagery or reasoning is the soul of the composition, often forming a kind of miniature narrative or drama, based on some captivating personification or allegory. It follows that in such cases the charm of the sonnet can be represented in a prose paraphrase, which will bring out clearly the significance of the conceit. With Shakespeare none of these things is true. His conceits are commonly the conventional ones; they are not characteristic of the finest of his sonnets; and the charm of his compositions will almost always disappear when the verbal and metrical body which he gave them is taken away. It is also a quality of his sonnet style—as readers familiar with the plays would expect—that he passes swiftly from one image to another, more often letting a number of conceits represent kaleidoscopically the mood of the poem than building it consistently upon a single one. For example take the interesting 125th sonnet, on the subject of love as concerned not with externals but with realities. It opens with the metaphor of an attendant bearing a canopy over some great personage, but passes swiftly to that of a building on an insecure foundation; then we change from the image of tenants who pay too much rent to that of gluttons who give up simple food for too much sweetness,—thence to an oblation of flour unmixed with inferior grades. And the final couplet, instead of recapitulating any of these, takes still another flight into the figure of an "impeached soul." This, to be sure, is an extreme instance; and on the other hand certain of the sonnets are composed on beautifully unified imagery. Of these one of the noblest is the 106th, on the familiar conceit that when ancient writers set forth the praises of beauty, they were really foreseeing, like prophets, the loveliness of the poet's beloved. Every line is here true to the controlling image, whose evolution is completed by the couplet at the close.

> When in the chronicle of wasted time
> I see descriptions of the fairest wights,
> And beauty making beautiful old rime
> In praise of ladies dead and lovely knights,
> Then, in the blazon of sweet beauty's best,
> Of hand, of foot, of lip, of eye, of brow,
> I see their antique pen would have express'd
> Even such a beauty as you master now.
> So all their praises are but prophecies
> Of this our time, all you prefiguring;
> And, for they look'd but with divining eyes,
> They had not skill enough your worth to sing:
> > For we, which now behold these present days,
> > Have eyes to wonder, but lack tongues to praise.

Coming now to look more closely at the real content of the sonnets, we shall doubtless do best to begin with those which are primarily to be viewed as exercises in the conventions of Renaissance lyric, and to pass to those which seem more individual than imitative. It is a natural assumption that in doing so we are also following, on the whole, the order of composition, though special circumstances might make this untrue in a number of cases. At the outset we observe a few sonnets whose only interest lies in the playful ingenuity of the poet's treatment of typical themes: the 128th, which toys with the fingers of a lady playing on the virginal; the 135th and 136th, which pun on the poet's name "Will," in connection with various Elizabethan meanings of the word; the 145th, another bit of word-play, so trifling in content that a number of critics refuse to believe it Shakespeare's; and the 153rd and 154th, parallel exercises in the re-working of a conceit, based on a classic myth, which came down to Shakespeare from an old Greek epigram. All these might have been the work of any of a hundred sonneteers for whom the form was a recreation of the lightest character. Of similar tone and style, but of somewhat more significance for its theme, is Sonnet 20, which sketches lightly, in the Italian manner, the portrait of a youth of such beauty and gentleness that he seems almost a lovely hermaphrodite, a mistake of Nature, whom the poet scarcely knows whether to call master or mistress of his love. For the Italians, as has already been noticed, such a poem would have seemed conventional enough, and Shakespeare treats it not with any suggestion of unnatural affection, but as a jest. Yet the theme was an exotic one, not naturalized in the English sonnet; and the presence in the collection of so many other sonnets having to do with a beautiful youth makes it natural to assume that its origin was personal as well as literary. So, for that matter, may have been the origin of almost any of the sonnets of these conventional types.

Chief, of course, among the themes common to all the sonneteers of the Renaissance, are those of Beauty and Love. We have seen how the two were related in the doctrines of the platonic poets; and, although most of the English love poets made but slight use of platonism, in the stricter sense of the term, save for occasional decorative purposes, they nevertheless maintained its general point of view toward the relationship of love and beauty. They also followed the Italians in being concerned with these themes in both sexes, not alone (though no doubt far more largely) with reference to woman. The word love, among the Elizabethans, was as naturally used between men as between man and woman; conversely, the word friend was common between lovers. When, therefore, in the collection of Shakespeare's sonnets we find the sex of the person addressed to be sometimes ambiguous and disputed, it is a matter of difficulty for his biographers but for literary interpretation normal enough. Call it, then, love or friendship,—the sonnets play on all the conventional aspects and conceits of devotion. In the 22nd the heart of the poet has taken up its abode in the beloved's breast, and he bears with him the other's heart instead. In the 24th the beauty of the beloved has been drawn on his heart, framed in his body, and hung in the shop of his bosom. In the 37th he views all the beauty, wealth, and wit of the beloved as his own by proxy. In the 46th his eye and heart dispute which is the more rightful owner of the beloved's image. In the 53rd he finds all other beauties to be but shadows or imitations (here perhaps is a touch of platonism) of the beauty of the beloved. In the 59th he wishes that the image of the beloved might in some way be transferred to a former age, that he might "see what the old world could say" of such a wonder. In the 68th, conversely, he views the beloved's beauty as an heirloom from better days, preserved by Nature in an age when artifical beauty prevails. In the 91st he finds all the glories which other men boast, according to their various tastes, bettered in "the one general best" of possessing the beloved. In the 99th he condemns the flowers for having stolen their color and perfume from the beloved's cheek and breath. In the 108th he reflects that he can find no new expression for his love, but, as in a liturgy, "hallows" the beloved's name in identical words day after day. In the 114th his eye, by a strange alchemy, changes the forms of even the worst objects presented to it into the "perfect best" of the beloved's image. It would be hazardous to try to say just which of these conceits were borrowed from Shakespeare's predecessors, and which of them he devised, in their present form, anew. But in poetic method they are all conventional.

This, however, is not the whole story. For in some cases the formal ingenuity of the composition is the principal thing, and the personal feeling which it professes to illustrate is rather assumed than felt; whereas in the greater number of the sonnets, even of this group, the poet has so saturated even the conventional imagery with lyric beauty and feeling that an impression of reality of experience dominates the whole. Whether this means more of "sincerity," as we often phrase it, than in the more awkward and merely formal sonnets, one cannot be sure; a lover inexpert in composition is not therefore less a lover. But the *effect* of sincerity is attained when the intellectual effort is submerged in the language of the heart. Nor are the conceits, even in themselves, of equal poetic value: some, like that of the exchange of hearts, or the warfare of eye and heart, are so superficial in character, so far from identifying themselves with any spiritual experience, that one naturally puts them in the same class with the protestations of one's correspondents on St. Valentine's Day. But others faithfully represent a significant reality. For example of this, take the notion that a great love seems to gather into itself all previous affections in the lover's experience, and to fuse in the beloved the identities of dear friends who have been lost awhile: this may be called a conceit, if elaborated formally, but it is a spiritual reality too. Shakespeare knew it as such, and glorified it in the 31st Sonnet:

> Thy bosom is endeared with all hearts
> Which I by lacking have supposed dead:
> And there reigns love and all love's loving parts,
> And all those friends which I thought buried.
> How many a holy and obsequious tear
> Hath dear religious love stolen from mine eye
> As interest of the dead, which now appear
> But things remov'd that hidden in thee lie!
> Thou art the grave where buried love doth live,
> Hung with the trophies of my lovers gone,
> Who all their parts of me to thee did give;
> That due of many now is thine alone.
>   Their images I loved I view in thee,
>   And thou, all they, hast all the all of me.

Over against the sonnets of devotion we must set two or three in what has sometimes been called the "anti-Petrarchan" manner, well known in Italian and French poetry of the sixteenth century. Here the poet, either playfully or satirically, rejects the artifices of the sonneteers of love, though elsewhere abundantly practicing them. The best of the English imitations of this type are found in Drayton's collection, as when he protests dashingly:

>Into these loves, who but for passion looks,
>At this first sight here let him lay them by!

Shakespeare's chief examples are the 21st, satirizing the professional maker of similes, who "every fair with his fair doth rehearse," and the 130th, in which the poet renounces, for his mistress, all claim to the beauties wherewith ladies are conventionally adorned. Going a step further, we come to the sonnets of "vituperation," in which a mistress is not merely refused the expected compliments but actually reviled. This type also had become familiar in Italy and France, and some find it represented in a few of Shakespeare's sonnets, the most disagreeable, on the whole, of any in the Elizabethan collections (see especially the 137th, 138th, the 141st, and the 150th). But these go so much further, in apparent realism and seriousness of tone, than any of the models that have been recalled as parallels, that to most readers they seem to belong not in the conventional but in the more personal class.

The evanescence of beauty is another of the dominant themes of the Renaissance sonnet, which brings it in tune with the elegiac element in the love poetry of every age. That youth should fade, that a lovely face "among the wastes of time must go," is the perpetual tragedy that touches us all, but poets most of all. For reasons of which we know nothing, Shakespeare found this theme particularly appealing. One might say that it gives more of unity to the body of his sonnets than any other, and suggests that a great part of them were written when he felt with special keenness the transiency of the precious things that go with youth. This has been made a means of argument, naturally enough, for one date or another, yet we know that the sense of growing old has little to do with the facts of the calendar. The grim autocracy of Time was a familiar subject of the poets, and Lucrece had devoted many lines to it in Shakespeare's version of her story; but in the Sonnets we have not only this shadowing, inexorable figure of Time, but a constant disposition on the part of the poet to count every wrinkle on his own face and every sign of fading bloom on the faces of his friends. Something, too, of a dramatic struggle intervenes, in which we become conscious of the figures of love and poetry contending against Time, now with less of hope, now with more. In the platonic philosophy this notion of the evanescence of beauty was connected with the interpretation of the reproductive instinct: love seeks propagation in order to perpetuate or renew the beauty of the beloved; and the protestations of lovers, throughout Renaissance literature, had made much of this material. Thus Venus, arguing with the cold Adonis, had echoed the reasoning of many a wooer of the other sex:

> By law of nature thou art bound to breed,
> That thine may live when thou thyself art dead;
> And so, in spite of death, thou dost survive,
> In that thy likeness still is left alive.
>
> (*V. & A.*, 171—4.)

In a series of seventeen sonnets, which stand at the opening of the collection, Shakespeare restudied this theme with more of variety and beauty than any other poet of the age, but in a new application,—not, as commonly, in the appeal of a passionate lover to the object of his desire, but in an appeal to a friend whose beauty the poet cannot endure to see fade without renewal. Doubtless the theme was suggested by an interest in some actual youth of marriageable age, but with what degree of personal feeling each reader must judge for himself.

Another means of defeating Time's designs against beauty was to invoke the powers of poetry, the art supremely capable of eternizing worthy things in fadeless lines. Almost every sonneteer of the age took up this story, finding the subject a means of combining the praises of love with the classical theme of the poet's work as "a monument more lasting than bronze"; and Shakespeare, as with other themes, took it up to give it something like final expression in his 55th and 65th sonnets.

> O fearful meditation! where, alack,
> Shall Time's best jewel from Time's chest lie hid?
> Or what strong hand can hold his swift foot back?
> Or who his spoil of beauty can forbid?

The answer is found in "black ink," in "powerful rhyme":

> 'Gainst death and all-oblivious enmity
> Shall you pace forth; your praise shall still find room
> Even in the eyes of all posterity
> That wear this world out to the ending doom.

The wholly conventional character of this doctrine may well caution us from supposing, as some have done, that Shakespeare was gifted with a noble prescience of his literary immortality, or from inferring, with one distinguished critic, that his sonnets must have seemed to him "more important and valuable than his plays." We know only that, like his masters, he was conscious that in the world of sense

> All passes; art alone
> Enduring stays to us,

and that he gladly devoted the wealth of his own lyric powers to friends whose beauty remains indeed, as he said, enshrined in his verse, though his enemy Time has ironically swept their names into oblivion.

But there is a conflict more important than that of Time with Beauty; it is that of Time with Love. The peril is that Time, in defeating Beauty, may defeat Love also; and poetry can do nothing to forestall this. The platonists had also their answer for this problem: it was that, though love is born of beauty, it properly tends to pass from the beauty of the outer to that of the inner world, and rises eventually to be a thing of the spirit. We have seen, in a former chapter, that Spenser made much of this doctrine; in his sonnets called the Amoretti, written (as many suppose) for his bride, he set forth not only her beauty but "the fair idea" of her "celestial hue." Shakespeare was not a platonist. He seems sometimes to make allusive use of concepts or phrases which the members of that school had contributed to current poetry, but he was not interested in symbolism, nor in transcendental interpretations of common experience. Yet he could not avoid the problem for which no answer save that of the inner life has ever been found. The deepest of his sonnets of love or friendship, then, are those which represent it as an inner experience triumphant over circumstance. In the 29th it triumphs over ill fortune and defeated ambition:

> When, in disgrace with Fortune and men's eyes,
> I all alone beweep my outcast state,
> And trouble deaf heaven with my bootless cries,
> And look upon myself and curse my fate;
> Wishing me like to one more rich in hope,
> Featur'd like him, like him with friends possess'd,
> Desiring this man's art, and that man's scope,
> With what I most enjoy contented least;
> Yet in these thoughts myself almost despising,
> Haply I think on thee: and then my state,
> Like to the lark at break of day arising
> From sullen earth, sings hymns at heaven's gate.
>   For thy sweet love remember'd such wealth brings
>   That then I scorn to change my state with kings.

In the 30th it triumphs over loss and sorrow. In the 123rd it triumphs over the ravages of Time, and again, in the 124th, over the accidents of Time's love or Time's hate. In the 116th all these triumphs are summed up in a solemn affirmation or credo, which might well stand at the close of the series, were the sonnets arranged in topical order.

> Let me not to the marriage of true minds
> Admit impediments. Love is not love
> Which alters when it alteration finds,
> Or bends with the remover to remove.
> O no! it is an ever-fixed mark
> That looks on tempests and is never shaken;

> It is the star to every wandering bark,
> Whose worth's unknown, although his height be taken.
> Love's not Time's fool, though rosy lips and cheeks
> Within his bending sickle's compass come;
> Love alters not with his brief hours and weeks,
> But bears it out even to the edge of doom.
>   If this be error, and upon me proved,
>   I never writ, nor no man ever loved.

Each of the sonnets in this group is, of course, a carefully wrought work of art, with a place in the traditions of the form. But none of them is conspicuously conventional, and their very lack of the common formulæ of the platonists, the Petrarchans, or the rest, seems to bring us to hear in them the authentic lyric voice of Shakespeare.

We have by no means exhausted the themes of the sonnets of love, but must note the remainder more rapidly. A considerable group concerns the subject of love in absence, including those based on familiar conceits already associated with that theme, such as the 27th or the 43rd, with others of deeper and more individual quality, like the beautiful 52nd, in which the time of separation is viewed

> as the wardrobe which the robe doth hide,
> To make some special instant special blest
> By new unfolding his imprison'd pride.

Wholly of this deeper sort are three or four sonnets on love in contemplation of death: the 66th, which enumerates, in Hamlet-like mood, all the ills which make life easy to renounce; the 71st, in which the poet begs to be forgotten, lest "thinking on me then should make you woe"; the 73rd, perhaps supreme in workmanship, which has already been quoted (page 127); and the 74th, wherein the poet's "better part" is promised to remain with his friend, when "the dregs of life" have been lost. Of quite another character are certain sonnets, some twenty in all, which represent love in estrangement. Here the conventional element is almost wholly wanting, and the personal note very strong; in particular, these poems are marked by an extraordinary spirit of self-submission, far exceeding mere forgiveness, despite the fact that in most of them it is implied that the cause of the estrangement lies wholly in the friend addressed. The poet, we are told (as in the 88th), will take sides against himself on behalf of the one he loves; whatever is alleged against him (in the 89th) he will not merely not deny, but will actually bring proof to support it. The sonnet immediately following these is the poetic climax of the group in question,—perhaps the most beautiful lyric of injured love in all literature:

>Then hate me when thou wilt; if ever, now,
>Now, while the world is bent my deeds to cross,
>Join with the spite of Fortune, make me bow,
>And do not drop in for an after-loss;
>Ah, do not, when my heart hath scap'd this sorrow,
>Come in the rearward of a conquer'd woe;
>Give not a windy night a rainy morrow,
>To linger out a purpos'd overthrow.
>If thou wilt leave me, do not leave me last,
>When other petty griefs have done their spite,
>But in the onset come; so shall I taste
>At first the very worst of Fortune's might;
>>And other strains of woe, which now seem woe,
>>Compar'd with loss of thee will not seem so.

Clearly we have now passed very largely out of the field of conventionalism in the sonnets, into that of individual lyric art; and there are several other groups or classes which seem even more conspicuously to represent the personal side of the collection. For example, we find a number of sonnets, related in a puzzling way to those just discussed, which imply fault, infidelity, or ill reputation on the part of the poet,—some of them sad yet relatively light of tone, like the 109th and 112th, others deeply serious, and saved from tragedy only by a note of reconciliation, like the 119th and 120th. Certain other groups resemble these sonnets in being not wholly intelligible without some knowledge of the circumstances that gave rise to them. Such are the sonnets on the dark woman, at once fascinating and repellent, those which apparently involve a story of the theft of the poet's friend by a false mistress, and those which concern a rivalry with one or more other poets in the graces of a patron, as noticed in the preceding chapter. For all these poems, to be sure, interesting parallels have been found. The Italians had written on women whose beauty was unconventional and whose character was unadmirable, on rival poets and fickle patrons, on men who depreciated themselves to honor their friends, and who freely forgave their friends for stealing their sweethearts. Thus, if Shakespeare knew intimately the poetry of his continental predecessors and contemporaries, it is true that he had no need to invent a single theme for his sonnets, even of the less usual kinds. But, aside from the doubtful probability of his having any such intimate knowledge, the sonnets we are now considering present little evidence of imitation and much of direct personal utterance. They are not among the best of the collection; they are not so lucid, so skilfully wrought, or so beautiful, as their author could easily have made them, had he been interested in them primarily as works of art. Their power consists in intensity of feeling and ironic realism, rather than in either intellectual or verbal charm. To most readers, then, they seem to show that a lyric form which Shakespeare originally practiced by way of imitative experiment, and later for the most finished expression of the great themes of poetry, he also came to use, purely for private satisfaction, in comment or correspondence on intimate experiences of himself and his friends.

Many of the sonnets have been omitted altogether from the foregoing survey, and cannot be recalled for consideration here. But there are two, standing quite in isolation from all the themes that have been noticed, that we must not altogether let slip. Each is a moral epigram in sonnet form,—mature, compact, and of powerful expressiveness, —which Shakespeare would seem to have composed in some moment of reflection, quite apart from the sonneteering habit. The 129th is on Lust, and might be viewed as a study akin to the verses on that theme in *The Rape of Lucrece*. It sums up all human experience on the subject, in fourteen lines which sternly say all that could be said in forty or four hundred. It would serve as motto for *Measure for Measure,* or epitaph for Edmund in *King Lear*. The 146th sonnet is an equally serious, but less impersonal and more lyrical, study of the soul imprisoned and starved by a sinful body. Again we are reminded of *Lucrece,* and the scene where Tarquin's soul has been captured and enthralled by the rebel subjects, the senses.

Shakespeare, striking here a note not of the Renaissance but of Christian renunciation and faith, bids his soul rally her powers, starve the rebels that herself may be fed, and so in the end triumph even over Death, whose dominion is of the body:

> Poor soul, the centre of my sinful earth,
> [Lord of] these rebel powers that thee array,[2]
> Why dost thou pine within and suffer dearth,
> Painting thy outward walls so costly gay?
> Why so large cost, having so short a lease,
> Dost thou upon thy fading mansion spend.
> Shall worms, inheritors of this excess,
> Eat up thy charge? Is this thy body's end?
> Then, soul, live thou upon thy servant's loss,
> And let that pine to aggravate thy store;
> Buy terms divine, in selling hours of dross;
> Within be fed, without be rich no more.
>   So shalt thou feed on Death, that feeds on men,
>   And Death once dead, there's no more dying then.

It is evident why it has been possible for critics to write so much of the sonnets of Shakespeare, and to quarrel with one another at every point. They have disputed about the date of composition as a single problem, whereas much may be said for indications of many periods of Shakespeare's development. They have debated whether the sonnets were personal or impersonal, and again have discovered proof on both sides. In some cases they have emphasized the conventional conceits in the sonnets,

[2] Unfortunately the text of this line is corrupt, having been mangled by the printer. The reading here given is suggested by the apparent contrast with "rebel"; some prefer "Thrall to," suggested by "made her thrall" in the corresponding passage in *Lucrece*. Perhaps in place of "array" we should read "warray," make war against. Notice also that "aggravate," in the tenth line, means simply "increase."

until one would suppose there was nothing else to find there; in others the essential originality of the poet has caused the elements of imitative art to be ignored. Even in the realm of appreciation there have been equally divergent views, ranging all the way from George Steevens's declaration that an act of Parliament could not compel readers for the sonnets, and Hallam's, that "it is impossible not to wish that Shakespeare had never written them," to Wordsworth's judgment that "in no part of the writings of this poet is found, in an equal compass, a greater number of exquisite feelings felicitously expressed," and the late George Wyndham's characterization of them as one of the "works of perfect art" in which, as tombs, "artists lay to rest the passions they would fain make immortal." For certain of the sonnets every one of these things is true. If all of them are really Shakespeare's, they show us every stage of development, and every mode of application, of his lyric art. Some are purely, even crudely, imitative of the affectations of the Renaissance. Some are powerfully expressive of individual feeling, but too largely the creation of special circumstances to stand by themselves as lastingly significant poems. But the best (and these no meagre handful, such as one culls from among the numerous commonplaces of the Elizabethan sonnet sequences as a whole) combine, like all great lyrics, personal feeling with content of wide and permanent significance; they challenge the affection of one generation after another, both by beauty of form and truth of thought.

It is also evident that the sonnets take us much farther, in the growth of Shakespeare's poetic powers, than the narrative poems. One thing which we should naturally look for we still fail to find,—any notable development of dramatic method. This is not because the sonnet gives no place for such elements; for both Sidney and Drayton made their sonnets highly dramatic, at times, as some modern poets have done. Shakespeare clearly was not interested in the form from that point of view. But in other respects, whatever their chronology, his sonnets show abundant growth of the important poetic qualities which were only faintly noticeable in the *Venus* and the *Lucrece*. The sense of accurate values both in the images of external experience and the details of inner emotional action; the easy adaptation of phrasing and rhythmic movement to the natural human utterance which the verse is to carry; the mastery of words, wedding their intellectual and sensuous functions so that image, thought, and feeling all spring miraculously at once from what had seemed a common implement of speech;—these things, which we sought out somewhat hesitatingly in the narrative poems, we find on almost every page of the Sonnets.

> Sap check'd with frost, and lusty leaves quite gone,
> Beauty o'ersnowed, and bareness everywhere.

> Then of thy beauty do I question make,
> That thou among the wastes of time must go.

> Rough winds do shake the darling buds of May,
> And summer's lease hath all too short a date.

> Then can I drown an eye, unus'd to flow,
> For precious friends hid in death's dateless night.

>   If thou survive my well-contented day,
>   When that churl Death my bones with dust shall cover.
>
>   Time doth transfix the flourish set on youth,
>   And delves the parallels in beauty's brow.
>
>   O how shall summer's honey breath hold out
>   Against the wrackful siege of battering days?
>
>   Spend'st thou thy fury on some worthless song,
>   Dark'ning thy power to lend base subjects light?
>
>   No longer mourn for me when I am dead
>   Than you shall hear the surly sullen bell.

These are a few of the verses which come to mind at once, aside from many still better beloved in the sonnets already quoted, wherein we find this supreme poetic craftsmanship, neither of the senses nor of the mind alone, which links these poems with the Shakespeare of the plays. The Sonnets are linked with the dramas even more profoundly by the signs of deepened experience. Whole areas of life lay behind the writing of the line

>   With what I most enjoy contented least.

And in the dark tumultuous passion of those few sonnets which we might gladly forget, because they seem too much like private documents of pain, one may discern the subjective form of experiences which Shakespeare transfigured in his objective rendering of tragic evil in the more sombre plays.

CHAPTER IV

THE CHRONICLE-HISTORIES

WHEN Shakespeare began his work for the theatre, the drama of national history was the most popular type upon the English stage. The victory over Spain, with other circumstances noted in an earlier chapter, had roused and united national feeling, especially at the capital, to an extent unapproached since the days of Henry the Fifth, and one can see evidences of a genuine popular passion for recalling England's past and interpreting it in the light of her great present. It has been computed that, for those who found the national lore in books, there were some forty works in print, up to the appearance of the second edition of Holinshed's *Chronicle* in 1586, which treated formally of English history. But the common citizen was more likely to acquire his knowledge in this field from popular tradition in ballad and romance, and, in the period we are now considering, above all from the popular stage. Thomas Nash could write, in 1592, that the subject-matter of drama for the most part "is borrowed out of our English chronicles, wherein our forefathers' valiant acts, that have lain long buried in rusty brass and worm-eaten books, are revived, and they themselves raised from the grave of oblivion."[1]

[1] *Pierce Penilesse,* Works of Nash, ed. McKerrow, 1, 212.

And twenty years later Thomas Heywood, defending his art in his *Apology for Actors,* enlarged on the same theme: "Plays have made the ignorant more apprehensive, taught the unlearned the knowledge of many famous histories, instructed such as cannot read in the discovery of all our English chronicles; and what man have you now of that weak capacity that cannot discourse of any notable thing recorded even from William the Conqueror, nay, from the landing of Brute, until this day?"[2]

The greater number of these chronicle dramas are lost to our view, having, no doubt, made small claim to literary form. Some idea of their numbers may be gained from the fact that Philip Henslowe, a single theatrical manager, recorded in his diary the names of some twenty-five plays on English history, between 1594 and 1600, no one of which has come down to us. It is impossible, therefore to say just what examples of the type Shakespeare had before him during his early years in London, or which plays are likely to have interested him most. The *Famous Victories of Henry the Fifth,* perhaps the earliest of the survivors, was doubtless among them. So, one would suppose, was the brief play of *The Life and Death of Jack Straw,* on the peasants' rebellion of 1381, and *The Troublesome Reign of King John,* which Shakespeare was presently to rewrite for his own company. These were crude performances, giving little suggestion of the nobler dramatic possibilities of the form. But not far from the year 1590 the group of "university wits" who seem to have been Shakespeare's immediate predecessors in developing the union of popular drama and poetry, Marlowe, Greene, and Peele, took up

[2] Shakespeare Society ed., p. 52.

the practice of chronicle drama with very interesting results. Peele produced *Edward the First*, a play naïve enough in structure and style, yet memorable for such heartening patriotic passages as this:

> Illustrious England, ancient seat of kings,
> Whose chivalry hath royalized thy fame,
> That sounding bravely through terrestrial vale,
> Proclaiming conquests, spoils, and victories,
> Rings glorious echoes through the farthest world!
> (I, i, 11—15.)

Greene adapted the form to historical fiction, and wrote the pseudo-historic story of *James the Fourth* of Scotland. Marlowe interested himself in the fall of Edward the Second, and in his play on that subject made the first chronicle-history which can be called at the same time a drama of character. These are works of known authorship; but it is not doubted that the same three writers accomplished more in the same field, of which we have uncertain traces over which the critics have labored with conflicting judgments. To Peele, for example, has been attributed *Edward the Third*, a play so much better than *Edward the First* that some would give a share in it to Shakespeare; and all three of the young dramatists, separately and in collaboration, have been made claimants to the old play which Shakespeare is thought to have revised as the First Part of *Henry the Sixth*. Marlowe, on the other hand, perhaps with some aid from Greene, has the strongest claim to the other two plays dealing with the same reign, which Shakespeare's company took over for revision. These were originally published with the titles *The First Part of the*

Contention of the two Famous Houses of York and Lancaster and *The True Tragedy of Richard Duke of York and the Good King Henry the Sixth.* We may be sure that in all these works Shakespeare found hints of still untried possibilities of the drama in chronicle form.

Now this form, one must realize from first to last, had lesser pretensions to be truly dramatic than the other important types of the age. Existing primarily for instruction's sake, and bound (not absolutely, but in general) to the sequence of facts as they had actually occurred, it implied a very different method of composition from pure comedy or tragedy,—a method which might be called epical first of all. In this respect it is linked with the old dramas dealing with the material of biblical story. Both the writers of the miracle-plays and the writers of chronicle-histories undertook, in the first place, simply to realize the narrative which they found in their source, to present the main sequences of events with some emphasis on their relative importance, and to fill out the details with which the more barren and pragmatic records of the chroniclers failed to satisfy the reader. In so attempting to satisfy the imagination, they pursued precisely the method into which a child, or one who narrates for children, naturally falls. For certain purposes this method, as has just been said, fills in details not provided by history; for others, it omits details in a manner often extraordinarily compressive. Thus in attempting to realize the history of the American Revolution, a child may conceive of a dialogue as taking place between George Washington and George the Third: they discuss the terms of the conflict, with more or less vividness and violence, and in the end the king yields to the general. If dramatized by the child, the story would undergo similar treatment. A battle of some days would resolve itself into a brief and intimate conflict; a treaty which in reality took months to negotiate would be disposed of in the exchange of a dozen words. Yet throughout, notwithstanding this compression, there would be an elaboration and a vivifying of incidents which history itself did not provide. Just so with the early makers of chronicle drama. Even in the days of the highest development of the form, the Elizabethans were content, for the most part, with exceedingly naïve processes whereby great events were brought close to them and made imaginatively impressive.

> Into a thousand parts divide one man,
> And make imaginary puissance,

said Shakespeare of the army of Henry the Fifth; and a moment later he refers to the method of

> jumping o'er times,
> Turning the accomplishment of many years
> Into an hour-glass.

No need to omit from such a drama the representation of a great battle: its essence could be found in a few soldiers, entering from opposite doors, and contending with effective physical realism. A soldier or two on the gallery of the inner stage might seem to be a garrison on a city wall. A king, as in childhood's pictures, would wear a veritable crown; and if he were deposed, he would take it off before men's eyes. The veiled threats and decorous recriminations of diplomatic documents would be translated into angrily shouted utterances, marked by all the frankness and picturesqueness of quarreling schoolboys in the street. These are some of the elements of what one might call the kindergarten method of depicting the course of history, characteristic of the chronicle drama which Shakespeare inherited.

Before going directly to his work, we should notice one more preliminary matter,—the relation of primitive structure to primitive characterization, in this chronicle type. The structure, as we have seen, is likely to be crude because it is based primarily on the mere succession of events, not on the causal relations which properly form a plot. The events of a reign, or even of a war, do not of themselves furnish matter for true drama, and the earlier writers of chronicle-plays made little effort to select and arrange them for artistic ends. The characterization, too, is likely to be crude because based primarily on types,—on the notion of a tyrant, a weakling, a patriot, a brave soldier, a coward; just as, for children, a character must take on the aspect of absolute goodness or badness. The two things are not, of course, connected by any inevitable law: it is possible to have a drama adequate in structure, but with characters of the merely typical sort, or one with highly individualized characters and little or no plot. But there is a tendency, especially in the historical drama, to find the two faults combined; and the correction of the one was intimately related to the correction of the other. That is, if the writer undertook to make his characters react upon one another like real people, instead of merely exchanging the commonplace utterances of their types, he was also likely to inquire how far the action of his play could be shown to be due to those reactions, as distinguished from the mere mysterious succession of incidents attributable to Providence or Fortune. The result would be a soundly plotted and effectively developed play. When Marlowe, studying the events of the reign of Edward the Second, saw the possibility of interpreting the king's fall as due in good part to certain elements of his character, something like a unified scheme of dramatic causation loomed in his mind. The resulting play does not, to be sure, possess a powerful plot, nor do its persons at all attain the rich characterization which we associate with Shakespeare. Yet Shakespeare probably found in it, as has already been hinted, the first notable example of the method which he was to develop in the dramatic interpretation of history. He also found in it a striking proof that a chronicle drama might become a true tragedy,—not merely the epic pageant of great personages in action, but the presentation of a fall from greatness to a doom which inspired pity and terror in the spectator.

But in talking of *Edward the Second* we are probably going beyond the date when Shakespeare had already begun his work in historical drama. His first opportunity to study Marlowe in this type was more likely found in the two plays devoted to the wars of York and Lancaster and the defeat and murder of Henry the Sixth; and his earliest dramatic writing may perhaps be discovered in the additions which he made to those plays in bringing them to the form which we know as the Second and Third Parts of *Henry the Sixth*. The evidence bearing on the precise facts of this revision is uncertain, and that concerning the revision of the old play which became the "First Part" is still more so, because no copy of it is extant. Because of certain passages in the First Part which are most readily interpreted as having been made for the purpose of leading up to already familiar scenes in the other parts, and for additional reasons which cannot be taken up here, it may well be supposed that Shakespeare's work in the Second and Third parts is earlier than that in the First;—in other words, that his company obtained their rights in the play dealing with the earlier portion of the reign, after they had already arranged for the revision of the plays dealing with its close. Some would even put Shakespeare's First Part as late as 1599. All this only adds to the difficulty of studying the development of his art in the chronicle form. But the important thing, on which there is substantial agreement, is that in all three parts of *Henry the Sixth* as we have them among Shakespeare's works, there is only his revision of other men's work, with certain additions original with him. These additions may amount to some seven or eight hundred lines out of the nearly 2700 of the First Part, though few critics would find so much of Shakespeare's there. In the Second and Third Parts they may rise to a proportion of between a third and a half of the whole, and seem to be accompanied by a thorough rewriting of a good part of the rest. That is, in the First Part we believe that we find Shakespeare's own verse in only a few distinctive scenes, whereas in the other two plays it constitutes the pervasive medium of the composition.

The old lost play which was eventually made over into the opening member of the trilogy may be supposed to have had for its main theme the wars in France, with the bril-

THE CHRONICLE-HISTORIES 155

liant exploits of Lord Talbot and the sensational career and capture of the Maid of Orleans. Perhaps, then, it was not concerned with the rise of the Wars of the Roses and the disintegration of Henry's sovereignty. At any rate, it is in the scenes which Shakespeare is thought to have added that the theme of the roses of York and Lancaster is introduced;[3] and if we include with them the latter portion of the first scene of Act IV, we may find in it a clue to his purpose in linking this play with the other two,—even if not (what some contend) a clue to his dominating idea in the whole group of chronicle dramas. This is in King Henry's speech of reconciliation:

> What infamy will there arise
> When foreign princes shall be certified
> That for a toy, a thing of no regard,
> King Henry's peers and chief nobility
> Destroy'd themselves, and lost the realm of France!
> (Lines 143—47.)

And again in Exeter's concluding words:

> No simple man that sees
> This jarring discord of nobility,
> This shouldering of each other in the court,
> This factious bandying of other favorites,
> But that it doth presage some ill event.
> (Lines 187—91.)

[3] The scenes most commonly ascribed to Shakespeare are II, iv and v; IV, ii-vii; and V, iii, line 45 to the end. (Those in Act IV, however, concerning the death of Talbot, are to be viewed as a revision of matter in the original version rather than as new additions.) We may plausibly include also among Shakespeare's contributions, in accordance with the view of his purpose above indicated, the closing lines of Act III (iv, 28-45), the latter part of IV, i (78-194), and the final scene (V, v), which seems certainly to have been added to connect the play with the second member of the trilogy. One is tempted also to attribute to Shakespeare the splendid verse of the opening speeches of Act III.

In accordance with this note, the death of Talbot, to which the remainder of the act is devoted, is represented to be directly due to the "jarring discord of nobility"; whereas the original version may very likely, since no such explanation is suggested in the chronicle, have shown the catastrophe merely as natural to the fortunes of war. In other words, there is some reason—admittedly inconclusive —to believe that Shakespeare reworked the stirring but isolated story of the wars in France so that it should form a more or less logical introduction to the plays which portrayed the civil wars as the characteristic features of the reign of a hopelessly ineffective king. That he did not do away with the crudeness of many of the scenes, and excise the outrageous caricature of the Maid of Orleans, is a vain regret which no modern reader escapes.

The other two plays from which the trilogy was drawn, and which for brevity's sake may be called *The Contention* and *The True Tragedy,* formed what amounts to a single composition, with unity of a certain sort, and were actually published, in one of the quartos, with a single title, *The Whole Contention.* The work opens with the conclusion of the treaty of peace and marriage which Suffolk, in the closing scene of Shakespeare's First Part, had been despatched to France to bring about, and it proceeds, through all manner of personal dissension and civil war, to the defeat of the King and Queen by the Yorkists, the murder of the former by Richard of Gloucester, and the accession of Edward the Fourth. Its main theme is the conflict of York and Lancaster, and the frankly didactic purpose of the earlier type of chronicle-history is well represented by such a passage as that in which the Duke of York explains his claim to the throne. Shakespeare left the lines practically unchanged:

> Edward the Third, my lords, had seven sons:
> The first, Edward the Black Prince, Prince of Wales;
> The second, William of Hatfield; and the third
> Lionel Duke of Clarence; next to whom
> Was John of Gaunt, the Duke of Lancaster;
> The fifth was Edmund Langley, Duke of York;
> The sixth was Thomas of Woodstock, Duke of Gloucester;
> William of Windsor was the seventh and last. . . .
> The third son, Duke of Clarence, from whose line
> I claim the crown, had issue, Philippe a daughter,
> Who married Edmund Mortimer, Earl of March;
> Edmund had issue, Roger Earl of March;
> Roger had issue, Edmund, Anne, and Eleanor. . . .
>   Anne,
> My mother, being heir unto the crown,
> Married Richard Earl of Cambridge, who was son
> To Edmund Langley, Edward the Third's fifth son.
> By her I claim the kingdom.
>   (2 *Henry VI, II, ii*, 10—47.)

Whether poetry does anything to better history, in such pedestrian lines as these, the modern reader may well doubt; but it is important to realize how representative they are of the humbler sort of process by which the chronicle was translated into verse.

Another highly typical element of the dual play is found in the broadly comic scenes which interrupt the serious course of history. At one point an old story of a beggar who professed to have been miraculously cured of blindness is introduced on the bare excuse of providing a bit of repartee to the disadvantage of Suffolk; at another, a trifling account, found in the chronicle, of a trial of arms between a master armorer and his servant is made into an effective farcial interlude with even less excuse. Of somewhat more serious purport, though even more humorous in detail, are the scenes depicting the Cade rebellion, wherein we seem to anticipate Shakespeare's later and more familiar sketches of the stupidity and violence of English mobs. "Thou has most traitorously erected a grammar school," says Cade, "to infect the youth of the realm, and it will be said to thy face that thou keepest men in thy house that daily reads of books with red letters, and talks of a noun and a verb, and such abominable words as no Christian ear is able to endure it. And besides all that, thou hast appointed certain justices of peace in every shire to hang honest men that steal for their living." One does not easily attribute scenes of this tone to Marlowe. Whoever wrote them, Shakespeare was content to take them over with little or no change; indeed they are so much of his own manner that it has been suspected that we have in them pieces of his own composition which in some way got into the published text of the old play.

As this suspicion implies, the problem of identifying Shakespeare's own work in the Second and Third Parts of *Henry the Sixth* is no less difficult, though for very different reasons, than in the case of the First Part. We have the older plays, but no one supposes that we have them in the precise form which Shakespeare used; just what he did, then, remains conjectural. In general, as we have seen, he appears to have rewritten the great part of his material, reducing it to his own fluent and—at this period—sometimes over-fanciful style. Thus his additions, where we can discern them, occasionally add to the beauty but detract from the directness or dramatic consistency of the text. At the close of the *True Tragedy*, the indomitable Queen Margaret, rallying her supporters for the final hopeless test, addresses them in a swift speech of less than a dozen lines. In Shakespeare's version (Third Part, V, iv), this is expanded to some thirty-five lines, forming, like many of the speeches in his early plays, a kind of lyric interlude, an almost operatic *aria*, only to be conceived of as indulging the fancy and the sense of beauty while the action halts. The element of characterization Shakespeare seems to have left pretty much as he found it. King Henry, however, who in the old versions is presented as a typically pious, kindly, and inefficient man (according to the chronicle), takes on something of a new richness and reflective dignity. Thus Shakespeare increased the king's soliloquy on the battle-field (Third Part, II, v) from a dozen lines to more than fifty, introducing a lovely lyric passage on the happy life of the countryman, over whom time passes with such kindly monotony:

> So many days my ewes have been with young;
> So many weeks ere the poor fools will ean;
> So many years ere I shall shear the fleece:
> So minutes, hours, days, months, and years,
> Pass'd over to the end they were created,
> Would bring white hairs unto a quiet grave.

Here one feels keenly the touch of magic which the lyric reflections of King Richard the Second were later to display more effectively.

In *Richard the Third* we come to the first of the historical plays which Shakespeare seems to have composed for himself, directly from the chronicle. The theme was far from being a new one, and the Shakespearean version of it is so closely connected with the plays on the reign of Henry the Sixth that some have supposed there was a sequel to the *True Tragedy* which was rewritten as that was. If so, it has been lost; and an actually extant play, called *The True Tragedy of Richard the Third,* Shakespeare made little use of. His play on Richard, however, seems actually more Marlovian than those which he made over from Marlowe's supposed work. The Marlowe that we think of when we call a manner "Marlovian" is not that of the maturer dramatist of *Edward the Second,* but of the writer of *Tamburlaine* and *The Jew of Malta,* who created characters by broad unshaded strokes of black and white (especially black),—incarnate forces rather than mixed human creatures, who boldly declared their purpose to carry out their tremendous will to the end desired, defying the heavens and mankind. The reality and the fascination of such persons were keenly felt by the Elizabethans, and not only in the persons of romance but in those of history, like Machiavelli, as we saw in a former chapter, and the crook-backed Richard of Gloucester. In the third of the old plays on the reign of Henry the Sixth, Marlowe seems to have sketched in the character of Richard, in full accordance with tradition, so that Shakespeare had only to take it over ready-made for the story of the brief reign of that wickedest of kings. Thus, in the third act of the *True Tragedy* is a soliloquy (revised by Shakespeare at the close of the second scene of Act III in the Third Part of

Henry the Sixth) in which the villain thus amply describes himself:

> Why, love did scorn me in my mother's womb;
> And, for I should not deal in her affairs,
> She did corrupt frail nature in the flesh,
> And plac'd an envious mountain on my back,
> Where sits deformity to mock my body,
> To dry mine arm up like a wither'd shrimp,
> To make my legs of an unequal size.
> And am I then a man to be belov'd?
> Easier for me to compass twenty crowns.
> Tut! I can smile,—and murder when I smile;
> I cry ''Content'' to that that grieves me most;
> I can add colors to the chameleon,
> And for a need change shapes with Proteus,
> And set the aspiring Catiline to school.

From this it is not even a step to the opening of Shakespeare's *Richard the Third*.

It was also characteristic of Marlowe's early work that such a character should be the protagonist of a tragedy which ended with the crash of his fall. The most primitive of tragic types, always dear to the child and to adults who preserve the child's point of view, is that concerned with the bad man who comes to a bad end, and the story of Richard of Gloucester was, of all the materials in the English chronicles, that best adapted to form such a story. The old play which introduced Richard's character was called, as we have seen, a tragedy, but it was the tragedy of the Duke of York and Henry the Sixth,—that is, the story of their tragic conflict,—and, ranging through the whole scope of that conflict, had neither unity of hero nor unity of action. Looked at superficially, the play of *Rich-*

ard the Third is the continuing chronicle-history dealing with the reign of Edward the Fourth, the deposition and murder of Edward the Fifth, and the reign of Richard. It begins with Henry the Sixth still unburied, and ends with the accession of Henry the Seventh. This is its aspect as chronicle-history. But in reality it is a tragedy, and the tragedy of a person. Historical events are compressed so rigorously as to give the reader the impression that Edward the Fourth died very soon after his accession, and that the rebellion against Richard followed immediately after his. One single thread of story, centered in one tremendous personality, is swiftly followed, with little or nothing of the usual method of digression for the mere sake of teaching history. Hence, despite the conventionality and crudeness of many of the elements in the play, it remains the only one of Shakespeare's chronicle-histories which has held the stage on its merits as an acting drama.

Of the old-time conventions which survive in *Richard the Third,* despite this impression of progress in structural art, the chief are the conception of the hero's character— its self-admitted, deliberate villainy—and the series of old-fashioned Senecan or Marlovian soliloquies in which it is set forth. Most of the soliloquies are in the first act, opening with the one which announces "I am determined to be a villain," and concluding with that wherein Richard desscribes his special art of hypocrisy :

> And thus I clothe my naked villainy
> With odd old ends stolen forth of Holy Writ,
> And seem a saint, when most I play the devil.
>
> (I, iii, 336—38.)

THE CHRONICLE-HISTORIES 163

By this time we are fully prepared to understand his conduct at every point that follows. Equally traditional and unrealistic are a number of scenes in which the emotional situation is expressed in a formally symmetrical fashion, with semi-lyrical utterance, as in an ancient Greek tragedy or a modern grand opera. Thus we have the extraordinary wailing quartet of Queen Elizabeth, the Duchess of York, and the two children of Clarence, in the second scene of Act II, and the long alternating dialogue of Richard and Elizabeth (much of it in the stichomythic or one-line speeches dear to the Greeks) in the fourth scene of Act IV. Somewhat similar, in the serious grotesqueness of its symmetry, is the great ghost scene at the close. Here, by setting the stage with the tent of Gloucester on one side and that of Richmond on the other, Shakespeare obtained just such an effect as the maker of a modern photo-play when he "cuts in" alternating views of two persons who are to be held simultaneously in the spectator's mind, though actually at some distance from each other. Thus the avenging ghosts alternately curse the sleeping Gloucester and bless the sleeping Richmond,—a stunning artifice, suggested solely, it would seem, by the chronicler's statement that "the fame went that [Richard] had the same night a dreadful and terrible dream," seeing "diverse images like terrible devils, which pulled and haled him."[4] This is a notable instance, then, of the conventional practice of filling in, for the chronicle drama, the outline given by history. On the other hand, for the method of condensing into a brief dramatic crisis what was historically much more intricate and deliberate, we find in this

[4] Boswell-Stone: *Shakespere's Holinshed*, p. 413.

same play the most extraordinary instance in Shakespeare: namely, the scene in which he daringly represents the fact of the marriage of Gloucester to the Lady Anne by showing the duke wooing her in the street beside the coffin of the king he had slain.[5] Gloucester's own comment,

> Was ever woman in this humour woo'd?
> Was ever woman in this humour won?

has been echoed by every reader of the play. The absurdity of the scene, from the standpoint of realism, is not precisely forgotten, but triumphed over through the intensity of the characterization of Richard's mind and will.

The statement just made may enable us to answer the question as to what, aside from its compact and impressive structure as tragedy, Shakespeare contributed to the rather primitive materials which we have found him using. Not much, this time, in the way of poetry. The verse of *Richard the Third*, whether truly dramatic or more lyric in character, is almost always effective for the poet's purpose, —often brilliantly so,—but errs again on the side of fluency, and shows little of typical Shakespearean beauty by way of compensation. Perhaps the most characteristic bit of style in the whole drama is not in verse at all, but prose,—the grim reflections on conscience uttered by one of the murderers of the Duke of Clarence. "It fills a man full of obstacles......It beggars any man that keeps it. It is turned out of towns and cities for a dangerous thing."[6] But Shakespeare's real contribution to *Richard the Third*

[5] I, ii, 49-225.
[6] I, iv, 142-46.

was Richard himself. This is a paradox, since we have seen that the character was a highly conventional one, and that Shakespeare did not try to make it otherwise. Richard remains an incarnate force rather than a human personality; but he is endowed not merely with the "will to power" which tradition prescribed for him, but also with a mind so agile, so intense, so almost beautiful in its malignant perfection, that one finds him actually appealing to both the esthetic sense and the sympathy,—as a beautiful python, or a beautiful machine-gun, might appeal. This lifts him above the convention of his type, and makes him seem real rather than made to order. For the same reason we think of him as less a descendant of the Jew of Malta than a forerunner of Iago.

A systematic study of the types of Shakespeare's chronicle plays is interrupted by *The Life and Death of King John*, which probably belongs at this point, though its date is quite uncertain. The play is not highly typical of anything, and must be passed over very briefly. It was a rewriting, by Shakespeare, of an anonymous play (published in two parts in 1591), *The Troublesome Reign of King John*, and he did not concern himself to correct the historical aberrations of his source by any independent use of the chronicles; hence it is the only one of the Shakespearean histories which is untrustworthy not merely in detail but in the large. The original writer made King John something of a hero of Protestantism, because of his quarrel with the Pope, but this theme seems not to have appealed to Shakespeare, and he found nothing which can be said to take its place. The events of the drama—the wars in France, the intrigues of the papal legate, the treaties made and broken—lead to no outstanding dramatic significance, and at the end the king dies as most men die, casually, without any such reason as makes a tragic plot. In reading the play, therefore, we seem to have reverted to a quite primitive sort of chronicle drama, less unified in effect even than the greater portion of *Henry the Sixth*. At the same time the poetic style is more mature, more characteristically Shakespearean, than that of *Richard the Third*. Of fresh characterization Shakespeare contributed very little, at least for any of the persons of historic importance, but he interested himself in Philip Faulconbridge, the legendary bastard son of Richard Cœur-de-Lion, and made his figure one that stands out from the rest like a piece of relief work on a background of tapestry,—a kind of incarnation, as some have thought, of the stalwart folk of England. He also heightened the pathos of young Prince Arthur, touched the maternal love of Constance with a bit of his magic, and occasionally wrote in a line or two which herald the poetry of greater days to come,—

> Life is as tedious as a twice-told tale
> Vexing the dull ear of a drowsy man;
> (III, iv, 108—9.)

or

> I am the cygnet to this pale faint swan
> Who chants a doleful hymn to his own death.
> (V, vii, 21—22.)

Otherwise, one feels that the play can have interested him but little.

For Shakespeare's real interest in the chronicle drama

must have come, about this time, to center itself in the story of the rise of the House of Lancaster, whose fall he had studied in his work on the reign of Henry the Sixth. One may conjecture that he pictured to himself the possibilities of an entire series of plays, beginning with the deposition of Richard the Second, including what he had already written on the coming of the house of Tudor to the throne, and perhaps continuing the story to some point discreetly chosen in the reign of Henry the Eighth. What is certain is that he found his supreme opportunity for chronicle drama in the events of the brief period from 1398 to 1415, making of them four great plays which together cover rather less time than he had traversed in *Richard the Third* alone.

The first of these plays was called *The Tragedy of Richard the Second*, a title which reminds us that Shakespeare once more found the materials of the chronicle falling into tragic form. The king with whose reign he was now concerned was, in fact, the second king of England to fall by deposition, followed by murder, and his fate invited some such dramatic study as Marlowe had given to the parallel case of Edward the Second. Here was tragedy —no doubt of that; but how different from the tragedy of Richard the Third! This king was not a villain; tradition had treated him kindly, on the whole, and viewed him as one led astray rather than evil in purpose. "He was seemly of shape and favour," wrote Holinshed, "and of nature good enough, if the wickedness and naughty demeanor of such as were about him had not altered it." But the chronicler goes on to note inexorably Richard's decadence into vice and tyranny. Shakespeare clearly interested himself in the question: what manner of man, young, attractive, well-meaning, who began his reign under happy auspices and with a loyal body of subjects, could ruin his opportunities, destroy his people's devotion, and throw away his crown? To this there are two or three possible answers of a very obvious kind, but he chose none of them. Instead, he conceived a character, without the aid of any sources of which we have knowledge, of an original and convincingly lifelike sort,—one who makes the tragedy of his fall a more complex and spiritual thing than any other historical play of the age. In other words, Shakespeare was here following, in some sense, the method of Marlowe in *Edward the Second*, as in *Richard the Third* he had been following the Marlowe of the plays of violence. King Edward, in Marlowe's tragedy, had been characterized with some independence; he was not a typical tyrant, nor were his fortunes the result of the mere play of force. Of Shakespeare's Richard the Second this is doubly true; indeed the earlier king fades into a comparatively colorless portrait by comparison. Richard is realized as a person in the sense which leads us constantly to speak of the characters of the later plays as acquaintances whom we should know anywhere, detached from their costume, background, or incidental action, and which is not equally true of any character in any earlier Elizabethan play. Indeed, on what may be called its inner side this drama reaches the highest point that the chronicle type attained. That is, it is less a story of external forces,—though ostensibly concerned with the usual themes of battle, murder, and sudden death,—and more a story of the inner life, than any of its fellows. At the same time in the matter of dramatic structure it shows a retrogression (like *King John*) from the standards of *Richard the Third*, following the looser methods of the old chronicle drama, and has never interested the people of the theatre as an effective acting play.

It is no part of our duty in this book to make an intensive study of the individual characters in the plays under review, but the importance of this one, taken in its chronological position in Shakespeare's work, makes it desirable to pause over it for a moment. Shakespeare's Richard is represented as a man who lives largely in the region of the imagination, and cannot—or will not—cope with realities. One may call him *par excellence* a poet. He utters himself more beautifully than any earlier character of the histories (though in Shakespeare's chronology Romeo and Juliet may have preceded him), with a blend of reflective and imaginative charm that look back to what we saw Shakespeare adding to the portrait of Henry the Sixth, and forward to Hamlet. Returning to his kingdom from the Irish campaign, when a dangerous rebellion is brewing, he salutes his England

> As a long-parted mother with her child
> Plays fondly with her tears and smiles in meeting,
>   (III, ii, 8—9.)

and believes that the very stones will take part with their sovereign against his enemies. When he is informed that Bolingbroke is strong in both substance and friends, he answers the warning by a simile, comparing the presence of the king with that of the sun that scatters darkness and crime when "he fires the proud top of the eastern pines."

When he hears of twenty thousand troops that have deserted him, he asks,

> Is not the king's name twenty thousand names?
> (Line 85.)

And when at last the gravity of his state really penetrates his imagination, he is still consoled by poetic emotion; he finds a "sweet way" to despair, and, at the moment when he should be rallying all his energies to the issue, cries:

> For God's sake, let us sit upon the ground
> And tell sad stories of the death of kings!
> (Lines 155—6.)

He is not only poet but dramatic poet; he has the keenest perception of the ironies of his misfortune, and is fain to dramatize them in brilliant little symbolic scenes. Realizing that his kingship is slipping away, he bids his courtiers put on their hats:

> Cover your heads, and mock not flesh and blood
> With solemn reverence.
> (Lines 171—2.)

At the ceremony of deposition he enjoys the dramatic effectiveness of the act of handing the crown to Bolingbroke, and goes on to weave a simile about it. His formal address of abdication (beginning "Now mark me how I will undo myself") is one of the great speeches of Shakespeare, worthy to stand beside the work of his golden age in the beauty and flexibility with which the tragic irony of the moment is expressed. The triumphant Bolingbroke is actually made to seem mean and unenviable, in contrast with the mastery of thought and feeling which his victim displays:

> God pardon all oaths that are broke to me!
> God keep all vows unbroke that swear to thee!
> Make me, that nothing have, with nothing griev'd,
> And thou with all pleas'd, that hast all achiev'd!
> (IV, i, 214—17.)

And the little drama comes to its climax, as a good drama should, with a stunning bit of action: Richard grasps a mirror in which he may gaze upon the once royal features, cries (echoing a famous line of Marlowe's *Faustus*),

> Was this the face that fac'd so many follies,
> And was at last out-fac'd by Bolingbroke?
> (Lines 285—86.)

and dashes the glass upon the ground. After this great fourth act the last one is an anti-climax; the murder of Richard seems so much less important than his deposition, that the thoughtful reader has but little interest in the scene which for the popular audience was the necessary catastrophe and conclusion.

Against this figure, from beginning to end, Shakespeare set that of Henry Bolingbroke, the practical master of affairs, who never allowed considerations of sentiment to intervene in his steady progress toward the throne. He watches all Richard's amateur dramatics with cold serenity, sure of the situation when the talking is over. When the mirror has been broken, and the tragic hero concludes,

> Mark, silent king, the moral of this sport,—
> How soon my sorrow hath destroy'd my face,

Bolingbroke replies, like one for whom this toying with words has no meaning,

> The shadow of your sorrow hath destroy'd
> The shadow of your face.
>
> (Lines 292—93.)

This is typical of his pragmatic attitude throughout the play. Perhaps Shakespeare had concluded that the triumph of the Lancastrian house was due to this grasp on realities. But if so, he intimates that such success was not without its ill omens. Henry, though no bloody villain of the old school, has nevertheless made his way to the throne through blood, and has his nemesis to follow him. The drama ends, then, not with a note of triumph, but with his remorseful purpose to go on a pilgrimage to wash the blood from his hand. If it was this play, as is believed, that the Essex conspirators arranged to have performed on their behalf, Shakespeare may well have been amused at their supposing that it was propaganda for rebellion; he may also have laughed profoundly when he discovered that the first printer of *Richard the Second* did not dare, or was not allowed, to include the great deposition scene in the quarto.

The enormous advance in art represented by the aspects of this play which we have been considering is all the more striking by contrast with older conventional elements which appear side by side with them throughout. Thus in contrast with the highly realized characters of Richard and Henry there are others of purely formal and typical character,—most notably, the queen. Besides the matter of characterization, there is a corresponding difference between the traditional and the maturer organic style. Mowbray, for example, in the first scene of the play, talks partly in old-fashioned epigrammatic couplets, which (like those of French classic tragedy) might easily be made effective on the lips of an impressive speaker, but are very far from producing the effect of actual human utterance:

> A jewel in a ten times barr'd up chest
> Is a bold spirit in a loyal breast.
> Mine honour is my life; both grow in one,
> Take honour from me, and my life is done.
>
> (I, i, 180—83.)

Compare this with the manner of Richard's most characteristic verse style (this, for instance:

> In winter's tedious nights sit by the fire
> With good old folks, and let them tell thee tales
> Of woeful ages long ago betid;
> And ere thou bid good night, to quit their griefs,
> Tell thou the lamentable tale of me),
>
> (V, i, 40—44.)

and one sees what a distance Shakespeare had gone in developing the capacity of verse to be *both* poetry and speech at once. On the other hand, at the moment of Richard's death—a scene in which Shakespeare may have had relatively little interest—the old-fashioned style is resumed. Perhaps it is appropriate enough; this is no time for musical reflective utterance. The king is at last fighting for his life with a burst of truly royal assertiveness, and is a traditional hero in a stage catastrophe; so Shakespeare permits him to perish, after all his great poetry, with some old-time ranting couplets on his lips that might have been written by any call-boy in the theatre. Besides the older formal and the newer conversational verse, we should also notice a few fine examples of the lyric interludes or arias which Shakespeare, as has already appeared, permitted himself to bring into his earlier plays. Of these the noblest is that put into the mouth of the dying John of Gaunt, in a scene wholly unsuggested by the chronicles, wherein the spirit of English loyalty is contrasted with the self-seeking of a decadent reign. Now, says the old duke, men dare to shame and spoil

> This royal throne of kings, this scepter'd isle,
> This earth of majesty, this seat of Mars,
> This other Eden, demi-paradise,
> This fortress built by Nature for herself
> Against infection and the hand of war,
> This happy breed of men, this little world,
> This precious stone set in the silver sea, . . .
> This blessed plot, this earth, this realm, this England!
> (II, i, 40—50.)

The play of *Henry the Fourth* is of a wholly different character. The reign of Henry did not present the outlines of a tragedy; on the other hand, Shakespeare's dramatic art was now at a point where he could not consider the making of a mere chronicle-history. Moreover, he had already sketched the character of Henry the Fourth, and it was not one to be especially inviting for further study. What, then, should he do with the story of the reign? The answer is twofold,—on the side of incident and on that of personality. The title-pages of the quarto editions of Elizabethan plays often aid us in conjecturing what the contents of the plays meant to their contemporaries, and those of the two parts of Shakespeare's next chronicle-history read as follows: "The History of Henry the Fourth, with the Battle at Shrewsbury, between the King and Lord Henry Percy, surnamed Henry Hotspur of the North; with the humorous conceits of Sir John Falstaff"; and, "The Second Part of Henry the Fourth, continuing to his Death, and Coronation of Henry the Fifth; with the humours of Sir John Falstaff and swaggering Pistol." This tells the greater part of the story. The only important thing which the makers of titles omitted was the part played by Prince Hal,—a rather serious oversight, one must admit, since he is the dramatic hero of both the plays. What Shakespeare found promising, then, in the reign of Henry the Fourth was, in the first place, the civil wars which filled the reign, like David's, with strife in punishment for the king's sins. The rebellion of the Percies, one of the chief of these troublous events, would furnish the rudimentary chronicle material for a play. In the second place, the youthful Prince of Wales, who as Henry the Fifth became England's greatest military hero, furnished the legitimate character interest for the period, an interest the more full of possibilities because of his traditional reputation as a scapegrace in the days before his accession to the throne. By a single happy stroke of fiction, altering the age of Harry Percy (who was actually a mature man at the time of the rebellion) to make him a coëval of the Prince, Shakespeare connected these two elements in a splendidly constructed dramatic whole: the Prince and Hotspur became the brilliant leading figures at the battle of Shrewsbury, which terminated the rebellion, and their contrasting characters formed the chief theme of the First Part of the play on its inner side. It would be difficult to exaggerate the sense of easy skill with which all this is accomplished, the interests of the old type of chronicle-drama being abundantly cared for, with all the fine details of war, alarms and excursions, single combats, and corpse-strewn fields, yet submerged, for the maturer spectator, in the study of the two fascinatingly contrasted types of youthful valor and ambition.

But this was not all, as the title-pages remind us. The legend of Prince Hal's fondness for disreputable companions had already given the author of an old anonymous play, *The Famous Victories of Henry the Fifth,* a hint for the mingling of comic fiction with the more serious story of his hero's achievements; and Shakespeare brilliantly followed suit. He conceived a richly comic, yet realistic, group of persons who are called, in the Folio list of *dramatis personae,* "irregular humorists,"—that is to say, amusing characters of an irregular course of life,— and developed for them a series of scenes which were not mere clownish interludes, such as often appeared in historical plays, but were interwoven closely with the serious portion of the dramatic structure and with the portraiture of the Prince.

Out of this comic portion of *Henry the Fourth,* as the whole world knows, came the chief piece of characterization which we associate with the play. The personalities of the two young Henrys are made intensely interesting, as we have seen, but they are not wrought out with any great subtlety or with that singular intimacy of understanding which we call characteristically Shakespearean; they are built up on a few simple concepts, easily discerned. Indeed from this standpoint there is no serious character in the two plays comparable with Richard the Second. But Falstaff! Coming into the story by the half legitimate process which we have just noticed, he rapidly grew in complexity and interest, until he became what we now recognize as one of Shakespeare's few greatest creations, and what some call the chief comic character in all literature. His original form and name were those of Sir John Oldcastle, a partly historical character who had been introduced into the play of the *Famous Victories,* and with whose personality Shakespeare daringly incorporated certain amusing features of the clown in the same play. When it became desirable to change his name (tradition says because of offence taken by members of the Oldcastle family), Shakespeare drew upon the also partly historical Sir John Fastolfe, who had appeared as a cowardly soldier in the Talbot scenes of *Henry the Sixth.* But none of these things explains how he became what he did,—coward, glutton, drunkard, libertine, buffoon, yet possessed of a joyous humor and a rich mental endowment which not only charmed Prince Hal but have captivated some of the most serious-minded of modern critics, despite their natural moral antipathy to Falstaff's qualities. Indeed his rich and magnetic personality has resulted in the evolution of a kind of legendary idealized Falstaff, whom some writers have proved to be really not a coward and a rascal after all.

The Second Part of *Henry the Fourth,* like most sequels, was doomed to be inferior to the first. For the chronicle portion, there was only the recrudescence of the Percy rebellion, to give opportunity for more scenes of war, and the further working out of the relations between the Prince and his father, in the scenes which approach the king's death. It seems clear that Shakespeare was somewhat concerned as to the problem of maintaining the comic reputation of the First Part, for Falstaff could never be as funny again as he had been; besides, it was necessary to the course of the chronicle-history that our sympathy with him and the other "irregular humorists" should diminish. The Prince was to become king, and his past to be put behind his back. Shakespeare therefore added to the familiar company of London rascals a new member, the "swaggering Pistol," who could be enjoyed quite without sympathy, and also an entire new group of comic figures in some *genre* scenes of country life, where we become acquainted with Justice Shallow and Justice Silence, together with the soldiers Mouldy, Wart, Feeble, and their companions. And he sought to turn the Falstaff story into a new type of comedy, which should harmonize with the serious theme of the play,—namely, one dependent on the disillusionment of the jovial knight, when, anticipating his greatest days on the accession of his friend Hal to the throne, he meets instead with discomfiture and rejection. This is always a legitimate theme for comic art, but it is normally enjoyed when applied to those whose expectations (like Malvolio's, for example) have been unwarranted, and with whom the sympathies of the spectator have not been allowed to ally themselves; and Falstaff is not one of these. Hence the closing coronation scene, in which all the old friends of the young king are rejected by him at the moment of their highest hopes, while it brilliantly accomplishes what the plot demanded, has proved very puzzling from the standpoint of the sympathies. The original audience was doubtless not so scrupulous as we are; but some modern readers are so offended that they will have none of virtuous King Henry the Fifth, after this cold-hearted scene. We cannot go into the matter adequately here: perhaps it is sufficient to remark that if Shakespeare is to be blamed, it is not for making Henry reject Falstaff, —an act suggested by the chronicle, and incorporated in the *Famous Victories*,—but for having made Falstaff too attractive to be rejected without a pang; and it is quite possible that he realized this keenly. Readers and critics take very different views of the processes of creative artists, and many feel that in the case of Shakespeare above all it is not to be supposed that he failed at any point to know just what he was trying to do, and to accomplish it perfectly. But there is still liberty to suppose that, in this period when human nature was revealing itself to Shakespeare in many fresh and wonderful ways, he may have found his creations growing under his hand quite beyond what he could have planned or hoped. We may conjecture, then, that he was himself astonished at the importance and charm which the character of Falstaff had developed, when its original place in the story was as a mere incident of the Prince's life in the under-world, and that he presently became aware that the dramatist, as well as the king, would have difficulty in getting rid of Falstaff satisfactorily. Such a view, at any rate, is pretty well borne out by certain details of the next play, *Henry the Fifth*.

To that play we must proceed at once, stopping only to

note that in *Henry the Fourth* the conventional elements of the chronicle drama, as we have studied them in the earlier specimens, have been reduced to the minimum. They may be found in a few scenes where the history of the reign is to be made clear, or a battle to be suggested by the swift primitive methods of the chronicle type. In like manner there are a few purely typical characters of the old-time sort, notably the two or three lightly sketched-in ladies of the serious part of the plot. But in general we have reached the point where the great majority of the characters are realized independently of traditional types. Rarely, too, does the style revert to the un-speechlike manner of the earlier period; but some of the exceptions are so attractive in themselves as to make us grateful for their survival. For instance, take the king's beautiful opening address on his purposed crusade, to be manned by soldiers

> Whose arms were molded in their mothers' womb
> To chase these pagans in those holy fields
> Over whose acres walk'd those blessed feet
> Which fourteen hundred years ago were nail'd
> For our advantage on the bitter cross.
>
> (I, i, 23—27.)

In *Henry the Fifth* Shakespeare may be said, from one point of view, to have gone further back into the primitive method of chronicle-history than he had done since the days of *Henry the Sixth*. Again there is no matter for tragedy, nor does the reign as a whole furnish any natural dramatic plot. The serious part of the play is soon discovered to be a kind of pageant of Henry as the ideal English king, with chief emphasis on his victories in

France. It is for this reason, then, that the structure was made to revert to the older method, admitting even such an intolerably undramatic speech as the Archbishop's exposition, in the second scene, of the Salic law. On the other hand, in the ease, the fiery energy, and the emotional unity with which its effects are gained, the play is not unworthy of its place at the close of the great series on the House of Lancaster. The wholly novel feature is the dramatist's outspoken taking of sides. In none of the other chronicle-histories has he given us a real hero, as he has given no pure villain save the traditional Richard of Gloucester. But the greatness and virtue of Henry the Fifth were as firmly fixed by tradition as the villainy of Richard. Said Holinshed in the chronicle:

"This Henry was a king of life without spot; a prince whom all men loved, and of none disdained; a captain against whom fortune never frowned, nor mischance once spurned; whose people him, so severe a justicer, both loved and obeyed, and so humane withal, that he left no offence unpunished, nor friendship unrewarded; a terror to rebels, and suppressor of sedition; his virtues notable, his qualities most praiseworthy. . . . . Never shrinking at cold, nor slothful for heat; . . very valiantly abiding, at needs, both hunger and thirst. . . . Every honest person was permitted to come to him, sitting at meal, where either secretly or openly to declare his mind. . . . . Of courage invincible, of purpose unmutable; so wisehardy always, as fear was banished from him; at every alarum he first in armour, and foremost in ordering. . . . . So staid of mind and countenance beside, that never jolly or triumphant for victory, nor sad or damped for loss or misfortune. . . . . For conclusion, a majesty was he that both lived and died a pattern in princehood, a lodestar in honour, and mirrour of magnificence; the more highly exalted in his life, the more deeply lamented at his death, and famous to the world alway."[2]

(*Shakespeare's Holinshed*, pp. 203—05.)

Shakespeare found, then, not a problem in character study, but a great personage to make vivid, less—as has been said—in the manner of drama than of pageantry.

The epic or pageant-like character of the play is found, on observation, to determine its structure. In contrast with any other of the dramas, the progress of events, though for the most part fairly true to chronology, is primarily topical; that is, the several parts of the action exist in order to illustrate the character of the hero, rather than because they are linked essentially to what precedes and what follows. Thus one may divide the play into a series of presentations of aspects of the king such as this: Henry as matured into manhood after his frivolous youth; as a serious student of national affairs and the duties of a king; as quick to maintain the dignity of his nation against insulting foes; as stern judge of the guilty in his own household; as incomparable leader of his men in battle; as the personal friend of the common soldier, and fellow-sufferer with him; as unfailing in courage when in straits; as devout and humble in time of victory. This outlines the play through the four acts which maintain an epical and emotional unity. Upon them Shakespeare lavished all his skill as maker of both effective scenes and effective verse, in working up the heroic portrait; he also introduced his first important piece of serious prose, in the fine dialogue of the incognito scene in Act IV, in order to represent the king on the fully colloquial level of his men. Then, with no squeamishness on the subject of anti-climax, he added the fifth act as a kind of a serio-comic epilogue, presenting the king in a comparatively unheroic aspect, as bluff and hearty Englishman wooing his queen. Here again the early play on the same subject gave him his cue: "Tush, Kate!" said the Henry of the *Famous Victories*, "but tell me in plain terms, canst thou love the King of England? I cannot do as these countries do, that spend half their time in wooing." From every serious historical standpoint these final scenes are incredible, of course; the mere notion that a British sovereign of the early fifteenth century was unable to speak French, which had barely ceased to be the formal language of the English court, Shakespeare must have known to be absurd. But the common Englishman of Elizabeth's day had a stalwart insularity, as we noticed in an earlier chapter, which made him suspicious of foreign manners and tongues; and Shakespeare, in portraying for him his favorite royal hero, stimulated the last full measure of devotion by representing that hero as confined to plain English—and English of a far more bourgeois, not to say vulgar, sort than he speaks elsewhere in the play—even in wooing his princess.

Another sign of the non-dramatic character of *Henry the Fifth* is found in the unaccustomed use which Shakespeare made of the prologue or "chorus" at the opening of each of the acts. Since the performance was to be one of pageantry, the limitations of his stage seem to have irked him more than commonly, or at any rate to have led him to meditate on the part which the spectator's imagination must play in pursuing the method of chronicle-history through scenes of such splendor and patriotic glory. Thus meditating, he devised a series of prologues in which the movement and objective vividness of epic poetry combine with the fervor of lyric, and which permit the author himself to comment on his work as in no other instance. In the first prologue the theme is the "imaginary forces" of the spectator, supplying what the "unworthy scaffold" cannot furnish. The second is used to note the passage of time between the acts, and to fill in historical matter essential to the understanding of the following scenes. The third does the same, but is more concerned to carry the listener through space, following the royal fleet across the channel. The fourth undertakes to supply the want of a stage adequately set for nocturnal atmosphere, and fills the beautiful scene that follows with "creeping murmur and the poring dark"; at the same time it breaks into a lyric outburst of praise of "the royal captain" of the host, and reiterates the apology for "the four or five most vile and ragged foils" that must represent the equipment of the armies at Agincourt. The fifth once more serves to o'erleap time and space (five years, in fact, if one pause to consider), and in passing, introduces the famous compliment to Essex, "the general of our gracious empress." Thus happily Shakespeare solved the problem of the loose and undramatic type which he could not now handle with the simple unconsciousness of an earlier period; and happy the actor-prologue who, in place of the usual doggerel verses provided to introduce a play, was privileged to recite these golden lines.

An audience which had become familiar with *Henry the Fourth,* and viewed this play as in some sense its sequel, must have had great expectations of comic matter, and again Shakespeare was faced with the question of how to dispose of the humorous companions of Henry's earlier day in keeping with the dignity of his kingship. The skill with which he answered it is beyond praise. First

THE CHRONICLE-HISTORIES

the old group reappears, Ancient Pistol now at their head, but they are little by little withdrawn from foreground into background, and from background into oblivion. Falstaff enters by hearsay, and by hearsay dies, in what one is tempted to call the cleverest scene—considering all the difficulties—that Shakespeare ever wrote.[7] Whether it is chiefly comic or chiefly pathetic can never be told; it is enough that Falstaff passes in a manner which is found appropriate both by readers who love him and those who have hardened their hearts to him, like the king. Nym and Bardolph now become more obviously rascals; the latter's fire is put out in the third act, and in the fourth we learn that Nym also has been hanged. Mistress Quickly, now Pistol's wife, dies early in the fifth act; her husband alone survives, and deserts the army for a life of crime. No one remains in view to remind either King Henry or ourselves of Prince Henry's tavern-haunting days. Meantime, Shakespeare introduced a new group of "humorists," wholly appropriate to the spirit and theme of the new play: the petty officers, headed by Fluellen, who represent the loyal provincial elements of Henry's army (Welsh, Irish, and Scots), and combine the mild amusement of dialect with the democratic effect of the scenes where the king mingles with them on so friendly footing.

When one passes from the spell of the brilliant pageantry of the play, and, linking it with its predecessors, reviews Shakespeare's work in the portraiture of Henry the Fifth, the result is likely to prove puzzling. Henry's words and deeds, as presented by the dramatist, are a great achievement, but the same can scarcely be said of the presentation

[7] II, iii.

of his character. It must often have been felt as a paradox that the greatest Englishman whom Shakespeare undertook to depict is by no means one of his chief creations. One difficulty may have been the very fact that the character was too fully made ready to his hand, and what he had to do was to reproduce it according to all the specifications. Another may be that he had an instinctive interest in people who fail, greater than in those that succeed. That he does not realize the personality as a vital whole, in the manner of his best work at this period, can scarcely be doubted. The most conspicuous example of this is his treatment of the legend that Henry had led a dissolute life in his youth, and suddenly surprised every one by the revelation of his better self. This is a most interesting theme, which a modern psychologic dramatist would delight to interpret, and which Shakespeare, even without the aid of modern psychology, might have worked up with brilliant success if he had studied it, so to say, from within. But he does not seem to have cared to do so. We find all manner of explanations of the paradox of Henry's youth, most of which were furnished by tradition of one sort or another. The first is what we hear from his own lips, in the first act of the First Part of *Henry the Fourth,* when he tells us (in a soliloquy obviously addressed to the audience) that he is being disreputable in order to break forth the more dramatically into virtue, when the time is ripe,—an explanation neither probable nor in any way to his credit.[8] Later in the same play he tells his father that his sins have been greatly exaggerated, but admits that he needs pardon ''for

[8] I, ii, 218-40.

THE CHRONICLE-HISTORIES 187

some things true.⁹ In the Second Part the Earl of Warwick explains that the Prince has been studying ill conduct just as one has, in acquiring a foreign tongue, to learn even immodest words which one has no intention of using.¹⁰ At the opening of *Henry the Fifth* the Bishop of Ely has another simile, based on the statement that

> wholesome berries thrive and ripen best
> Neighbor'd by fruit of baser quality,¹¹

which is very doubtful horticulture, and certainly far from true in human culture. In the same scene the Archbishop of Canterbury represents the change, quite inconsistently with these other explanations, as a real reformation, saying that

> Consideration, like an angel, came
> And whipp'd the offending Adam out of him.
> (Lines 28—29.)

We should perhaps not worry over these conflicting statements about the Prince, if his own personality, as portrayed in the plays, gave some single consistent explanation of the matter. But it does not; and one is forced to the belief that he acted as he did because the tradition of his change of conduct was so popularly interesting. The same want of vital characterization appears in the wooing scene, where we have noticed that Shakespeare condescended to make the king appear quite other than the courtly and finespoken prince that he had been hitherto. And it is most

⁹ III, ii, 26.
¹⁰ IV, iv, 68-75.
¹¹ I, i, 61-2.

serious of all in the rejection of Falstaff. The latter problem has sometimes been explained on the ground that Shakespeare was faithfully representing Henry the Fifth as the son of Henry Bolingbroke, thinking only of self and its interests when occasion required; while an occasional reader has even gone so far as to suspect that the dramatist secretly despised his hero, and ironically portrayed his faults in a kind of psychological cipher for the discerning observer, while seeming to glorify him before the people. This, of course, is to attribute to Shakespeare a type of art quite modern in temper, of which he never gives any unmistakable sign. The probabilities all lie elsewhere. As Falstaff, having no right to greatness, attained it, dramatically speaking, by the mysterious processes of creative art, so Henry, having every claim to it, displayed it with brilliant formal success yet failed of it as a spiritual creation. Shakespeare made him a magnificent figure in his pageant, but did not quite make him a living man.

In the truest sense *Henry the Fifth* marks the close of Shakespeare's work in English chronicle-history, though it must be noticed that in *Macbeth* and *King Lear* he was drawing from the same sources and carrying on what seemed superficially to be the same methods. Then, apparently after his career as active dramatist had closed, he reappeared as part author of the late play of *Henry the Eighth*, a chronicle drama born out of due time. It is agreed that Shakespeare's portion of this play is pretty much confined to some six scenes,[12] and it is fairly well agreed that the author of the remainder was John Fletcher.

[12] Those attributed to him are I, 1 and ii; II, ii and iv; III, ii (through line 203); V, 1.

THE CHRONICLE-HISTORIES 189

Just what happened no one can say: whether Shakespeare had begun to write a play on the reign of Henry the Eighth, and at the request of his company allowed the younger poet to use such of the scenes already in manuscript as might prove convenient, or whether there was more of real collaboration. A prevalent tendency toward the former view is due to the unsatisfactory results. However composed, the play of *Henry the Eighth* is more than atavistic in returning to the disunity, the astonishingly haphazard and piece-work methods, of the early translators of history into drama. It is neither tragic nor comic; it has neither plot, nor hero, nor proper conclusion. Its only outstanding theme proves to be the birth of Elizabeth as the result of the union of Henry the Eighth and Anne Boleyn; and why this should be introduced by scenes which tend to make that union contemptible, or why it was chosen for celebration in the reign of King James, there is nothing to show. Shakespeare's portion of the play is chiefly interesting for its use of his late, intricately wrought and close-packed style, which we shall notice more carefully in another chapter, and for his presentation of the nobly tragic figure of Queen Katherine. The latter is often viewed as a kind of replica of his portrait of the injured Hermione in *The Winter's Tale*. It seems impossible that he should have approved the fluent but conscienceless work of Fletcher (Fletcher was always both fluent and conscienceless) in this curious revival of chronicle drama; one may venture to imagine him as thinking it grimly appropriate that the play happened to bring about the destruction of the great theatre which had been built for better days.

CHAPTER V

THE COMEDIES

NO such clearly defined type was ready for Shakespeare's use in the field of comedy as in that of chronicle drama. There was, of course, a considerable development of old-time popular comedy, based in good part on broadly farcical material, not to say horse-play, and without the elements of literary form. There was also a cultivated tradition of comedy in the manner of Plautus, practiced especially at school and college. The most recent and interesting experiments, when Shakespeare began his work, were modifications of these. Greene and Peele had undertaken to write comedy of popular appeal, but in more or less literary form, based on romantic legendry,—the former in *Friar Bacon and Friar Bungay,* the latter in the *Old Wive's Tale;* on the other hand, John Lyly had developed the school drama in court plays for his boy actors, in which the possibilities of elegant and witty prose dialogue were shown for the first time on the English stage. But in general, the union of poetry and comedy was still quite unrevealed; so also was the realistic comedy of manners, involving both the representation and criticism of common contemporary life. These were to be the great contributions of Shakespeare and Jonson to their age.

The chronology of Shakespeare's early comedies is unfortunately a matter only of conjecture, nor is it certain that all the work of his first period was preserved. But it is well agreed, as our list of plays indicated, that in the first years of his authorship we may put three typical experiments in comedy, and in the second period the great series of five plays which stand at the head of the romantic and poetic comedy of the whole world, together with two minor performances (*The Taming of the Shrew* and *The Merry Wives*) in variant types. It is also generally assumed that *Love's Labor's Lost* represents his earliest extant work in the comic realm, though here the matter is complicated by the fact that our text of the play appears to be a "revised and augmented" version, probably made some seven years after the original writing.

Before going further into the comedies themselves, it may be worth while to pause for a preliminary word or two regarding the types into which comedy will always naturally fall. The deepest distinction, stated in extreme form, is between low or farcical and high or thoughtful comedy,—the former characteristic of the child, and of childish minds of whatever age, the latter of maturity. One need not stop to consider the difficult question of the ultimate origin or nature of the comic; no matter why a man who falls on the ice, or into the mud, is a comic figure; we know that he is. Every one will laugh at him, save the few in whom a highly developed sense of sympathy inhibits the normal reaction. But we all know, even when we laugh, that this is comedy of a low order; the child will find it the more amusing, the more wholly childlike he is, and the adult less and less amusing, according as he is really mature. On the other hand, if we suppose the man who falls on the ice or into the mud to be an extremely well-dressed person, who is known to be vain or sensitive in point of dignity, the comedy instantly changes. Its special aspect is now of a kind to appeal less to the childish and more to the mature spectator; it involves, in Meredith's now classic phrase, "thoughtful laughter"; though still in part comedy of farcical action, it is also comedy of character. If we now remove the physical experience, and substitute an incident of the same emotional value, whose form is actually the *result* of the character's inner nature,—the discomfiture of a rascal, perhaps, in the presence of one who has found him out,— we shall have gone the whole distance from the lower to the higher type. Actual drama, naturally enough, rarely presents either farce in its purity, wholly destitute of character shading, or character comedy wholly above the region of farce.

One further distinction: the comic spirit not only has these higher and lower interests with respect to thought and action, but in the thoughtful type it is marked by very divergent moods. Looking at the ridiculous material which life presents, it may take either a critical or a sympathetic attitude; its laughter is distinguishable as satiric or friendly. And the dramatist, even though his personal point of view seems to be hidden in the objective presentation of his story, cannot avoid this choice of moods. Like our acquaintances, the makers of plays impress us as laughing predominantly in the one tone or the other. If they run to excess in either direction, we begin to call them names, such as cynical or sentimental; and we perceive that the satiric type of laughter tends, when it goes very far, to destroy itself, being lost in a sneer, and that the sympathetic type may also be choked out by an excess of sentiment losing itself in a tear or a sigh. Comedy has, in fact, frequently perished by both these means. In its legitimate forms, then, we may distinguish not two but three principal kinds: farcical, thoughtful-satiric, and thoughtful-sympathetic or romantic.

The dramatists, of course, neglect to conform their work accurately to these discriminations: whoever did so would make an inferior play. For the best art, like the best type of personality, is not found at the extremes, and we should be sorry to dwell very long in the company of persons incapable of indulging in both thoughtful and thoughtless laughter, or of persons lacking in either the critical or the sympathetic spirit. Certainly the Elizabethans had no love for unmixed types, and their fondness for multiple plotting gave the dramatist special opportunity to combine different elements of comedy in the same play. Their habit, too, of combining prose and verse, or alternating scenes in the one form and the other, contributed to the same end. It was their love of poetry which beautifully counterbalanced their equal affection for uproarious farce. Shakespeare himself represents a good proportion of the possible mixtures; nevertheless, like other writers, he exhibits the natural dominance of one or another type and mood, and it happens that his three early comedies may be viewed as representing our three distinctive types. The *Comedy of Errors* is provocative for the most part of thoughtless laughter; *Love's Labor's Lost* of thoughtful laughter, primarily critical or satiric in tone; while the

Two Gentlemen of Verona is romantic, inviting to laughter by many of its situations, but always to sympathy with the persons concerned. As we shall see, it was only the third type which proved to have lasting interest for Shakespeare: it remained for him, in the later years which we associate with his chief triumphs in comedy, to combine more effectively than in the *Two Gentlemen* the element of thoughtful characterization with that of romantic sympathy. One may think it curious that he never returned, after the early experiment in *Love's Labor's Lost,* to comedy concerned with the satiric criticism of contemporary manners; perhaps the rise of Ben Jonson's genius in that field conspired with his own taste in turning him away from it. He touches such themes lightly, but only at long intervals, in the comedies of the romantic kind. On the other hand, from first to last he wrote nothing so serious as to find no room for elements of primitive merry-making farce, and nothing so farcical that some element of thoughtful characterization did not intervene.

The origins of *Love's Labor's Lost* (no matter what one means by origins) are suprisingly obscure. It is less imitative than Shakespeare's early histories and tragedies, and does not take an obvious place in the evolution of any current dramatic fashion, though in some ways it is clearly related to the court plays of Lyly. The plot is more nearly original, so far as known evidence goes, than that of any other Shakespeare comedy, and is marked by a fine youthful ingenuity. The play seems ill adapted to the popular stage, and the first edition, published 1598, adds to the title the words, "As it was presented before Her Highness this last Christmas"; but we have no clue

THE COMEDIES

as to what audience its original composition had in view. One or two of the characters, notably Holofernes the pedant, suggest (almost uniquely in Shakespeare's dramatic work) an intention to caricature familiar contemporary persons, but there have been no satisfactory identifications. On the other hand we identify very clearly the main objects of the author's satiric fun: they are the literary and social affectations of the period, and especially the affectations which are involved in the use of *words*. To toy with words, as we have seen, was characteristic of almost every writer of the time; but it was especially characteristic of Shakespeare that he could toy with them and then make fun of himself and all the rest for doing so. Between two and three hundred puns or other verbal quips have been counted in *Love's Labor's Lost,* and it would be hazardous to try to separate them into those which Shakespeare himself enjoyed and those which he threw in as mere burlesque. Almost every kind of word-mongery is both practiced and ridiculed in the play: puns, quips, and conceits; bombastic and hyperbolic art-prose just then fancied in England under influences coming from Spain; alliteration and other forms of decorative tone-color; pedantic classicism, full of Latin phrases and etymologies; and sonneteering of the Petrarchan school. Or, take Biron's own classification:

> Taffeta phrases, silken terms precise,
> Three-piled hyperboles, spruce affectation,
> Figures pedantical. (V, ii, 406—8.)

The character of Don Armado exists especially for the ornate prose run to madness; Holofernes for the show of classical learning; and most of the other characters illustrate all the rest. One might say of the whole company what Moth did of the schoolmaster and the curate: "They have been at a great feast of languages, and stolen the scraps."

Underneath this superficial comedy of contemporary fashion is the deeper irony of the main plot, wherein Shakespeare struck one of the chief notes of world-comedy, the theme of aspirations and professions incompatible with the facts of life. The immediate instance is the folly of youth renouncing love, which Biron sums up in saying, "We cannot cross the cause why we were born." And in Biron's personality the satiric perception of the folly is incarnated, as well as the experience of it. This doubling up of comic significance in a single person we shall find to be most characteristic of Shakespeare. In the early portion of the play (perhaps throughout, in the original version) both the theme of love and the character of this ironic student of it are treated very lightly; all is in poetic form, but the poetry does not penetrate far below the surface of the feelings, and we laugh, as has been said, with but little sympathy with any one concerned. But at the close of the fourth act Biron breaks forth in a magnificent serious recitative on the power of love, which it is evident was added in the late revision of the play, and which seems suddenly to lift the whole action to a somewhat higher level. This is the passage beginning,

> But love, first learned in a lady's eyes,
> Lives not alone immured in the brain,
> But, with the motion of all elements,

> Courses as swift as thought in every power,
> And gives to every power a double power,
> Above their functions and their offices.
>
> (IV, iii, 327—32.)

And again, at the close of the play, Biron's lady Rosaline, who hitherto has seemed no less frivolous a person than the rest, turns serious too, and imposes on her lover the strange penance of spending his humor for a twelvemonth on sick and crippled folk in hospitals. Her reason is the profoundly significant one that in this way he may learn something of the difference between true wit and a mere "gibing spirit":

> A jest's prosperity lies in the ear
> Of him that hears it, never in the tongue
> Of him that makes it; then, if sickly ears,
> Deaf'd with the clamors of their own dear groans,
> Will hear your idle scorns, continue then,
> And I will have you and that fault withal.
> But if they will not, throw away that spirit.
>
> (V, ii, 871—77.)

One wonders how many of those in the company of Her Highness, at the court presentation of this play, had a glimpse of recognition, in passages like these, of an interpretive genius that reached far beyond the superficial merriment of the comedy.

Aside from Biron, the more serious characters in *Love's Labor's Lost* are presented with little realism or individuality. The king and the princess are a perfectly respectable king and princess, no more; and their ladies and gentlemen are characterized, for the most part, with equal conventionality. Armado the braggart rhetorician is a fascinating person, but a type (and a caricature) rather than an individual. Holofernes the schoolmaster, who we have seen may have been drawn from life, has some real individuality, but again it is that of caricature. One does not complain of this: there is nothing, in the greater part of the play, to depend in any way upon character other than that of the typical sort; and therein its youthful quality appears. For the rest, we can only pause to notice how many dramatic or theatrical devices Shakespeare introduced into this comedy, from one or another contemporary convention, which he was later to use again with variations worked up with more highly developed art. There is a clever masque, and a pageant which makes a little play within the play, and a scene of wooing in masked disguise, and a scene wherein soliloquies are overheard by concealed listeners, and some trifling but happy scenes with a merry-witted clown, and a scene or two of contrast between the humor of stupidity and the humor of intelligence, —all these things being sources of comic success which we know better in the later plays.

The *Comedy of Errors* marks a decided advance in dramatic technique, and something of advance in dramatic style. Here Shakespeare took the droll plot of Plautus' *Menechmi,* added to its intricacy and drollness (for example, by adding twin slaves to twin masters), and carried forward an exceedingly difficult series of complications in scenes that develop swiftly and with perfect clearness. So far as mere plotting went, on the side of farce, he showed that he had already fully learned his trade. And for style, though from the nature of the piece there is less of

THE COMEDIES

poetic beauty than in *Love's Labor's Lost,* there is a closer approach to realism of dialogue, and an abandonment of the many youthful artifices of lyric form that impair the dramatic effect of the text of the earlier comedy. Despite these advances, the *Comedy of Errors* often impresses a reader as the most primitive of the plays,—an effect due to its almost wholly farcical nature. A comedy dependent upon the assumption that twin brothers look so much alike that their very wives can make no distinction between them, and upon the further incredible assumption that these brothers have happened to come into possession respectively of twin slaves equally impossible to tell apart, asks nothing in the way of either characterization or ideas to make it all that it should be. No doubt it would be possible—and Shakespeare made the experiment later, in *Twelfth Night*—to study the fortunes of a pair of twins whose characters were so different that the contrast of their personalities, taken together with the likeness of their persons, developed into high comedy instead of farce. But this would be to ask more than the occasion required; and those who seek for fine distinctions between Antipholus of Ephesus and Antipholus of Syracuse are engaged in a gratuitous search for what Shakespeare was not concerned with. On the other hand, it is true, even here, that he was not content with wholly characterless farce. The servants, like most of the humbler characters in the early plays, have somewhat more of individuality than their masters; and Adriana, wife to one of the masters, is endowed with much more reality and personal dignity than her prototype in the Latin source. Furthermore, the presentation of the aged parents of the principal characters does something to raise the piece above the level of farce, the pathos of their story being sketched in, as framework to the main comic action, in a mood of humaneness which is distinctively Shakespeare's. Aside from touches like these the play is unique among his works in its almost entire dependence on the interest of plot; we remember it neither for realism, characterization, satire, poetry, nor romance.

Both these initial comedies, then, stand somewhat apart from the main lines of Shakespeare's dramatic evolution: they represent the two chief comic joys of youth, critical burlesque and astonishing farce. But in the third, the *Two Gentlemen of Verona,* we are at the real beginning of his career in comedy. Here he tested the possibilities of treating in comic form the materials of continental romance, in which the theme of love was entwined with adventure, and thereby developed a dramatic type which was to prove of the greatest importance in his later career. Love and adventure: these are not in themselves the normal materials of comedy, since it is supposed to concern itself primarily with matter more familiar, more rational, more subject to moral judgments,—just as poetry is not the normal medium of comedy, because of its want of harmony with the realistic and the rational. It was in the two great forms of metrical and prose romance, beloved both in the Middle Age and the Renaissance, that these themes of love and adventure found their chief expression, as they do in prose romance to this day. But the Italians first, and later some English playwrights, had made the experiment of translating the matter of the romances into popular drama. Greene, for example, was doing it with

Ariosto's *Orlando,* apparently just as Shakespeare was beginning his work for the stage. And in some of his original comedy, referred to at the opening of this chapter, Greene had experimented effectively with the problem of combining dramatic humor with the gentler passions of romance. In particular, his fancy for heroines who engage in rather bold adventures but retain their Arcadian simplicity of spirit and purity of feeling may have given suggestions to Shakespeare of which the *Two Gentlemen* shows us the first fruition. If so, Greene was certainly not made happier by the obvious fact that in his imitator's work the possibilities of romantic comedy—the vital union of narrative technique with poetic seriousness—were newly and brilliantly revealed.

Shakespeare evidently found the story of this play in a Spanish source, Montemayor's romance of *Diana,* though whether directly or through a lost intervening play we do not know. As with Plautus' story of the twins, he seems to have deliberately complicated the action, increasing its difficulties for plausible representation, as if to satisfy both the eagerness of his audience for abundance of narrative material and his own eagerness for experimentation in dramatic technique. Thus he added to the adventures of two rival ladies and a changeful lover the story of a faithless friend, and made that friend's faithlessness as downright and unreasonable as it well could be. The result is an aggregation of fascinating improbabilities which come upon us, one after another, with the casual charm of the world of romance. In the *Comedy of Errors* the improbabilities had largely depended upon an initial hypothesis to which we became accustomed as the play proceeded, but here they accumulate their daring demands upon credulity from one act to another. Modern readers are most likely to balk at the concluding scene, in which Valentine not only forgives the unfaithful Proteus but even offers to resign his lady to his suddenly penitent friend. To an Elizabethan audience this was not so extraordinary a proceeding as it appears to us, since—as we saw in a former chapter—the doctrine of the superiority of man's love for man to his love for woman was familiar in the Renaissance; a certain Italian play, called *The Duel of Love and Friendship*, had this for its principal theme. At the same time one cannot overlook the fact that Shakespeare made little effort to work out either the repentance of Proteus or the renunciation of Valentine by means of plausible characterization or any other device for the concealment of the bald miracles of romance. The fact that he made his changeable hero to bear the symbolic name of Proteus is in itself an incidental evidence of the "stock" nature of the character; indeed no character in the play can be said to attract our interest for himself as distinguished from what happens to him.

If there be an exception to this last statement, it is found in Launce the clown-servant,—one should perhaps rather say, in Launce and his dog. In a sense this character also had already become a convention of the stage, but Launce is somewhat more than a type; as he describes to the dog his parting from his family, and seeks to dramatize the scene with the aid of his shoes and other convenient objects,[1] we are conscious of his interest as a person, and —if we happen to have read Shakespeare's later plays—

[1] II, iii, 1-35.

of his significance as precursor of still more individual clowns to come. Indeed that is likely to be characteristic of our feeling regarding a great part of the *Two Gentlemen*, even more than in the case of *Love's Labor's Lost*,—how full it is of experimental elements which Shakespeare repeated so much more effectively a little later that the world has largely forgotten the preliminary sketches.

The next comedy, the *Midsummer Night's Dream*, might be said to interrupt the direct evolution of the comic type in Shakespeare's hands, though from one point of view it forms a happy link between the *Two Gentlemen* and *The Merchant of Venice*. It is like the preceding comedies in its regal indifference to probability and detailed characterization,—in being a kind of glorious romantic farce; but since it is a "midsummer night's dream," with a setting and associations which withdraw it from the normal tests of plausibility, there is an effect of consistency and causation quite wanting in the others. Romance is now working in a region of perfect freedom. But this cannot help in the development of real human comedy, which lacks such freedom by being bound to the common human world; hence the play, while a masterpiece, is felt to be what Armado would call a "delightful ostentation, or show, or pageant, or antic," rather than a normal drama. There can be little doubt that the *Dream* was made for festal purposes instead of for the regular stage, and every reader will believe, even in the absence of proof positive, that it was first presented in connection with some great wedding, —such, for example, as that of the Earl of Derby, which was celebrated at Greenwich Palace at a time (1594) when the play may plausibly be dated. The patent reference to the Queen, in the beautiful passage on the "Vestal throned by the West,"[2] makes it seem equally certain that the occasion was to be one where Her Highness would be present.

The result, if one should judge it from an outline of the play, is a wondrous hodge-podge: matter from Athenian tradition, as handed down through Chaucer's *Knight's Tale;* English fairy-lore on the one hand, and English village realism on the other; the classic tale of Pyramus brought from Ovid and turned into howling farce as dramatized by the boors; constant flights from the real earth to fairyland, from ancient Greece to modern Britain, from ravishing poetry to clownish mirth. Never was there a wedding graced with such wealth of fancy as the Earl of Derby's—or whose ever one may prefer to guess; never was what has been called the vaudeville spirit of English drama so satisfied and so glorified. And when one considers closely, the art with which the diverse materials are wrought into one fabric is another and still more notable achievement of Shakespeare's technique. First we have a framework, fit for a noble and serious occasion, depicting the noble and serious matter of the marriage of Theseus; and into the framework is presently set the plot of the tangled loves of four Athenian young people. This plot might itself be handled as serious romantic comedy, and so it seems to begin; but it is made to pass into the forest where the fairies dwell, and soon they are entangled with it, and made to determine its course by mere fantasy and magic. Love, for this part of the play, proves to be a matter of "quips and cranks and wanton wiles," though eventually

[2] II, 1, 155-68.

restored to the level of normal human happiness. Further, into this inner portion of the play there is introduced the under-comedy of the six workmen,—Quince, Snug, Bottom, and the rest,—made pertinent by the circumstance that they also are planning for the marriage of Theseus; and presently this under-comedy also is drawn into the forest and into fairyland. By this means Bottom becomes by miracle the object of Titania's passion, and love, on this level, is a matter not merely of fortune and fantasy, but of grotesque ephemeral lunacy. This is the complication, unparalleled in comic art. The dénouement is swift and beautiful: the charm dissolves, the love wrought of madness fades, the proper human affections resume their power; we pass out of the forest into daylight and common earth, and Theseus, in the great speech at the opening of the fifth act, queries whether what is reported of the happenings in the wood is not a mere "fairy toy" of the fancy, and suggests that lovers, lunatics, and poets are all of a class, and equally incredible. We then have the wedding pageant as produced by the clown-workmen,—a reworking, it will be noticed, of Armado's pageant of the Worthies in *Love's Labor's Lost;* Shakespeare even repeats the detail of representing the chief persons as giving gracious welcome to the crude efforts of "tongue-tied simplicity," thus gently linking the farce-scene with the dignity of its setting. Following the clown-play there is a court dance, the "bergomask," and the stately exit of the noble lovers, closing in the framework with which the play began. The audience supposes that the noble Theseus has said the last word. But no; for the fairies, forgiving the duke for disbelieving in their existence, come suddenly upon the stage to render the epilogue to his play, outdoing his courtiers' dance with one of their own, and leaving their blessing upon his house and his bridal bed. Surely, on the lighter side of the imagination, poetic comedy not only has not excelled this composition, but could hardly hope to do so.

There is an interesting paradox in the element of characterization in the *Dream*. Commonly, we say, farce-plots give us little individuality of character, and need none; it is the thoughtful drama of higher seriousness which must be rooted in personality. But we have already seen Shakespeare's early tendency to study the art of vivid portraiture more in his minor characters than in the major persons. This comedy goes much further in the same direction. Its serious personages, Theseus and Hippolita and the four lovers of the principal plot, are but faintly individualized, and speak always the mere language of their type, while the fairies and the clownish workmen, theoretically the most purely typical of persons, are made astonishingly vivid and lifelike. Bottom we know as a real individual, more certainly, perhaps, than any character that Shakespeare had thus far created. Titania and Puck we are more likely to think of as having existed in identical form through ages of tradition; but, while this is true in a very general sense, we do not find them thus definitely portrayed when we search into the sources of Elizabethan fairy lore. Shakespeare seems, indeed, to have defined and determined their personality, not merely for his own play but for all later time.

We cannot pause to consider the poetry of this play. It is, of course, a rich and notable contribution to the form of comedy, for the type in hand; but since the type is a minor and isolated one, the style of the *Midsummer Night's Dream* is not a part of the evolution of Shakespeare's comic style. The lyric element is exceedingly large; such early habits as the abundant use of rhyme reappear in proportions which Shakespeare had already discarded in other dramas; and we do not discover an advance in his characteristic art of presenting veritable speech in the form of poetry. For this advance we turn to the next comedy, *The Merchant of Venice,* which in the logical evolution of the type, as was already observed, follows the *Two Gentlemen of Verona.* Here for the first time, at least in Shakespeare's comedy, we find that perfection of dramatic utterance, conferred almost equally upon all the persons in the play, which rarely attracts attention to itself because so plausible as mere speech, but bears the dialogue upon an unfailing stream of poetic form and poetic beauty. For example of this we should not go to the great speeches, —Bassanio's on "outward shows" or Portia's on the quality of mercy,—but to some normal and relatively commonplace utterance like this:

> You know me well, and herein spend but time
> To wind about my love with circumstance;
> And, out of doubt, you do me now more wrong
> In making question of my uttermost
> Than if you had made waste of all I have.
>
> (I, i, 153—57.)

This finely modulated style adds, too, to the impression of reality in character and action. When we no longer hear the chiming couplets, the undramatic lyrical arias, or the traditional sonorous rants of the older manner, we are likely not to recognize so readily the older mannerisms of characterization or conduct, even when they exist.

The fundamental fact about *The Merchant of Venice* is its quality as a romance. Indeed it is so complete a specimen of the type that one may hesitate to say in just what sense it is to be called comedy. Love and adventure again make up the principal matter, drawn from two ancient stories of wholly diverse origin,—that of the three caskets and that of the pound of flesh,—which may already have been united in the work of an unknown earlier dramatist. A third element, dearer to Shakespeare even than to his age, the theme of manly friendship, was precisely fitted to link these two stories into one. But this is not all; never was the Elizabethan love of multiple plotting better furnished with "God's plenty" than here. Shakespeare added the Lorenzo-Jessica story as a further link between the fortunes of Jew and Gentile, and then threw in the little sub-comedy of the bridal rings, as if (perhaps) he found the sum of all the rest too prevailingly serious. As usual, the complicating of the plot was accomplished with no qualms respecting essential probabilities; one might almost say that the dramatist piled one improbability on another, daringly watching to see whether the structure could be so delicately balanced as not to topple with a crash. The pound of flesh was hard enough in itself to bring into the legal system of a rational community; the three caskets were ill fitted to a story of real human love; and when one adds the coincidences, the successful disguises, the extraordinary helplessness of the Duke—and of everyone else save Portia, with a number of minor strokes of fortune not needful to recall, the result is a tissue of absurdities all the more incredible from the fact that no supernatural causes are introduced to account for them. It is curious, too, that Shakespeare does not concern himself to develop the details of the play so as to avoid difficulties, as he might easily have done,—to show just how Bassanio changed from a fortune-hunter to a true lover, and a reflective moralist to boot, or why Antonio suddenly became so amiably helpless and incapable, after a vigorous career as man of affairs. He was content to let all such things take their course according to the authority of "once upon a time," and to let even character, instead of forming the story, be formed by it as in the kingdom of romance.

Why is it, then, that all these things are barely noticed by the ordinary reader, still less by the ordinary spectator, of the play? And why is it—to associate with this question one that has already been raised—that we commonly call *The Merchant of Venice* a true comedy instead of an extravaganza or a romance? One or two of the reasons are matters of course. Shakespeare's technique is such, by this time, that he disguises the irrationality of his plot by skillful evolution, by the blending of the unplausible with the plausible, and the placing of emphasis so that the reader shall remember what he is desired to remember, and forget what he had better forget. The style, too, as we have seen, is developed to a point of naturalness which carries what is said to a similar point of credibility. And above all, the characterization has a vividness which seems not merely to make the action real because the people are real, but even to persuade us that the action is the logical outcome of the characters. This is the first of Shakespeare's plays in which most of the serious persons are individualized with some depth and distinctness, and in which we find few or no figures treated in the merely conventional manner. Not all, of course, are depicted with equal care; one need not be ashamed to confuse Salanio and Salarino in personality as well as in name. Many of the parts, too, belong to types familiar enough in times past: Launcelot the clown is restudied from Launce of the *Two Gentlemen,* Bassanio will be represented readily by whatever actor won the favor of the audience as Valentine, and Shylock will be made up like Marlowe's Jew of Malta,—all seeming familiar enough on their first appearance. But as the play proceeds they grow upon us as newly created persons,—Bassanio more than Launcelot, as Shylock more than Bassanio. Above all, as it is hardly necessary to observe, the character of Portia takes on a wholly new quality which not only makes it seem that the play arises in good part out of her personality, but interests us even more in herself than in what she does. This last is more than can be asked of a heroine of romance, and is the chief answer to the question why even the serious part of *The Merchant* has a proper place in the field of comedy. Portia interprets life in the comic spirit, at the same time that she embodies the points of view of poetry and romance. She is the first of the great series of Shakespeare's heroines of which this is true, and when we set her beside the comparatively colorless ladies of the earlier plays, we are filled with wonder as to what had happened to reveal this new kind of incarnation of romantic comedy to its creator. One type of student conceives that a profoundly individual woman must have come into Shakespeare's life, whose manysidedness he busied himself henceforth in trying to portray; another imagines that he had discovered a boy actor so much more mature and capable in spirit than those for whom conventional female parts were commonly necessary, that he set to work to give him matter worthy of his powers. In any case, from now on we find the combination of goodness, charm, and capacity chiefly associated with women.

With this we should have to leave the play, were it not for a difficulty of a peculiar kind that has thus far been avoided in discussing it. Instead of being troubled by the question whether it is romance or comedy,—types which at any rate are not contradictory in character,—a number of persons in recent times have been troubled by the question whether it is *tragedy* or comedy, a much more serious matter. The trouble can be traced pretty definitely to the modern practice of creating "star" parts in the theatre, according to which the chief personage in *The Merchant of Venice* proves to be Shylock. The leading actor cannot be blamed for finding the Jew far more interesting than Antonio or Bassanio, and there is no harm in having a villain for hero, if the story ends, as here, with his discomfiture and punishment. But the tendency of such a process, at best, is to carry us over into the tragic field, even when no sympathy is developed for the villain; and if the villain-hero is made really appealing, the problem becomes difficult. This, as every one knows, is what has happened with Shylock. It is a plain matter of history that in the days of Shakespeare Shylock was represented as a typical hook-nosed rascal of a Jew, bigoted, usurious, and revengeful; there is even some good reason to suspect that he was a partly comic character, to be jeered at by the populace like his occasional original on the street. The Elizabethan audience despised him, and were quite untroubled by suspicions that anti-Semitism was an unworthy thing. By the same token, they had no fear that Antonio, in his treatment of the Jew, did not exhibit quite the spirit becoming to a Christian,—a fear which deeply affects many moderns, whose ethical sense is better developed than their historical. These modern spectators go to a performance in which a great actor takes the part of Shylock,—a stately, gray-bearded personage, exhibiting something of the noble dignity of his race; they are impressed, despite his vices, by the ill treatment he receives at Christian hands; and when, at the close (for the light-hearted fifth act is commonly omitted), he stands before them a pathetic and broken old man, phrasing his defeat in simple eloquence, they feel—and have every reason to feel—that this is tragedy, the tragedy of Shylock. If this were the whole difficulty, and the problem were due solely, like some other Shakespeare problems, to modern perversions of the dramatist's intent, we need consider it no further; but the matter is more complicated. The actor is to blame for the emphasis which makes Shylock's fate the chief feature of the latter part of the play, but he is not wholly to blame for raising the problem of sympathy.

On this matter of sympathy two things may be said, both of which happen to be of some general significance for the student of Shakespeare. In the first place we have to recognize that this is one of the instances where the lapse of time, with its accompanying changes in social thinking, has wrought havoc with an author's material. The utter and irreconcilable animosity of Jew and Christian was the simple datum of Shakespeare's sixteenth-century story, and he accepted it, interpreting it for the matter-of-course attitude of his audience, with no more occasion to study independently the social problem involved than to study the constitutional character of the laws of Venice. The story demanded that the spectator's sympathies should be all against the Jew; the play would cease to be either comedy or romance if they were not. To conceive, therefore, that Shakespeare was in any way seeking to interpret the general question of racial or religious prejudice is a pure hallucination. But the passing years, with the growth, in most Christian countries, of an attitude toward the Jew at least a step nearer Christianity than that of the sixteenth century, have reversed, in large degree, the sympathetic attitude toward this portion of *The Merchant of Venice*. To just this extent the play is spoiled; there is no help for it; Time has thrown one of its main constituents into the wallet on his back. But again, this is not quite all. The modern actor, most would agree, is not wholly without warrant, in the text of the play itself, for something of his sympathetic interpretation of Shylock. Not to go into the more disputed matters, such as the significance of the Jew's references to his dead Rachel, there is no getting over the fundamental humanity of his great speech, "Hath not a Jew eyes?"[3], with the rest of its bitter but unanswerable reasoning, or the fundamental pathos of his final words—

> Nay, take my life and all; pardon not that. . . .
> I pray you, give me leave to go from hence.
> I am not well.
> (IV, i, 374, 395.)

[3] III, 1, 60-69.

Somewhere, somehow, there has crept into the character, originally formed of much the same stuff as Marlowe's Barabas, an element of human reality which was wholly wanting to Marlowe's play,—although, since that was a tragedy, such an element might more safely have been introduced than into the comedy of *The Merchant*. Shakespeare, one may suppose, had now reached the point where he could not well present a character in some detail without endowing him with that vitality which awakens sympathy as real people always properly awaken it, no matter what their sins; and in Shylock he carried this vitalizing process to a point which positively endangers the total effect of the play. Perhaps he did so deliberately, because he could not resist the impulse to sketch in a bit of gratuitous pathos, or to develop that element of the grotesque which the union of the pathetic and the ugly, the grand and the base, always creates. Perhaps Shylock grew on him unawares, and he was troubled, as we suspected he was in the case of Falstaff, by the appealing qualities of the man. But here, at any rate, he had no need to labor to find a solution, since there is no reason to suppose that his audience felt Shylock's pathos strongly, as they must have felt Falstaff's charm. It was posterity that was to perceive the problem of Shylock; whether Shakespeare had any foresight of the fact—this were to consider too curiously.

After *The Merchant* the natural course of the romantic comedies is again interrupted, if our chronology be right, by certain minor experiments in variant types, which we can notice only briefly. *The Taming of the Shrew*, even apart from the question of its type, would scarcely assist us in the study of Shakespeare's comic development, since it is a rewriting of an older anonymous play, and even in its present form is believed to contain a good many scenes which are not Shakespeare's. The old play, *The Taming of a Shrew*, contains, like the later one, an introduction or framework plot (that of Christopher Sly, before whom the main drama is supposed to be performed), a principal plot (that of the shrew), and a sub-plot (that of Bianca). It is clear enough that Shakespeare rewrote the introduction and the portion containing the story of the shrew; apparently a collaborator—or, as some have conjectured, the writer of an intermediate lost play—revised the Bianca story, along the lines of numerous familiar Italian comedies of intrigue. The main portion of the play, dealing with the taming of Katherine, is a rollicking farce, strongly English in atmosphere despite the professed Italian setting; Shakespeare seems to have contributed little to its substance save the vivified personality of the tamer. Petruchio, indeed, is the only fully characterized person in either main plot or sub-plot, and if the play seems to be something more than a farce it is because we acquire a real interest in himself as well as in his riotous actions. The chief opportunity for character study which the story furnished, namely, the matter of the shrew's inner nature and the reasons for its ultimate change, is wholly neglected; we see Katherine converted only from the outside,—as quite befits the spirit of the piece. It is also appropriate to the same spirit that the drama should be singularly destitute of poetry. Nothing in it is so Shakespearean as the portrait of Christopher Sly in the induction, and he disappears after the opening of the second scene of the main play, in a very curious and provoking manner. Properly he should have remained visible in the gallery or upper stage, watching the comedy performed in his honor, making occasional comments like those that followed the first scene, and resuming his own story at the end. The usual assumption is that the revisers, perhaps because they needed the upper stage for other purposes, decided to have him fall asleep and be carried out by the attendants, trusting the audience to lose interest in him henceforth; but it is also possible that something more of his part was lost from the copy from which the play was printed. In any case, no one can fail to regret that we have missed Shakespeare's further development of so real a personage.

At this period Shakespeare's principal attention was probably devoted to the plays on Henry the Fourth and Henry the Fifth; we are therefore to think of the Falstaff story as, in a very real sense, the next of his comedies. And there may be some natural connection between the study of realistic English humors in the Falstaff group of characters and the unfinished sketch of Christopher Sly. Certainly Shakespeare's work in this (for him) new field of comedy was warmly welcomed, and that welcome led him to write one whole drama of native humors, *The Merry Wives of Windsor*. There is a familiar legend that this piece was composed at the request of the Queen, who desired to see Falstaff in love. The tradition arose too late to be called authentic, but the spirit of it is sound: *The Merry Wives* is obviously a farce made to satisfy a demand— whether from the throne or humbler sources—to see more of the pleasant rascals who had made the two parts of *Henry the Fourth* almost more comedies than histories. Shakespeare devised a composite plot of domestic intrigue, allied to many familiar fabliaux, novelli, and continental comedies, brought into it the fat Sir John as the comic villain to be frustrated in his ill designs, and also, with much ingenuity, found places for other old acquaintances, —Dame Quickly, Pistol, Bardolph, and Nym. The realistic village atmosphere, which he had sketched so swiftly and charmingly into the Shallow scenes of the second *Henry the Fourth,* now develops elaborately as the background for the whole action, giving us a hint of what might have happened if he had thrown any large portion of his workmanship into the field of prose naturalism instead of poetic romance. But one does not feel that his heart was in the performance. Modern readers have taken it especially hard that the Falstaff of the *Merry Wives* is so frankly disgusting a person, with his sensualism more to the front, and his wit certainly less so, than in the historical plays. But this is in good part because, as we saw in the preceding chapter, Falstaff has charmed the moderns into idealizing him quite absurdly. If he were to be in love, it could only be the kind of love in which the *Merry Wives* displays him; and, that theme once introduced, he must either be made to come to discomfiture and disgrace or to win a success marked by the cynical immorality of many a continental tale of kindred type. Shakespeare unhesitatingly chose the former alternative, and made the comedy unsympathetic in mood. The only regrettable thing is that one of so agile a mind as Falstaff should find his threefold defeat so largely in the physical realm: a ducking, a beating, and a bout of pinching demean the prince of humorists rather sadly. This main farcical action was enriched by Shakespeare, as we should expect, with a wealth of accessories, and with a partly romantic under-plot, dexterously interwoven with Falstaff's at the end, in a kind of anti-masque or burlesque fairy pageant. Spectators who remembered both the *Midsummer Night's Dream* and *Henry the Fourth* must have gone beside themselves with joy when they perceived that here was another magical forest, with Falstaff for wandering lover, Pistol playing as Puck's kinsman Hobgoblin, and Dame Quickly as Titania!

With *Much Ado about Nothing* we return to the regular course of Shakespeare's comedy, ready to be dazzled by the brilliancy of the great trio of plays that crown this period of his work. The first of them gives us the prettiest example of multiple plotting which we have found thus far, and exhibits a technical achievement in the structure which perhaps remains unexcelled, among all the plays, save by *Twelfth Night*. Two chief plots, of fairly equal importance, as in *The Merchant of Venice,* develop at first with apparent indifference to each other, but are cleverly linked at the opening of the second act and fully intermingled at the opening of the fourth. The dénouement is accomplished by the introduction of still a third story, that of Dogberry and his companion in the clown scenes. One forgets the intricacy of the design because of the skill with which it is executed. But the two main plots, that concerned with Hero's marriage and that of Benedick and Beatrice, retain their distinct interests throughout the play, and remain rivals, in an unusual sense, for chief place. The former is properly the chief, and determines the main course of the action; but the latter rises into the first place in the mind of almost every spectator. The reason is significant. The Hero plot is another bit of conventional

THE COMEDIES

romance, derived from an Italian novello, with a dark-browed misanthropic villain to interrupt, temporarily, its happy course. The Benedick-Beatrice plot is unconventional, with much of realism and satire to set off the romantic spirit effectively, and by the intense and vivid characterization of its persons comes to live in the memory far longer than the scenes—superficially more thrilling—of Hero's story. Thus we are enabled to observe, side by side, the plotting of pure romance and of high character comedy, each temporarily isolated but combined with its fellow in the whole design.

The temptation to go into the details of *Much Ado* must be resisted, but we are justified in pausing over a single significant matter in each of the main plots. The romance plot, with Hero, Claudio, and Don John as its chief persons, might easily form a tragi-comedy; that is, it brings about so serious a situation that it threatens to arouse the tragic emotions, and the wickedness and pathos of Hero's wrongs approach the point of spoiling the light-hearted pleasure proper to comic art. Readers who allow themselves to dwell unduly on this portion of the play sometimes refuse to be comforted by the dénouement, complete as it is. Yet *Much Ado* is true comedy, nevertheless; and why? It is partly a simple matter of technique, which any one may follow out for himself, if he cares to notice how Shakespeare keeps the threatened tragedy from producing, even for the time being, the effect of a really serious matter.[4] But the deeper explanation is that the

---

[4] It is suggestive, in this connection, to contrast Hero's assumed death with that of Hermione in *The Winter's Tale;* in the latter case the spectator is intended really to believe that she is dead, and to experience an extraordinary revulsion of feeling on her return to life.

persons in this plot are so slightly characterized that the mere action keeps us in the not too thoughtful region of romance, where we are assured of ultimate happiness. Hero is an excellent young woman, and we wish her well, but are not deeply concerned with the sufferings of her spirit. Claudio is—we may go so far as to say—an excellent young man, though some readers can never feel that the play ends happily so long as Hero is left in no better hands. Such readers are scrutinizing his *character* too closely. If Shakespeare were scrutinizing it, something would be made of its faults, and the story would develop accordingly; but Claudio is barely a character,—he is a figure in the romance. And the villain Don John, who takes us back to the earlier days of the drama by the naïveté of his rascality, announcing frankly, "I am a plain-dealing villain," and not tempting Shakespeare to plan any real motive for his deed,—we know that he also is simply an effective stage figure, existing to complicate the plot and to be discomfited as soon as everything is ready. Certainly no man cares for his soul; there is no Shylock problem here. Whether Shakespeare did this deliberately, perceiving that the effect of this main plot would be impaired, instead of enhanced, if he permitted too vividly human persons to carry out its movements, or became so promptly interested in the persons of the other plot that he left these in their pristine romantic vagueness, any reader may judge for himself.

On the other hand, the startlingly vivid characterization of Benedick and Beatrice at once marks the height of Shakespeare's comic period as fully upon us. No one knows whether he had a definite source for their story, but it is obvious that it was a re-working of that of Biron in *Love's Labor's Lost.* The initial conceptions of the two heroes, and the methods of their introduction to the reader, are almost identical; and the concealment scene of the early comedy of course proves to be the germ of the great concealment scene in the second act of *Much Ado.* Yet the differences are as important as the identities. In a sense the scene just referred to is brilliant farce; it can be fully enjoyed only when seen on the stage, or by the aid of unusually keen visual imagination, so that Benedick's presence before the eyes of the audience, and his apparent (but only apparent) concealment from those who discuss him, may be realized in every detail. But of course it is much more than farce, because three-fourths of the fun is due to our knowledge of Benedick's character. In the earlier play this element of thoughtful laughter was not wholly wanting, but it was due to the situation in which the court of Navarre had placed itself, rather than to any individual qualities of the king and his gentlemen. Shakespeare's new version of the situation, now wholly without artificial formality but born solely of Benedick's conception of himself as predestined to die a bachelor, takes us far into the heart of comedy. Again, what happened to Biron and his companions was simply the revelation of the fact that they were in love; but what happens to Benedick is a transformation. From a rather ungallant wit he becomes a chivalric gentleman. All this applies equally, and at certain points with increased force, to the daring repetition of the situation in the third act. The personality of Beatrice is now the thing that makes it possible, makes it significant as comedy, and makes it a transforming fact for her nature. At this point one should also notice the contrast between her inward taming (it is she who uses the word,—"taming my wild heart to thy loving hand") and the mere spectacle of the taming of the Shrew.

One is tempted to think of Shakespeare's progress in comedy, during this period, as being in large measure a dream of fair women, so unresistingly does he permit their personalities to dominate the plays,—Portia, Beatrice, Rosalind, Viola. The step from Beatrice to Rosalind, slight enough in some ways, brings us back to the point where the moods of comedy and romance are combined in a single person and a single plot, instead of being presented side by side. In *As You Like It* Shakespeare made still another experiment in his favorite art of retelling stories already told, and took over the contents of Thomas Lodge's pastoral novel *Rosalynde,* which had been written nine or ten years before. The pastoral fashion of the Renaissance is one of its most characteristic modes, and had affected every form of English literature since the days of Spenser's *Shepherd's Calendar* and Sidney's *Arcadia.* On the stage its influence was less important than in novel and lyric, but there were charming elements of conventional pastoral machinery in some of the court plays of Lyly, and more realistic English ones in popular pseudo-history plays dealing with the legends of Robin Hood. All these types were familiar to Shakespeare, and there is some evidence of his having derived suggestions for *As You Like It* not only from Lodge's novel, his immediate source, but from the *Arcadia* and from recent Robin Hood plays. Clearly, however, he was not much interested in the more formal side of pastoralism. In his youth he might well have found pleasure in reproducing something of its classical symmetry and daintiness, as we may conceive from hints in *Love's Labor's Lost* and *A Midsummer Night's Dream;* but he now finds it suggestive chiefly for the realistic charm of outdoor atmosphere, and for the possibility of once again carrying his action into a happy forest where anything may happen. The story of *Rosalynde* gave him a fresh blend of love and adventure, a new opportunity for using the favorite device of a heroine disguised as a boy or man, and an action which could be both complicated and disentangled in Arden Forest. The original cast of characters furnished him with the principal persons of the play, and also with the more formally pastoral sub-plot of Silvius and Phebe; and to these he added the clown-pastoral of William and Audrey (named, it will be noticed, to mark their realism), so as to have fun with the more artificial aspects of country life at the same time that he employed them. Even to these three groups of lovers and their kindred he added other characters, for good measure. One was Jaques, who may have been suggested by a brooding melancholy shepherd in the *Arcadia*, but whom Shakespeare made a good-natured caricature of the blasé Elizabethan traveler, world-wise and world-weary,—or, in Jaques' own phrase, wrapped "in a most humorous sadness." Another was Touchstone the clown, whose type, of course, has already become familiar, but who takes on a somewhat greater seriousness, a deeper wit, than his predecessors, and is more intimately engaged in the fortunes of the chief persons; hence he links the lighter and more serious elements of the drama in a new way. The result of all this is what we have found elsewhere in Shakespeare, a kind of hodge-podge, viewed from the standpoint of severer schools of formal unity and consistency; yet all these characters seem rationally met together in Arden, through the combined magic of the author's structural design and his contagious romantic sympathy.

It is no part of our privilege to analyze the outstanding character of Rosalind, or the extraordinary charm with which Shakespeare handled the complications resulting from her meeting with Orlando in male disguise. Readers who know the situation only from Shakespeare, unfamiliar with the treatment of similar devices in other romances and dramas of the age, must take it on faith that the delicacy, the sincerity, the mingled merriment and dignity, of the lovers' intercourse under these conditions, are conspicuously peculiar to the author of *As You Like It*. But further, regarding Rosalind, we must note the special degree in which she incarnates, like Portia, Shakespeare's blend of the spirit of comedy with that of romance. She speaks much of the time in prose; no other heroine of the romantic plays makes any such use of it outside of rather low-pitched comic scenes. Beatrice's saucy prose we remember; but Rosalind's, while not altogether wanting in sauciness, is very different. It appears to express her personality with special aptness. She can be in love, and make fun of being in love, at the same moment. "Men have died from time to time, and worms have eaten them, but not for love";[5]—and while she says this, she is head over ears in love, herself. "Love is merely a madness," she further tells Orlando; "and, I tell you, deserves as

[5] IV, i, 107.

well a dark house and a whip as madmen do'' [a painful little glimpse into the methods of Elizabethan alienists!]; "and the reason why they are not so punished and cured is, that the lunacy is so ordinary that the whippers are in love too."[6] Again—and this we may perhaps more definitely call her creed—she tells us that she holds equally in despite an excess of melancholy and an excess of laughter: "those that are in extremity of either are abominable fellows."[7] So true is all this to the spirit of the play, and to that of Shakespeare's comedy as a whole, that if Rosalind said much more by way of general comment on life, we should listen to her very carefully, suspecting that we were almost at the point of hearing Shakespeare himself. (In this connection it may be worth while to recall that it is *not* Rosalind, but the melancholy Jaques, who says that all the world's a stage, and gives the brilliant but cynical outline of the human drama of growing old.)

It is only fair to admit that the last act of *As You Like It* is disappointing. This is not the first time that we have found Shakespeare relatively indifferent to the effect of his conclusion; indeed he rarely closes a play on its highest level; but in this case the dénouement seems to emphasize curiously the incongruity of the materials of the comedy, which in the preceding acts had been willingly forgotten. It is even a bit slovenly in its manner of patching things up. The bad duke, who had long ceased to be an object of interest, is converted with astonishing suddenness; and what is more serious, Orlando's brother Oliver, whose malevolence we have scarcely been able to forget, is not only

[6] III, ii, 420-24.
[7] IV, i, 5.

reformed as suddenly, but betrothed to Celia, that the set of happy couples may be complete. To some this seems an unpardonable turn; there is more question of Celia's married happiness than of Hero's with Claudio. But such readers mistake the spirit of the under-plots. As with Claudio and Hero, none of these minor characters has been made a matter of individual concern; the inner romance, the romance of personality, is all Rosalind's and Orlando's. Oliver and Celia, Silvius and Phebe, Touchstone and Audrey,—these wed, not because of what they are, but as figures in the pastoral pageant. The last act, then, is to be enjoyed as one enjoys a comic opera, to which a great part of its technique is very similar. If Shakespeare has led us into the mood of thoughtful comedy, for a time, through the rich characterization of the heroine and the reflective beauty of a number of the principal scenes, he bids us here throw it swiftly aside, and join lightly in the masque of Hymen: otherwise we shall be left standing outside with Jaques, the only unsatisfied spectator.

Of *Twelfth Night*, the last of its group, there is little to say which has not been said already of other plays, so far, at least, as its principal story is concerned. It is the crowning example of Shakespeare's willingness to use again not merely the matter of other men's writings but his own. The complications resulting from the resemblance of twins he had treated in one of his earliest comedies; those due to the adventures of a maiden disguised as a young man had been used in two or three others, and in one of these the maiden had carried a message from the man she loved to her rival in his affections, while in another a woman had fallen in love with another woman whom she mistook for a man. It was in an Italian story, once more,—but one which had been used in an English novel and perhaps also in a play,—that Shakespeare found the means of weaving all these situations into one great résumé of the matter of romantic comedy. The form was that of a kind of double plot, the story of the twins Viola and Sebastian, and the story of the Duke's love for Olivia; but this was woven into fascinating unity by Olivia's love for Viola, and Viola's for the Duke. Here, then, one pair of lovers could not be left in the background, as merely accessory to the other, like Oliver and Celia. Both ladies are therefore characterized with clearness and detail, though the younger of course has the right of way as mistress of the romance. It is only Sebastian who is neglected; we know him not for himself, but only for what he looks like and what he does,—and that is precisely what the plot demands. Beyond this it is enough to say that almost everything that had been done in earlier comedies is here done a little better. The exposition of the opening scenes is Shakespeare's finest technical work of its kind, up to this time. The scenes dependent on Viola's disguise are not quite so amusing as those of like character in *As You Like It,* but they are elaborated with richer emotional and poetic significance. The farcical situations resulting from the resemblance of the twins come to their height in the great scene of the duel between Viola and Sir Andrew, which of course is not by any means merely farce, but character comedy of the keenest quality also. The unity of the action (again excluding all question of the under-plot) is superior to that of any comedy since the *Two Gentlemen of Verona,* and its dénouement so far above that of *As*

You Like It as to imply a wholly different type of art. And the whole is suffused with poetry more beautiful for its own sake than any since *The Merchant of Venice;* even the clown sings such lyrics as "O mistress mine" and "Come away, Death." Whether one counts Viola a finer creation than Rosalind is a matter of taste. It is characteristic that she does not speak in Rosalind's spicy prose; gaining in poetry, she may be thought to lose a bit in intellectual charm. At any rate, one would hardly say of her, as of Rosalind, that she comes close to speaking for Shakespeare's own point of view.

The only queries that concern the perfection of *Twelfth Night* lie in the under-plot, the story of Malvolio. Not that its execution falls short of the rest; every one of the comic characters is individualized with complete and delightful vitality, and their scenes are plotted as effectively as the more serious ones. But the Malvolio story has a hazardously slight connection with the chief portion of the play; the two are never inextricably interwoven, in Shakespeare's usual manner. What is somewhat more troublesome, Malvolio's story, like Hero's and like Shylock's, seems to some persons to become too serious a matter for comedy. His ill treatment, farcical in itself, is raised by the vitality and the dignity of his character to something like the painfulness of tragic art. This difficulty, like the Shylock problem, is characteristically modern, and may be thought to flatter our fineness of feeling in contrast with the more boyish capacity of the Elizabethans to enjoy horse-play even to the point where it was far from seeming playful to one of the persons concerned. No one can delude himself, as in Shylock's case, into the belief that

Shakespeare *meant* this story to be tragic. It is either all good sport, or outrageous both dramatically and otherwise. Again we must divide the blame between Time, as responsible for some increase of humane sensitiveness on the part of the English-speaking world, and the modern actor who makes Malvolio a leading and an over-serious part. Lamb gives a brilliant account of Robert Bensley playing it with "richness and dignity," looking, speaking, and moving "like an old Castilian," and concludes, "I confess that I never saw the catastrophe of this character while Bensley played it, without a kind of tragic interest." The maturer portion of a modern audience may sometimes be observed to endure actual suffering, during the scenes where the steward suffers most, while the younger—or otherwise less developed—spectators are enjoying themselves hugely, as Shakespeare wished them to. The affair is a delicate matter to judge, and has been complicated by the fact that some readers view Malvolio as an arrant hypocrite, others as a disagreable but wholly virtuous soul, still others as a deliberate type of the race of Puritans whom Shakespeare desired to bring to judgment. Two remarks must here suffice. The first is, that if Shakespeare desired to caricature Puritanism in Malvolio, he ignored many tempting opportunities to make his purpose clear; the second, that if the buoyant cheerfulness of *Twelfth Night* is to be preserved for us, it is imperative that the steward shall not be interpreted as a person of too great moral dignity or importance.

To return for a moment to the principal portion of the play, it is worth noting that it forms a kind of summit or acme, not merely of Shakespeare's art in romantic comedy, but of his presentation of the theme of love on its happier side. The Elizabethans had a common word, *fancy*, which properly and more commonly meant an illusion or a passing caprice, but was often applied to youthful love, because it came—and sometimes went—in so illusory and capricious ways. It was engendered in the eyes: so said the singer in *The Merchant of Venice*, and this was good doctrine, since fancy came through the captivating perception of beauty. It distorted all things else in the interest of its object; even Duke Orsino, when under its power, admitted this:

> So full of shapes is fancy
> That it alone is high fantastical. (I, i, 14—15.)

But as the experience grew into something deeper, maturer, and more lasting, it was likely to drop this term for the nobler one, love. Now it is the aspect of love *as fancy* with which the comic spirit is most concerned,—its tricks, caprices, illusions, and humors,—and this we have seen Shakespeare reveling in, throughout even the relatively sympathetic comedies. *Love's Labor's Lost* treated it with an ironic touch, as a wanton wrecker of men's resolves; the *Midsummer Night's Dream* made it the sport of fairies and the creature of their magic juices; in *Much Ado* irony was again emphasized, as two young persons who had scorned love's power were suddenly swept into its control; and we have seen how Rosalind agreed with Theseus in counting it a kind of hopeless universal lunacy. In *The Merchant of Venice*, to be sure, love is treated more seriously; indeed Portia's great speech of self-dedication ("You see me, Lord Bassanio, where I stand")[8] in itself

[8] III, ii, 150-67.

is quite unexcelled, from this point of view, in any of the plays; yet after all love plays but a small part in *The Merchant*, compared with friendship. *Twelfth Night* fills the stage with the streaming forces of love and beauty, and the poetic mood seems to make them matters of dignity and inner worth. Not that the tricks of "fancy" are gone,—it still shows us its familiar swift, irrationally transforming ways,—but we are made to laugh less lightly, and to sympathize more intimately. It is also true that the possibilities of love's sadness are sincerely hinted in this comedy, as in none of the others. One may doubt whether Portia, Beatrice, or Rosalind would suffer long or deeply, even if love proved transient; their emotional equilibrium and intellectual resources would go far to keep them carefree. But with Viola (as we might know merely from her lovely lines on the maid that never told her love) it would be a more serious matter. With this in view, one remembers with some sadness that she is the last of Shakespeare's heroines of love who is not made to suffer bitterly —until we come to Miranda at the very end of the list.

The first editors of Shakespeare included four other plays, besides these that we have been considering, among his comedies; but they are marked by such distinctive elements that it seems preferable to reserve them for another type and another chapter. As for "Love's Labor's Won," mentioned by Meres in his list of the comedies, who knows whether we have considered it or not? It may have been revised or renamed as *The Taming of the Shrew, Twelfth Night,* or *All's Well that Ends Well,* or through some ill fortune may have perished irretrievably.

CHAPTER VI

THE TRAGEDIES

IT IS an ancient and never-settled question why mankind finds pleasure in a form of art concerned, like tragedy, with such matters as crime and suffering, which give little pleasure, or pleasure of an ignoble kind, to those who have to do with them in actual experience. The problem cannot be discussed here, but one is reminded that it is pertinent in a special way to the age of Shakespeare. That age, despite its vivid sense of the color and joy of life, its willingness to revel in all pleasures that the earth could give, and its eager realization of a newly enlarged and fascinating world, was as devoted to the literature of suffering as to that of pleasure, and its tragedy became its greatest dramatic form.

Two or three aspects of this interest, if not explanations of it, may be briefly noticed. One was the childlike love of vivid sensation, so characteristic of every form of Elizabethan art; from this standpoint we may say that the men of that age went to see a tragedy as a boy would gladly go to see a collision between two motor-cars or locomotives, if the accident could be foreseen. A somewhat deeper aspect is the interest of personality. The Renaissance developed this in many ways, and, as we have seen, by no means failed to take account of the evil in human nature: this, while a distressing, was also a fascinating feature of mankind. From this standpoint, then, we may say that the Elizabethans went to see a tragedy as any of us would go out of our way to see a vial which we were told contained a distillation of the most deadly poison known to chemistry, or a serpent whose fangs produced the most dangerous venom of the tropics. A third aspect of tragedy, rather more attractive and more creditable to its amateurs, is its relationship to poetry. For the conditions of the Elizabethan drama this, it is clear, would be highly important. Poetry sometimes becomes a vehicle of comedy, but it is a kind of triumph over natural incompatibility when it does. Of tragedy, however, it has been the normal vehicle, and the passions with which tragedy is concerned have in almost every age stimulated poetry to its highest reaches of beauty and power. Of this the age of Sophocles and that of Shakespeare are, of course, the supreme examples. The Elizabethans, then, found in tragedy a means of satisfying at once their interest in vivid sensation, their curiosity respecting the darkest corners of the human mind and heart, and their love of surging eloquent verse.

Before taking up Shakespeare's tragedies by themselves, let us pause, as we did in approaching his comedies, to notice one or two distinctions that concern tragic types. The fundamental distinction is the same as in comedy,— that between mere outer action and action which takes its meaning from within. In other words, we find types of tragedy corresponding, on the whole, to farce on the one hand and high comedy on the other, to the thoughtless and the thoughtful kinds of laughter. If two locomotives meet on a bridge, and are hurled to destruction, there is a shock and a catastrophe which in one sense may be called —and will be called—tragical; yet obviously it is of the lowest order of significance. If we are acquainted with men who were killed in the crash, the tragic sense is more intimately touched, yet still without involving dramatic values. "Simply to be affecting," said Goethe, "is the worst of all objects of tragedy. One must know why, how, and to what end one is affected." If, with this in mind, we imagine that the dead men had been the closest friends, or the bitterest enemies, and if in the moment of their death the friendship or the enmity was revealed in a final sublimated form, we shall at once perceive the presence of something which lifts the incident into the realm of tragic significance. Even so, the story might still be centered only in the remarkable sequence of events; but just so far as the narrator concerned himself with the *persons* of the story as the real subjects (not the mere objects) of the catastrophe, the reader's interest would be correspondingly directed, not chiefly to the physical violence, the external destruction, but to the inner life of the sufferers,—what they were, first of all, and last of all what happened to them. Yet no matter how far this interest might be emphasized, a childlike reader would still be chiefly interested in the external, the crash of the collision itself. Tragic drama, then, normally begins with the crude interest in catastrophe, and rises to that which is spiritual. This is what happened in the Elizabethan age, and we shall see how largely Shakespeare was concerned with the evolution.

One may also note, for tragedy as well as comedy, some distinctions of points of view or moods. Tragic drama without sympathy, corresponding to comedy of the purely critical sort, we should hardly look for; yet something like it has actually been developed in modern times. The Elizabethans made no such experiment. But the sympathies may be directed one way or another, and may also be related in very different ways to the moral judgment. When we have been made intimately acquainted with the victim of a catastrophe, we may have so identified ourselves with him as to share keenly in the defeat, loss, or pain in which he was submerged; or, it may be, we have been made to develop an antipathy which leads us to view his fate with grim satisfaction. The fate of Bluebeard may be tragic, but it is too keenly desired to cause a tragic sigh or tear; and not only keenly desired, but clearly deserved. On the other hand, if the catastrophe has seemed to bear no relation to the victim's deserts, if it suggests the triumph of evil over good, or the irrational crushing out of innocence, the tragic pain may rise even to excess, so that we query whether the experience is not intolerable. With all these moods, and these varying adjustments of sympathy to judgment, the Elizabethan makers of tragedy experimented; and Shakespeare among them.

When he began his work for the stage, the Senecan play, as we saw in a former chapter, was the strongest influence affecting English tragedy. This was marked by its emphasis on deeds of villainy and revenge, by ghosts and other supernatural horrors, physical violence even to the point of gruesome and revolting detail, and passionate ranting utterance on the part of both offenders and sufferers. At the same time it had a semblance of literary form and maturity, giving space for reflective soliloquies and other harangues which implied both rhetorical elaboration and something of philosophic thought. It was therefore precisely suited to the infancy of Elizabethan drama, when that drama was made for an audience equally fond of rhetorical and physical violence, of lyric beauty, learning, and bloodshed. The chief representative of the type was Thomas Kyd, of whose *Spanish Tragedy* we have already had a glimpse.[1] Kyd designed his story to appeal to all the various kinds of tragic sensibility, save only those which depend on intimate and lifelike characterization, and made some approach to creating one vital and sympathetic character, in the person of a father who goes mad from grief over the murder of his son. Scarcely a writer of tragedy in the whole succeeding era fails to show evidence of having studied Kyd's crude but effective art. Meantime there had also arisen the star of Marlowe's tragic genius, exhibited most characteristically in *Tamburlaine* and *The Jew of Malta*. This young Titan made his chief advance upon the type of Seneca and Kyd in centering tragedy in a dominant, all-absorbing personality, possessed of an indomitable will at war with its environment. The element of sympathy still remained comparatively dormant. Marlowe did not take sides with or against his heroes: he presented them in all their towering ambition or villainy, and thrilled the spectator with the crash of their fall. One was not asked to suffer deeply on their behalf; but the tragic significance of the human will was revealed in a new and epochal way.

These were the men whose works Shakespeare evidently

[1] See the epilogue, quoted on page 65.

THE TRAGEDIES 237

studied in the early period of his workmanship. He seems, however, to have written only one or two formal tragedies until near the acme of his career, so that we have no means of tracing the evolution of his work in this type from imitativeness to independent mastery. Unfortunately, too, the first of the Shakespeare tragedies, as commonly listed, is of disputed authorship; while both the first and the second are of disputed date. *Titus Andronicus* was performed and published in 1594, but may have been revised from one or more earlier plays, and just how much of it is Shakespeare's no wise man will dare to say; it has been held to be wholly his, to be wholly the work of others, to be his revision of others' work, and to be other men's revision of his. *Romeo and Juliet* was published in 1597, with the statement that it had "been often, with great applause, played publicly"; its original composition some would carry back two or three years only, some to the very beginning of Shakespeare's career. Under these circumstances we cannot dogmatize about the early course of his tragic art. Its origins, however, are sufficiently clear.

The story of *Titus Andronicus* is a pseudo-historical tale of the late Roman empire, of unknown origin, and in the play is treated first of all in the manner of chronicle-history. Indeed it is important to remember that for the Elizabethans there was no clear distinction, at any time, between what we call history-play and tragedy. But in this drama one soon discovers that there is to be little concern for the fortunes of the Roman empire; the interest depends on private passions of lust, malice, and revenge. These passions are developed with all the horrid characteristics of the school of Seneca and Kyd, save only the element of the supernatural; there is no ghost or portent in the play. Physical horror is carried to a point which even Kyd did not achieve; mere murder becomes a trifle; mutilation is practiced as a fine art; and from the dreadful myth of Atreus, which Seneca had gloated over in his tragedy of *Thyestes,* the dramatist borrows the incident of a revenger's feeding to his enemy, at a banquet, the flesh of the enemy's children. It is worth noting, however, that the Shakespearean version of this horror, unlike the Greek and Latin stories, makes it the deed not of a rational hero, but of a madman.

It is characteristic of this type of drama that it should make but slight appeal to the sympathies, despite the great accumulation of suffering. The Senecan dramatist does not undertake to present a personality with whose point of view we are to identify ourselves, so that we shall suffer with him intimately. And so here: Titus, the chief sufferer, begins his part in the play with an act of outrageous cruelty of his own; he is only one of a whole world of brutes. Hence the tragic quality remains, for the most part, on the low level of sensational interest in the mere crash and fury of the action. Nevertheless the creator of Titus, taking a hint from Kyd's experiment in developing sympathy with the mad father of *The Spanish Tragedy,* nurtures a similar irrational but growing pity for the wretched father whose cruelty returned upon him a thousandfold. The madness of Titus, whether its details are from Shakespeare's hand or another's, is a matter to which the student of Shakespearean drama must give close attention. It is at once sensational, pathetic, and—at times— comic. In real life this is true of all madness, and the mixed mood which it produces in any spectator is keenly remembered by any who have had experience with it, apart from such intimate personal relations as make it wholly painful. The Elizabethans were in this respect realists beyond even ourselves. Hence they freely represented on the stage all the emotional reactions of madness at once, as they freely allowed themselves to feel them in common life. The climactic scene of Titus' insanity[2] is one in which he conceives that he can reach the gods by arrows shot into the heavens, a message being attached to each for the particular deity addressed. Such a conception, in itself, might be merely pathetic; but when the shooting is fully displayed on the stage, and the madman's companions are made to join with him, saying (for instance)—

> My lord, I aim a mile beyond the moon;
> Your letter is with Jupiter by this,

we are conscious that for the more thoughtless spectators the scene is becoming uproariously comic, while very few, even among ourselves, would restrain a smile. Yet underneath it all are the pathos and the tragedy of Titus' lot. This is one of the mixed moods which Shakespeare found inherent in the esthetic of his time, and whose artistic possibilities he was later to raise, in *King Lear,* to the highest conceivable point.

But Marlowe, as well as Kyd, had been studied before this tragedy was written; and into the welter of thrilling persons and deeds, tossing to and fro under the winds of ignoble passion, Shakespeare introduced a Marlovian prince

[2] IV, iii.

of the will, who dominates all the other evil forces like a Satan. He appears in the unpromising guise of a black Moorish camp-follower of the Gothic host, as Marlowe's study of the same type was found in a Maltese Jew. The latter had described himself thus:

> As for myself, I walk abroad o' nights
> And kill sick people groaning under walls:
> Sometimes I go about and poison wells. . . .
> Being young, I studied physic, and began
> To practice first upon the Italian;
> There I enriched the priests with burials, . . .
> And every moon made some or other mad,
> And now and then one hang himself for grief.
>
> (*Jew of Malta*, II, iii, 176—200.)

With not a little more to the same effect. The Aaron of *Titus* undertakes to outdo his prototype:

> Even now I curse the day—and yet, I think
> Few come within the compass of my curse—
> Wherein I did not some notorious ill,
> As kill a man, or else devise his death,
> Ravish a maid, or plot the way to do it,
> Accuse some innocent and forswear myself,
> Set deadly enmity between two friends,
> Make poor men's cattle [fall and] break their necks,
> Set fire on barns and haystacks in the night,
> And bid the owners quench them with their tears. . . . .
> Tut, I have done a thousand dreadful things
> As willingly as one would kill a fly,
> And nothing grieves me heartily indeed
> But that I cannot do ten thousand more.
>
> (V, i, 125—44.)

This, of course, is a rather crudely typical character, naïve enough in its implications and appeals. But the poisonous power of Aaron's personality, combined with the awful imperturbability of his indomitable will, is no trifling matter, as we confront it in the play; he is given elements, too, of common human reality which were scarcely within Marlowe's grasp. Our chief interest in him, however, is in looking forward to the transformation of the type in Shylock and Iago.

These are some of the matters which make one forget, for the moment, the mere brute violence, the gratuitous reeking gore, of *Titus Andronicus,* though they could never make the play tolerable to see upon the stage. There is also some incongruously beautiful poetry of the early Shakespearean type, which shows where the writer mercifully forgot the dramatic situation for the moment, to indulge the rhetorical possibilities of its pathos.

> Alas, a crimson river of warm blood,
> Like to a bubbling fountain stirr'd with wind,
> Doth rise and fall between thy rosed lips,
> Coming and going with thy honey breath. . . .
>
> Oh, had the monster seen those lily hands
> Tremble, like aspen-leaves, upon a lute,
> And make the silken strings delight to kiss them,
> He would not then have touch'd them for his life!
>   (II, iv, 22—25, 44—47).

Lines like these make it seem not without significance that *Titus* appeared in the same year with *The Rape of Lucrece.*

Romeo and Juliet shows Shakespeare concerned with the poetic beautifying of tragic matter of a totally different sort. To this he was led by his interest in Italian romance, and in the theme of love as a dominant dramatic motive: one might say, indeed, that *Romeo and Juliet* is the darker side of *Two Gentlemen of Verona.* If Fortune had frowned on true love, instead of taking sides with it, the fate of Valentine and Sylvia might have been that of their unhappy successors in the same city; it was not the characters, in either case, which of themselves made for a fortunate or tragic outcome. Italian romance, as we have seen, had already been experimented with in English drama, but less in tragedy than comedy. One or two Senecan dramatists had undertaken to blend their tragic type with stories redolent of beauty and pathos in the Italian manner, and to show Fortune at war with love. Most notably, Kyd himself was probably one to make the experiment in a play called *Soliman and Perseda,* whose authorship is not fully proved. In this work Love, Fortune, and Death form a chorus to the tragedy, and not only discuss but seem to control by their arbitrary power the fates of the lovers. At the close Death would appear to be triumphant even beyond his wont, since some eighteen characters lie dead upon the stage; no human voice remains to pronounce the final word. Yet Love, in the epilogue, declares that he will never yield to death, and even denies that his adversary has bereft his victims wholly of their love:

> Thou didst but wound their flesh, their minds are free;
> Their bodies buried, yet they honor me.

The substance of this allegorical conception one might say is made over by Shakespeare into the flesh-and-blood reality of *Romeo and Juliet.* If the play had been wrought out in the Kyd tradition, it might have opened with some such ominous figures as Strife or Fortune heralding the lovers' doom; but instead it begins with a gusty burst of familiar life, the tumult of a street brawl, which, though seemingly more comic than serious, actually presents the fundamental tragic cause, the feud of the two houses. Nor is there in the whole play any of the machinery of the old tragedy of revenge, though the plot gave ample opportunity for it. Both for this greater directness or realism of method, and for the tragic use of all the riches of romantic poetry, the dramatic nature of *Romeo and Juliet* was essentially new.

The story was an old one, found in familiar French and English as well as the Italian versions. Shakespeare took it chiefly from a rambling narrative poem which had appeared only two years after he was born, Arthur Brooke's *Romeus and Juliet;* there is some evidence also of his having derived suggestions from a dramatic version, now lost. His alterations from the sources are relatively few, though to the student of Shakespeare's technique they are of no little significance. The dominant impression, when one compares Brooke's poem with the play, is that Shakespeare took the story as he found it, one of youthful love smitten down by fate, but elevated and purified the emotional values to an extraordinary degree. Hardly a character is added; none save Mercutio is developed newly; even the Nurse, who seems to many readers so Shakespearean, had been sketched in some detail by Brooke. Romeo's first love affair, for Rosaline, which in the hands of certain critics is explained by more or less profound psychological laws, has its sufficient reason in the fact that it was a part of the story: the hero's sudden endowment of fatally undying passion was the more astonishing and tragic because it came upon him when he was already an acknowledged devotee of another lady. In like manner the concluding reconciliation of the families is one of the data of the play.

Nor can it be said, as we say so often in the case of other dramas, that Shakespeare remade the story by creating personalities out of which it seems to rise. None of the important characters, to be sure, is lifeless or tamely conventional; but all save Mercutio are less individuals than types. If we were to walk in the golden weather of old romance, that "chronicle of wasted time," we know that we should meet many a Romeo and many a Juliet; we should not be sure of recognizing Shakespeare's lovers by any salient trait or action,—only if they spoke we might know them, from the combined purity and passion of their utterance. It is not precisely a fault of the play that this effect, as of types, dominates it; should we not wish Shakespeare, before reaching the period marked by the intense individualization of his characters, to have given us these eternal types of youthful beauty and love? If their tragedy arises from their personalities, it is only in the sense that it depends on those universal characteristics of love in youth,—passionate loyalty and headlong rashness. The tragedy is not of character, but of fate. That there may be no mistake about this, the sonnet-prologue tells us that we are to follow the course of "a pair of star-cross'd lovers." Here Shakespeare, no doubt consciously, combines with his romantic material something of ancient classical method and mood. As in Greek tragedy, we are not intended to follow the story with eager curiosity as to how it will terminate; we know from the first that the actors are doomed. What we are to watch for is the means by which Fortune spreads her nets for their feet, the means by which they struggle to avoid them, and the lovely flaming colors of passion which their alternating moments of joy and despair bring into their faces, their hearts, and their speech. When they seem nearest deliverance, Shakespeare unresistingly follows his source in making the final stroke of fate one of the merest chance, so completely unrelated to the principal action that the tragic plot seems actually to be forgotten or destroyed. That is, the catastrophe proves to be due not to the feud between Montague and Capulet, after all, but to the accidental detention of a hitherto unheard-of person. This turn of the action has been severely (and in a sense quite incontrovertibly) criticized, from the standpoint of formal dramatic art; but it may be viewed as only heightening our tragic impression of the lovers as hopelessly at the mercy of Fortune's whims.

Since this is clearly a tragedy of the sympathies, inviting no moral judgments either for or against the principal characters, the upshot is a mere sense of pathos and of pity, not of any stern recognition of the reign of law;— that is, if we call it the tragedy of the lovers. It might, of course, be considered as the tragedy of the houses of Montague and Capulet, in which case the moral is plain, and the reign of law equally so—were it not for that final bit of accident. But no spectator does view it as anything but the tragedy of Romeo and Juliet. It is therefore much to our purpose to ask, why do we not feel more crushed with helpless sorrow at the close? There are several possible answers. One has just been hinted: there is the matter of the feud, its final judgment and atonement, to intimate that the lovers have not died wholly without moral cause, or in vain. Another is the sense of love as triumphant even in the face of death,—an old, old means of reconciliation with tragic fact, ever effective and ever new. When Romeo cries,

> O, here
> Will I set up my everlasting rest,
> And shake the yoke of inauspicious stars
> From this world-wearied flesh,
> (V, iii, 109—12.)

we hear no note of defeat, but the voice of something which Fortune cannot touch. It is also true that our suffering is mitigated by the comparatively low degree of individual characterization which we have seen this play exhibits. One is able to mourn with a sweet sadness, but not too poignantly, over the death of youth and beauty seen as lovely types. For the same reason Ophelia's death is faintly moving, never felt as intolerably sad; but it is not so with Desdemona's or Cordelia's, nor with that of a real friend who died yesterday. Just so far, then, as we conceive Romeo and Juliet to be typical rather than personal, the beauty of their end is greater than its pain. And this means that the whole drama may well be viewed as emotionally akin to a tragic opera, when contrasted with the more intimately affecting tragedies of Shakespeare's later period. It is quite tolerable and within reason that an opera should have been made of it, and that Romeo and Juliet should die uttering the strains of Gounod's music in a long duet,—as that Tristan and Isolde should pass in the music of the *Liebestod,*—whereas the attempt to make an opera of *Othello* was folly. Music suppresses personality, but expresses and exalts the simple, large, typical emotions, of which youthful love is the most universal and the least individualized. Therefore *Romeo and Juliet* is musical, even as Shakespeare left it.

What has just been said makes it clear why this tragedy is so largely lyrical in style. That is not the whole story, of course; there is an element of broad prose realism, as in every play that Shakespeare wrote. But the serious portion of *Romeo and Juliet* is so written as to make room at any point for the method of the *aria,* and sometimes for the lyric duet; the great examples need hardly be mentioned, since they are close to the tongue of every lover of English poetry. More generally, the style of the play marks it as at the point of transition between Shakespeare's earlier, more conventional and rhetorical, period, and the more individual and dramatic period that we have found beginning with the time of *Henry the Fourth* and *The Merchant of Venice.* Here, as in *Richard the Second,* both styles stand out very plainly. At one extreme, take the astonishing outburst with which the placid Friar Laurence is made to announce a fine morning as he strolls in his garden:

> The grey-eyed morn smiles on the frowning night,
> Chequering the eastern clouds with streaks of light,
> And fleckèd darkness like a drunkard reels
> From forth day's path and Titan's fiery wheels.
> (II, iii, 1—4.)

At the other, Mercutio's lines when wounded to the death:

> Help me into some house, Benvolio,
> Or I shall faint. A plague o' both your houses!
> They have made worms' meat of me. I have it,
> And soundly too.
>
> (III, i, 110—13.)

But at its best, as always, the verse combines the effects of realistic speech and impassioned poetry:

> Ah, dear Juliet,
> Why art thou yet so fair? shall I believe
> That unsubstantial Death is amorous,
> And that the lean abhorred monster keeps
> Thee here in dark to be his paramour?
> For fear of that, I still will stay with thee,
> And never from this palace of dim night
> Depart again.
>
> (V, iii, 101—08.)

This we recognize as faintly predictive of the great lyric-dramatic speeches of *Othello*, *Lear*, and *Macbeth*.

At this point the reader should really be asked to turn back to the chapter on the chronicle-histories, and look again at the paragraphs on *Richard the Third* and *Richard the Second*. For those two plays, which belong chronologically between *Romeo and Juliet* and *Julius Cæsar*, have a place among the tragedies quite as truly as among the histories; and they "look before and after," to the days of the tragedy of villainy on the one hand and the tragedy of failure on the other. *Richard the Third*, it will be recalled, belongs (like *Titus Andronicus*) to the era of Kyd's ghosts and revengers and Marlowe's evil-purposed supermen. *Richard the Second* marks the beginning of Shakespeare's interest in men who fail, and fail in spite of being attractive, well-intentioned, and in some sense able. Henceforth the fortunes of this type form his chief tragic theme, and his great tragic period opens with his use of it in *Julius Cæsar*.

It was by no means a novelty to present the deeds of the great men of antiquity, as well as of modern history, on the Renaissance stage. Matter of Greece and Rome had been dramatized more in France than in England, and the life of Julius Cæsar in particular; but for England we have evidence of at least one Cæsar drama in Latin and one in English. Shakespeare, while he may have borrowed trifles from such lost plays, certainly made his version independently, from the greatest of all his literary sources, Plutarch's *Lives*. This he treated, first of all, in the manner of a source for chronicle-history, and to many of his audience *The Tragedy of Julius Cæsar* must have seemed to be a drama of the same type as *The Tragedy of Richard the Third*. But the differences lay in the nature of the source. The English chroniclers were concerned primarily with the course of history, and with the characters of individuals only incidentally to that subject; but Plutarch was concerned primarily with the characters of great men, and with the course of history only as it flowed around them and threw their outlines into prominence. He was not only biographer, too, but philosopher, and set out thoughtfully upon the task of tracing the causes of visible events in the springs of human motive. Hence Shakespeare found the *Lives* singularly congenial to his own maturer interests; and, whereas in translating Holinshed into drama he had chiefly to supply character interpretation to fit the data of the action, in dramatizing Plutarch he had chiefly to determine the series of actions which should bring out the elements of personality most effectively.

The structure of *Julius Cæsar* was designed in a curious manner. In advance everyone would have anticipated that the tragedy would be modeled either on that of *Richard the Third,* depicting first the rise of the hero to the height of his power, then his fall and death as the concluding catastrophe, or on that of *Richard the Second,* beginning late in his life and devoting the whole play to his decline and fall. On the contrary we find that Cæsar dies almost precisely in the middle of the play, and that the rest of it is devoted to the fall of his murderers. This is the external peculiarity, and marks a structure so singular that some have supposed —quite gratuitously—that the play was made up from two originally separate dramas, one on Cæsar's fall, the other on his revenge. But the internal peculiarity is even more significant: it turns out that the reader is interested not chiefly in Cæsar, but in Brutus who slew him, and that in the latter part of the action, even at the moment of observing that Cæsar's spirit walks abroad and is taking its revenge, we are made to view Brutus as the tragic hero. In other words, while technically and ostensibly the tragedy deals with Cæsar's fall and his revenge, actually and spiritually it deals with Brutus' apparent success and his early failure.

Plutarch had presented the two great men impartially, devoting a separate life to each; and Shakespeare in one sense is impartial also. It is true that he diminishes Cæsar's personal greatness, in a manner which has offended some readers in every generation. For this he had some warrant in Plutarch's account of the hero's last years, and also in a stage tradition of a Cæsar who fell because he had arrogantly sought to lift his head higher than the gods permit to mortals. To so present Cæsar was clearly in the interest of the special emphasis upon which Shakespeare had determined, whether we look at the action or the emotional effect of the play; and in the same interest Brutus was ennobled a touch beyond what the source indicated. Yet the total attitude remains impartial. Shakespeare seems to have keenly perceived the irony that lurked in the story of the conspiracy and the triumvirate; if there were doubt, his resumption of the theme in *Antony and Cleopatra* would make us sure. Cæsarism falls (we now call it Kaiserism, with the aid of an unusually happy etymology) because it is incarnate in a personality that is losing its grasp on the facts; and idealism presently falls because incarnate in another personality that proves to be less in touch with the facts than Cæsar. Hence the ever blind and selfish mob on the one hand, and the selfish but far from blind politicians of the triumvirate on the other, find opportunity for one more experiment in imperialism. All this Shakespeare presents with his usual concreteness; there is no abstract political philosophy, to make the play less a drama; but one sees that the writer is even more thoughtfully interested in the ineffective moral idealism of Brutus than he had been in the ineffective imaginative idealism of Richard the Second.

It is scarcely necessary to ask, as we did at the close of *Romeo and Juliet,* why the catastrophe of *Julius Cæsar* does not sadden us more. Here there is no mystery of fate; there is but little effort to touch the sympathies with profoundly moving pain or pity. The judgment is satisfied that all happened as it must have happened. None of those who failed could have succeeded: history rarely reveals itself as more intelligible, even if ironic, in its progress. We may mourn for Cæsar, if the glamour of his greatness has touched us appealingly; we can scarcely fail to mourn for Brutus, though it has hardly been possible for us to acquire for him any passionate regard. Thus intelligence, rather than the capacity to suffer, is demanded of the spectator of this tragedy; and one sees why it may be called as nearly perfect as any that Shakespeare made, yet at the same time is one of the least powerful.

Except for this want of emotional intensity, the style of *Julius Cæsar* is near the crest of Shakespeare's mastery of his instrument. In the battle scenes the old method of chronicle-history is revived, but with a mature skill quite foreign to the earlier examples. There are no purely conventional scenes nor conventional characters. Portia is hardly more necessary for the purposes of the play than were the women of *Richard the Second* and *Henry the Fourth,* but her reality in contrast with their faint existence as stage figures is all the more notable. And for the student of Shakespeare's craftsmanship his rewriting of an already noble composition is an endless delight. Of this the classic example is found in the orations of Brutus and Antony in the Forum. "Brutus and his confederates," wrote Plutarch, "came into the market-place to speak unto the people, who gave them such audience that it seemed they neither greatly reproved nor allowed the fact." "Afterwards, when Cæsar's body was brought into the market-place, Antonius, making his funeral oration in praise of the dead, according to the ancient custom of Rome, and perceiving that his words moved the common people to compassion, he framed his eloquence to make their hearts yearn the more."[3] From such hints as these were born the speeches which still form the world's masterpieces in the dramatic representation of oratory. Nor at any point in the play can one suspect either a missing or a wasted word.

If *Julius Cæsar* seemed somewhat paradoxical in the difference between its ostensible type and its actual interest and effect, *Hamlet* intensifies the paradox tenfold. Here the principal fact is that the play was Shakespeare's outstanding success on the stage as a tragedy of blood and revenge, and that it remains, in the view of the modern world, his supreme achievement in the study of the inner life. To this day, indeed, it can be presented to an audience of the young, the untutored,—one might add, to the deaf, or those ignorant of the English tongue,—and maintain itself solely as an acting play, filled with thrilling sensationalism and rising to a crash of elemental objective violence at the close. Yet at the same moment the more reflective spectator listens eagerly for the actors' words, would scarcely complain if the stage were eclipsed in darkness,—at least if Hamlet's face could be seen,—and at the end could give only an imperfect account of the details of the plot. What is still more serious, critics and professors persist in discussing the play with reference to a thousand matters which do not trouble the spectator at all, and almost every thoughtful person, from Coleridge to the youth who has most recently discovered his soul, offers us an in-

[3] *Shakespeare's Plutarch,* ed. Brooke, i, 103, 137.

dividual interpretation, based on his belief that there is a touch of Hamlet in himself.

To return to the primary facts, *Hamlet* is now agreed to be the result of the rewriting of an older play which was probably called by the same name and written by Thomas Kyd. We should perhaps be willing to give more for the recovery of this lost *Hamlet* than even for some lost work by Shakespeare himself, since it might enable us to see just what happened in the development of its story in his hands. But we have the story in the form in which it came to Kyd (descended from a Danish chronicle to a French collection of tales), and we know enough of his work to conceive the general manner in which he must have told it. From his point of view it was typical matter for a tragedy of revenge, a type most of whose elements we have seen in *Titus Andronicus,*—crime, intrigue, revenge, bloodshed, and madness. To these characteristic features there would commonly be added, as in *The Spanish Tragedy*, the appearance of a ghost inspiring or directing the revenger. It is also very possible that we have evidence as to Kyd's version of the Hamlet story from a surviving German play of the seventeenth century, whose outlines seem more likely to have been taken from his play than from Shakespeare's. If this is so, we are confirmed in the suspicion that it was Kyd who introduced the ghost of the murdered man and the madness of Ophelia. Shakespeare probably added nothing of importance to the action, but concerned himself, as usually in this period, with the question, Of what manner of people could this story be true?

Now the old Hamlet story was very simple in outline. The brother of a Danish sovereign openly murdered the king, winning his throne and his wife. The young son of the dead man bided his time, and, that he might not be suspected of planning revenge, pretended to be insane, and thus obtained access to the closely guarded tyrant; in the end he slew his father's murderer, and acceded to the throne. Kyd, as we have just seen, probably changed the plot by making the murder secret, in order to have it revealed by a ghost; and at the same time it became necessary for him, just as in *The Spanish Tragedy,* so to delay the revenge, by an intrigue plot, that the catastrophe would not occur too soon. He also, of course, changed the outcome to a tragic one for the prince: in this type of play no important character could survive. If we inquire (with a look forward to Shakespeare's version) just how the delay was effected,—that is just why the prince did not accomplish his revenge sooner,—the altogether probable answer is that Kyd did not make this clear. Certainly in *The Spanish Tragedy* he did not make it clear, and we have seen that in his version of *Hamlet* he probably omitted the very feature of the plot which made revenge a difficult matter; that is, the king had now no such reason to be on his guard as he had in the original story. Nor is *The Spanish Tragedy* the only Elizabethan play of revenge in which delay, protested against by one or another character, but still imperfectly explained, is noticeable; it might almost be said to be a conventional detail of the type. If there was action enough, and eloquence enough, the audience would not be disturbed by what our more critical theory of the drama would call imperfect motivation.

At any rate, this difficulty, such as it was, Shakespeare took over with the play, and seems to have made little effort to get rid of it; or, if he did make the effort, he failed. For to this day we do not know, when we stop to ask, why Hamlet's revenge was delayed so long. There are a hundred theories about it, devised in the studies of critics, but the only certain thing about the "mystery" is that no theory can be right which was not obvious to the audience that first saw the play of *Hamlet* performed, and which does not remain obvious at any adequate performance. Some persons believe that Hamlet was hindered in his action by objective circumstances; others—much more numerous— that he was hindered by something within himself. Either view is harmless if it helps the holder of it to enjoy the play, but the play does not itself present either view with clearness. There are minor matters which it also fails to make clear: why Hamlet treated Ophelia as he did; why the king was so disturbed by Hamlet's "Mouse-Trap" play, but not by the dumb-show which revealed its action; and why Hamlet made no use of the advantage gained by the "Mouse-Trap" performance. In other words, when the details of this great tragedy are scrutinized with frankness and at leisure, it is seen to be a very imperfect composition; —greatness and perfection, littleness and imperfection, are by no means necessarily wedded. The imperfection may be due in part to accidents in the transmission of the text, for we have three different editions (two quartos and the folio version), no one of which can be regarded as final. But the difficulties seem to lie deeper,—in the older (and already popular) play which Shakespeare rewrote with extraordinary success but apparently with no such concern for consistency as if he had dramatized the story at firsthand.

Fortunately, if we drop our critical measures and microscopes, all this does no harm. For the spectator as spectator, *Hamlet* is a satisfying play, and the brilliant action conceals its own defects: this must have been so at first, and is so still. And for those who are something more than spectators, Prince Hamlet himself is their exceeding great reward. We all know what happened in the evolution of this character, though we cannot say just how or why: that a traditional figure in a conventional tale of blood revenge came to take on, in Shakespeare's mind, the attributes of a personality at once the most individual and the most representative among his creations. The most individual,—for there is a quality in Hamlet's voice and in his mind which we know and love as we know and love the voice and mind of our nearest friend, and could never mistake for another's. And the most representative,—for his perceptions of the tragedy of his existence are so extraordinarily universal in their nature, so little wrapped up with the mere circumstances of his story, that they seem to be every man's experiences of the mystery and the disillusion of the human lot; hence, as has already been noticed, one after another reader feels that Hamlet is like himself. No theory has been able to hurt him; no actor can spoil him. We listen eagerly for every word he utters; the audience in the theatre is restless until he comes on the stage,—no matter what *happens*, the interest, the humor, the wisdom, the suffering, the poetry of the drama are summed up in him. Hence most persons, if they once allow themselves to be troubled with the old problem of the reason for his delay, feel certain that, no matter what the answer is, it lies in Hamlet's personality. And in some sense they are doubtless right. Whatever happens in Shakespeare's story, as distinguished from Kyd's, must be due to Hamlet's mind and heart. Only somehow Shakespeare did not adequately link this inner source of the action, as in other plays, with its outer details. For this omission two explanations, at least, have been given; the choice between them will depend on one's whole conception of the processes of the dramatist's art. One is, that Shakespeare saw the inconsistencies of Kyd's melodramatic tragedy, despaired of avoiding them without undertaking more changes than the familiarity of the story now made practicable, and set himself, with all his technical skill so to conceal them that they remained unnoticed for some two hundred years. The other, that he began the revision with only a conventional drama of crime, ghost, delay, revenge, in mind, but soon found his hero so strangely alluring on the subjective side that he threw his whole energy into depicting that personality, and let the details of the objective action take their more or less negligent course. To some persons, of course, a belief in either of these possibilities seems the heresy of a decadent world.

The extraordinary place which the Prince's personality occupies in the drama may be said to be symbolized by the impressive series of soliloquies, characteristic especially of the earlier half of *Hamlet,* which many readers instinctively call to mind first of all. The fondness of the Elizabethans for the soliloquy has already been noticed, in connection with *Richard the Third;* they used it frankly as a conventional means of avoiding the limitations of the dramatic form, which forbids the author to tell us what his characters are *thinking,* as distinguished from what they say. That is, the Shakespearean soliloquy is a glimpse into the mind of the speaker, and often may best be thought of as not even uttered aloud. For this reason Lamb objected, soundly enough, that the soliloquies of Hamlet are ill fitted for presentation on the stage, where the actor "comes and mouths them out before an audience, making four hundred people his confidants at once." They introduce us to that inner aspect of the Prince of which he gives but fleeting revelations to other men, and, in particular, show us that his nature had been shocked into melancholy and disillusion, before there was any intimation of his father's murder, by the stain on the character of his mother. From this an infection of the soul spread swiftly, making all womanhood, his own manhood and all mankind, even the earth and the o'erhanging firmament, seem foul and pestilent. Here lies the inner tragedy so fascinating to every soul and every generation which has in like manner been tempted to generalize from its own bitterness to a ruined race and a disfigured cosmos. But this aspect of *Hamlet,* as has already been hinted, is exaggerated by studious readers, who connect the soliloquies with the dramatic action more closely than Shakespeare did, and give too little heed to the latter part of the play. For in the fourth and fifth acts the action is one of fairly normal intrigue, with the vigorous development of conflict between the Prince on the one hand and the King and Laertes on the other,—a conflict in which the hero, like the typical hero of tragedy, destroys his enemy, saves his soul and his cause, but gives up his life. It is a very modern illusion that the main theme of the drama is a problem of spiritual weakness; the normal spectator, unspoiled by theories, has always found it a brilliant objective story of conventionally thrilling events. Yet the hero, as we have seen, imposes his personality upon his story, or—so to say—steps out from its action and strangely tempts us to consider it as made only for himself.

Passing a thousand things which tempt further discussion, we can pause only to notice the remarkable character of the comic elements intermingled in this tragedy. This intermingling, of course, is one of the most familiar Elizabethan practices, and Shakespeare in varying ways followed the practice in all his tragedies. *Romeo and Juliet* represents the most popular and primitive method, with its large number of comic scenes of different kinds,—most of them based on the traditional theme of the clownish humor of servants, and many of them serving as pure interlude scenes, with no essential place in the action. Shakespeare never repeated this generosity. In *Julius Cæsar* he barely made a place for the expected clown in the brief part of the cobbler in the opening scenes, and in most of the remaining tragedies he followed a similar plan, allowing for a single clown scene,—perhaps two,—linked with the serious action though in broad contrast of tone. In *Hamlet* we find the usual scene near the close, with the "first gravedigger" as chief humorist. But this, of course, is far from being all the comedy in the play. The greater portion arises from Hamlet himself, the only one of Shakespeare's tragic heroes who is a humorist and a wit. His assumed madness gives him the opportunity to play both parts, and to be the satiric clown to his own tragedy. Thus serious matters turn swiftly to comic, as they pass through his consciousness, with a result by no means light-hearted, but rather ironic in effect. Polonius cannot be pompous and complaisant, Rosencrantz and Guildenstern cannot be con-

THE TRAGEDIES

ventionally agreeable, Orsino cannot be elegant, Ophelia cannot even be maidenly,—all are made mean and ridiculous by Hamlet's reactions. This is the function of a great part of the prose in the play: it destroys the poetic mood, deliberately, as a rapier might prick a bubble. The clown-scene in the graveyard, which at first we might suppose to be only an interlude, changes its tone when the Prince enters, and furnishes another opportunity to the mordant acid of his wit. "That skull had a tongue in it, and could sing once." "Why may not imagination trace the noble dust of Alexander, till he find it stopping a bung-hole?"[4] This is enjoyed as comedy to-day, as at the first performance, yet at the same time we recognize it as belonging to a profoundly serious element in Hamlet the prince and *Hamlet* the play. The eighteenth century, which did not approve or understand the mixed moods of the Elizabethans, omitted the graveyard scene from the stage. We count it a characteristic bit of Shakespeare's genius; but we commonly omit the ribald comedy of the songs in Ophelia's mad-scene (which Shakespeare probably took over from the older play) as going a step too far in the mixing of moods, and feel justified in making the scene wholly pathetic. Laughter is a strange and hazardous thing; one age, as one person, refuses it to that which has easily won it from another.

Othello presents a contrast to *Hamlet* at almost every point. Where the latter play was relatively formless, and turns out to be obscure in action the more one studies it, this is rigorous and clear, and almost as swift and concentrated as a Greek tragedy. While *Hamlet* was full of those

[4] *V*, 1, 83, 225.

mixed moods which the eighteenth century called "Gothic," and made us to pass back and forth from fear to laughter, —from sensational interest in the action to sheer intellectual pleasure in the hero's mind, nor ever knowing where we should end till the end had come,—this is terribly simple, and moves inexorably toward a catastrophe which is foredoomed from the beginning and brought steadily nearer with the relentlessness of a coiling serpent. *Hamlet* presented a contest between good and evil on fairly equal terms, with superior intellect on the side of goodness, and a certain final sense of "a divinity that shapes our ends"; while in *Othello* the contest is intolerably uneven, with intellect on the side of evil, and a dominant impression that the destinies themselves have joined also to crush out innocence and faith. Hence this play has inspired, on the one hand, such a statement as Macaulay's, that *Othello* is "perhaps the greatest work in the world,"[5] and on the other the saying of the chief American editor of Shakespeare, "I do not shrink from saying that I wish this tragedy had never been written."[6]

For the story Shakespeare turned again to the field of the Italian novel, finding it, in all probability, in a French version of Cinthio's *Hecatommithi;* and when we examine the source we are astonished, as in other instances, almost equally by the imitative and the transforming elements of the play. The main outlines were in the novel, and the three chief persons: a Venetian lady, a black and passionate but noble Moorish general, and a villainous ensign of the Moor's staff. Of the ensign the novelist wrote that he was

[5] *Essay on Dante.*
[6] Furness, *Othello,* New Variorum ed., p. 300.

"a man of handsome figure, but of the most depraved nature in the world...... Despite the malice lurking in his heart, he cloaked with proud and valorous speech and with a specious presence the villainy of his soul with such art that he was to all outward show another Hector or Achilles.'"[7] Here, evidently, is a hint for a study of villainy very far away from the typical dark-browed, self-confessed evil-doer of *Titus Andronicus* or *Much Ado*. There is also in the novel a hint of the tragic possibilities that lie in the marriage of a dark-skinned Moor with a Venetian lady. By this it is not implied that Shakespeare or his audience was concerned with the problem of racial character or conflict in the large; they knew no such question from the standpoint of anthropology or sociology, but could not be altogether ignorant of its occasional significance for individuals. Cinthio represents his Desdemona as telling her husband, "You Moors are of so hot a nature that every little trifle moves you to anger and revenge," and his villain as hinting to the Moor that his wife "has taken an aversion to [his] blackness."[8] All this Shakespeare made use of, just far enough *not* to suggest anything beyond the personal experience; at the same time he accepted and transfigured the novelist's brief sketch of a love that was sufficient to overcome the racial disparity. Not only so, but, instead of presenting this love baldly as a datum of the play, which we must accept on faith, he took pains to depict it in its inception and growth. The whole matter of the Moor's color is solved in Desdemona's simple saying, "I saw Othello's visage *in his mind*,"[9]—a saying which, if

[7] New Variorum ed., p. 378.
[8] *Ibid.*, pp. 380, 381.
[9] I, iii, 253.

one chose to philosophize it, might yield solutions of many a race problem of larger scope.

The principal situation and intrigue thus given, Shakespeare conceived three persons who should not only make the dreadful story possible, but should redeem it from what seemed a hopelessly foul and sordid tragedy of the baser passions, to something of commanding power and nobility. What manner of man could love his wife devotedly, and, not being jealous by nature, could nevertheless come to believe in her guilt without a shred of real evidence, and thereupon slay her with his own hand? What manner of woman, pure as snow, could nevertheless lay herself open to suspicion of infidelity, and by every word and deed blindly tighten the net in which she was being enmeshed? And what kind of man, seemingly open-hearted and a friend to all his fellows, with no real cause of complaint against these other two, could nevertheless undertake deliberately to poison their love and ruin their lives? These are the questions the poet undertook to answer; and the result is found in three dramatic creations unsurpassed in vitality and tragic power by anything in the literature of the world. The plausibility of the play, triumphant over all but insuperable difficulties, is as usual due in good part to Shakespeare's swift and sure-footed technique; but it is still more a matter of characterization. When we become conscious of what Othello is, and of what Desdemona is, we perceive that they alone, of all persons on the earth, could undergo precisely this experience. Nor can we easily imagine, even if others should undergo it, that we could so love and honor any other two as we are made—perhaps in despite of our will—to love and honor these. The beauty of blind barbaric passion, and the beauty of blind childlike purity, linked by a helpless but indomitable love,—never was there such a tragic chord as this to sound on the strings of the heart.

The only mystery is Iago, whose villainy has been found perplexing, in part because of Shakespeare's insistence on complicating the character in discrimination from the old-time simple, transparent bad man. Cinthio's villain is an absurdity: we are told that he plotted his crime from the sole desire to win Desdemona for himself, yet he proceeds to arrange for her murder, and to take the chief part in carrying it out. Iago proves to be, like the Marlovian princes of evil, an artist in villainy, loving it, in a sense, for its own sake as well as for the power it gives him, yet—like real men—realizing this only gradually, and never quite admitting the fact even to himself. In an extraordinary series of ten soliloquies he permits the audience to overhear the workings of his mind, incidentally suggesting such different reasons for his intrigue that the critics have been at much pains to try to reconcile them. We cannot here go into the matter, to argue either for or against the consistency of Shakespeare's intention. It is clear enough, however, how far he had gone from the conventional art of the early tragedies, in the direction of a kind of characterization which suggests the complexity of life itself. Certainly at this time he was deeply interested in the place of evil in human nature and experience,—of what old-fashioned people and theologians call *sin*. He made no effort to expound a theology or a philosophy concerning it, but, like every maturing mind, saw it to be a much more obscure and complex matter than it appears in the childlike process which labels all things clearly as white or black. He also represented moral evil as being, in place of the caprices of Fortune, the chief source of tragedy, while at the same time he made the element of chance to conspire with it strangely in bringing about tragedy's fatal ends.

The style of *Othello* has all the adequacy and reality of that of *Julius Cæsar* and *Hamlet*, with tenfold increase of intensity and beauty, where this is demanded by the scene. Foulness, as well as beauty, here comes within its scope to a degree hitherto unrevealed, and Shakespeare's language distils each to its very alcohol. For the one, we may recall Othello's greeting to his wife on his arrival at Cyprus:

> O my soul's joy!
> If after every tempest come such calms,
> May the winds blow till they have waken'd death!
>
> (II, i, 186—88.)

For the other, his despairing representation of his love as having become "a cistern for foul toads to knot and gender in."[10] Two notable types of prose appear in this tragedy. One is characteristic of Iago,—dry to the point of dessication, because every particle of normal human sentiment has been withdrawn from it, reducing it to an ignoble rationalism. "Virtue! a fig!......Our bodies are our gardens, to which our wills are gardeners." Love "is merely a lust of the blood and a permission of the will."[11] The other type is Othello's when he is gone clean mad with

---
[10] IV, ii, 61.
[11] I, iii, 322, 339.

THE TRAGEDIES 267

the agony of his conversion to unfaith: "Ay, let her rot, and perish, and be damned to-night.... My heart is turned to stone; I strike it, and it hurts my hand."[12] For emotion at this point of intensity, poetry cannot be made sufficiently intolerable. When the feeling becomes more nearly tolerable, it finds relief—for both Othello and ourselves—in the eternally mitigating and consoling powers of rhythm, strong to represent suffering, but suffering under control:

>   Had it pleas'd heaven
> To try me with affliction; had they rain'd
> All kinds of sores and shames on my bare head,
> Steep'd me in poverty to the very lips,
> Given to captivity me and my utmost hopes,
> I should have found in some place of my soul
> A drop of patience.
>   (IV, ii, 47—53.)

It is notable, however, that at this point in his workmanship Shakespeare's great pieces of verse cannot be isolated and read by themselves. There are no arias, no lyric interludes; all is intensely dramatic. Even the crowning burst of poetry,—one of the supreme achievements of the English tongue,—Othello's death speech, cannot be uttered by itself and for its own sake; it must be taken with the moment and the scene.

In passing to *King Lear* we remain in the atmosphere of desolating evil and pain, and the same time enter upon a confused and stormy action as different as possible from the prevailing unity and clearness of *Othello*. *Lear*, in fact, is the most Elizabethan, the most "Gothic," of Shakespeare's plays. In multiplicity of plot, extravagance of

[12] IV, i, 191-94.

action, and unprecedented mixing of moods, it ministered to all that was most barbaric in his contemporaries' desire for action and passion. Yet, paradoxically, there is no Shakespearean hero who reminds us so much of the heroes of Greek tragedy as King Lear: in his towering arrogance, his combination of regal dignity with weakening passion, and the sufferings which he undergoes in falling from greatness to the poorest estate, he is a fit companion for Ajax or Œdipus. One might say that in this play Shakespeare omitted no means of tragic power or pleasure which any dramatist had conceived, save only that of unity.

The story of Lear was found in the chronicles of British history, and the play doubtless had the appearance of chronicle-drama. An earlier play on the subject was called *The True Chronicle-History of King Leir and His Three Daughters,* and Shakespeare is supposed to have made some use of this, though he composed a wholly new drama instead of rewriting the old one. But the old play was not a tragedy: it ended with the success of Cordelia in restoring her father to his throne, and this was the ending warranted by the whole tradition. Shakespeare's wrenching of the outcome to that of a tragic catastrophe is one of the most curious facts in the whole story of his use of narrative sources; one would give much to know his reasons. It might, of course, be a sufficient explanation that tragedy, of a more or less violent and bitter sort, was proving the most successful type of drama on the stage at this period, or that Shakespeare was just now in a sombre mood, at odds with happy endings. It is probably sounder to suppose that he perceived in Lear the possibilities of an impressive hero whose nature might best be made so essentially tragic that only catastrophe could properly result. In the chronicle, the story was of the nature of romance, and the *Winter's Tale* enables us to see how Shakespeare might have treated it as dramatic romance. But the king, as he grew in the dramatist's mind, was unworthy of any less powerful emotional effects than those proper to tragedy.

Another curious feature of Shakespeare's method in this play is the addition of a secondary plot, that of Gloucester and his sons, drawn from an incident in Sidney's *Arcadia*. *Lear* is the only one of the tragedies with a distinct underplot, and the effect is to divide the interest in a rather perplexing way. At least two reasons for the experiment suggest themselves. It may be thought that the degradation of the king, and his ill treatment by his daughters, though intensely moving to the sympathies, are inadequate as material for a truly dramatic plot; hence that Shakespeare associated with this story an intrigue which is more substantial if less intense. Again, it is clear that to set beside the story of Lear's sufferings from the cruelty of his daughters that of Gloucester's sufferings at the hands of his son may be said to intensify the dark sense of the power of evil in human affairs. We now have three villains instead of one, and when they ally themselves an intrigue of terrifying proportions is developed. Nevertheless probably few readers find the plot of *Lear* as impressive as that of *Othello*, or the combined villainy of Goneril, Regan, and Edmund as terrifying as Iago's concentrated malignity. On the modern stage the action remains confused, instead of being cleared up, like that of most of Shakespeare's plays, merely by proper performance. On the stage of its own time, where imagination swiftly set each scene in accordance with the spirit of the lines, and where the action could hurry from one place, one time, and one mood to another, the complex movement of *King Lear,* accumulating tragic matter as it goes, like a tumultuous flood after a cloudburst, was doubtless more intelligible and impressive. Modern actors wisely hesitate to put it on. "The Lear of Shakespeare," said Lamb, "cannot be acted"; and he was thinking of nothing more than the personality of the king. "The contemptible machinery by which they mimic the storm which he goes out in, is not more inadequate to represent the horrors of the real elements than any actor can be to represent Lear."[13]

The play, then, moves in the imaginative realm in a somewhat different sense from any other: Shakespeare does not attach it to common life so closely as is his wont. At the outset he makes no effort to attain plausibility through preparation and character detail. We must accept the passionate irrational king, with his odd plan for dividing the kingdom, and the devoted yet strangely cold and reticent Cordelia, as data not to be inquired into but taken on poetic faith. When once we do so take them, they grow upon our sympathies in the usual wonderful way; but they never quite come out into the daylight of familiar life. The farm-house where the king takes shelter from the storm does not seem a common English farm-house; "Gloucester's castle" (which exists only in the modern stage directions) is vaguely located as in some land of myth or dreams; even familiar Dover cliff takes on a mysterious eerie look. This, then, the only one of the tragedies whose action lies in England, seems further from the real

[13] *Essay On the Tragedies of Shakespeare.*

England than any other. It takes hold of common life only because its theme is the perpetual common tragedy of the cruelty of youth to age. The pathos of the suffering which results from this cruelty Shakespeare heightens by every device of plotting and poetry, so that even without the usual sense of objective reality we are caught up into the strange world of pain, and our hearts are broken with the king's.

The catastrophe is abrupt, and singularly unprepared for. In *Hamlet* and *Othello* Shakespeare had introduced accident as accessory to the main course of tragic cause and effect, but he now reverts to the method of *Romeo and Juliet,* and makes it the suddenly determining factor of an action which had come to seem full of hope. That Cordelia should die is doubtless necessary to the tragedy of the king; without the loss of her, his cup of suffering could not be drained, or the nemesis of his arrogance have its perfect work. But that her death should come about with so little of sound dramatic preparation is the most serious of all the instances of Shakespeare's disposition to let the close of an action take care of itself.

The comic elements of this tragedy add to its strange Gothic greatness, like the grinning gargoyles on a solemn cathedral. Lear's madness, of course, is made one source of them,—an element which Shakespeare added to the original story. It is doubted by some critics whether an audience can ever have laughed at antics so unutterably pathetic in their essence as his; but, so far from having to go back to the Elizabethans for proof to the contrary, we shall find that any audience will laugh at them to-day, if they are presented with realism,—even with the text ex, purgated of its broader lines. But this, of course, does not mean that the pathos is obscured: it may even be heightened by the spectator's shamed sense that he is laughing indecently. Shakespeare also added the fool, his highest development of a process with which he had been concerned throughout his career, of making the originally irrelevant clown an interpreter of the spirit of his drama. And for good measure he threw in the assumed madness of Edgar, whose behavior we know was one of the popular features of the play among its contemporaries, since the title of the first edition refers specifically to "the unfortunate life of Edgar, and his sullen and assumed humor of Tom of Bedlam." When we find blended in one scene the growing madness of the old king, the partial madness of his fool, and the pretended madness of the outcast, and over them all the shades of night and a howling tempest, we realize the strange and almost terrifying means to dramatic power which the conventions of Elizabethan tragedy put into Shakespeare's hands. One wonders if he could have gone much further in their use, and have kept his own seemingly unshakable sanity. Then a little later, as we pass out of all this sound and fury into the calm of the scene of the king's recovery, and hear the utterly simple lines (certainly among the most pathetic ever penned),

> Pray do not mock me.
> I am a very foolish fond old man,
> Fourscore and upward, not an hour more or less,
> And, to deal plainly,
> I fear I am not in my perfect mind,—
>
> (IV, vii, 59—63.)

we can only "consider, and bow the head."

The two tragedies just reviewed are the most painful that Shakespeare wrote, as they are among the most poignant representations of pain in all literature. As to which of them is nearer to seeming intolerable, there may be some difference of view. In *Othello* the suffering is more wholly undeserved, for the first scene of *Lear* makes us ready to believe that both the king and Cordelia have sowed for themselves the seeds of tragedy. It is also true that the crushing of Desdemona is peculiarly hard to bear because of her childlike unresistance; Lear is at least a man, though his age and weakness go far to bring about the same impression. On the other hand, Desdemona's moral triumph, in the self-devoting lie with which she dies, and Othello's recovered mastery of himself and the situation, at the moment of his suicide, conspire to give us a sense of *sursum corda*, a lifting up of the heart, which in some measure atones for what they and we have suffered. Something like this would be our answer if we should try to say why we could endure to read the play a second time; and in *Lear* there is no such compensation. Finally, in both tragedies we are, after all, spared the worst. In each of them there has been an awful conspiracy against love, and love has survived it. "Many waters cannot quench love"; Iago learned this, and Edmund.

The next tragedy, *Macbeth*, must again have seemed to Shakespeare's audience to be a chronicle-history, and it was actually written from the chronicle. Something—one guesses it must have been the desire to celebrate the accession of a Scottish king of England—led Shakespeare to open his Holinshed to the *History of Scotland*. There he found the story of "one Macbeth, a valiant gentleman, and one that if he had not been somewhat cruel of nature, might have been thought most worthy the government of a realm"; how, shortly after the end of a war between the Scots and the Danes, as he walked one day with Banquo (traditional founder of the house of the Stuarts), Macbeth met with "three women in strange and wild apparel, resembling creatures of the elder world," one of whom presently cried out, "All hail, Macbeth, thane of Glamis!", the second, "Hail, Macbeth, thane of Cawdor!", and the third, "All hail, Macbeth! that hereafter shall be King of Scotland." And how, after the first two prophecies had been strangely fulfilled, "Macbeth, revolving the thing in his mind, began even then to devise how he might attain to the kingdom......But specially his wife lay sore upon him to attempt the thing, as she that was very ambitious, burning in unquenchable desire to bear the name of a queen."[14] From this one sees how the whole drama began to unfold itself in Shakespeare's mind. It became, of course, a personal tragedy, not a chronicle drama; but there remain in it one or two survivals of the chronicle method, which are puzzling unless one remembers the old type. The chief of these is the long dialogue of Macduff and Malcolm, in the fourth act, which has little concern with the course of the tragedy as such, and is commonly omitted on the modern stage. From the standpoint of the chronicle-history of Scotland, the matter of Malcolm's succession to the throne was one of the important final steps in the action, and the conversation, reproduced almost literally from Holinshed, was in itself effective. Nevertheless it may be thought odd that Shakespeare should have permit-

[14] *Shakspere's Holinshed*, pp. 23-25.

ted it to intrude upon a tragic story so concentrated and intense. Perhaps it was becoming plain that the action of the play was insufficient to reach the normal length; for as we have it, *Macbeth* is so much shorter than Shakespeare's other dramas that it has been conjectured to be an abridgment.

As tragedy, the play recalls us to the type exemplified in *Richard the Third*. That is, it deals with villainy; and the first part of the action shows us the hero's rise to the throne through bloodshed, while the latter part depicts his fall. But how great the contrast between the two dramas! In studying it, we are observing the essential elements in the growth of Shakespeare's art from its immature and imitative days to those of his free and incomparable mastery of its powers. The central distinction might be said to lie in the identification of the poet and the reader (or, the dramatist and the spectator) with the tragic hero. Every one feels that in the story of Richard the Third Shakespeare is standing outside the villain, showing us his deeds and—to some extent—his thoughts, with extraordinary vividness and intensity, yet never bringing us into such intimate relations with him that we seem ourselves to be thinking his thoughts with him, and even, in a strange vicarious way, to be sharing in his deeds. The same thing is true of Goneril, Regan, and Edmund, and even of Iago, who represents the highest possible point to which the objective and unsympathetic representation of evil could go. No reader says to himself, "Under like conditions, I myself might do as Iago did"; but the thoughtful reader has some such shuddering notion respecting Macbeth. For here, if the drama has taken its proper hold upon us, we so follow the course of his inner feeling and motive—not merely the lines of thought by which he designs or justifies his deeds—that we are strangely identified with him, and cannot view him as a monster whose destruction may be watched with equanimity. The means by which this result is accomplished cannot be traced here in detail. The principal point is that Macbeth is presented to us at the outset in a nobly attractive form, and is actually, in some sense, a good man. Allied with this is the fact that he not only perceives, but actually *feels*, the vileness of the evil which he makes his own, both before and after he has adopted it into his bosom. It has been debated whether he has a conscience, but the debate, like many others, would seem to be largely a matter of definition. Certainly Macbeth had no such conscience as developed into true contrition, or what evangelical theologians call saving repentance. But if by conscience we have in mind the primitive and etymological meaning of the word, a vivid inner consciousness of the nature of the evil to which one is tempted, Shakespeare pours all the resources of his art into the representation of that consciousness in Macbeth. He is even conscious, like Faustus, that he has sold his soul to the devil ("mine eternal jewel given to the common enemy of man"); in other words, Shakespeare is depicting, without any of the old religious symbolism of the Faust legend, the same inner tragedy which Marlowe had treated in a more childlike way. All this helps to identify Macbeth with every man who has said to himself, with Ovid, "Video meliora, deteriora sequor," or with St. Paul, "What I would not, that I do."

The soliloquies of the tragedy are a significant means to the same end. We have become familiar with the overheard reasonings and confessions of villains, presented by the Elizabethan convention of the formal soliloquy, in the case of Richard, of Iago, and of Edmund. It is hardly necessary to point out that in Macbeth's we see not merely *plans* in the making, but evil thoughts and purposes in the making, instead of ready made; and they struggle against that sense of their vileness which we have already observed. All this makes for sympathy of a kind hitherto hardly known in tragedy of villainy. Something like it was accomplished in ancient Greek tragedy, as in the story of Orestes; but the greater expansiveness of the Elizabethan dramatic structure, permitting the development of character through the lapse of time, gave Shakespeare a technique which the Greeks did not possess. Finally, for these means of developing sympathy with the villain-hero, there is his wife. We have seen the origin of Lady Macbeth in the passage quoted from the chronicle, and it bears out the theory that one of her chief functions is to diminish, in some degree, our sense of Macbeth's moral responsibility for his deed,—a use all too freely made of her sex since the fall of Adam. Shakespeare, as the comedies showed, was disposed to represent the union of goodness and efficiency as characteristic of woman; but in tragedy this powerful and beneficent combination was bound to be disturbed. In Desdemona the tragic action was possible only because of the heroine's possession of extraordinary goodness with extraordinary *in*efficiency; one knows that Portia or Rosalind, in Desdemona's place, would very soon have found the way out. In Goneril and Regan, on the other hand, Shakespeare had studied womanhood extraordinarily destitute of goodness, becoming thereby "the most dreadful cause" of tragedy; and he carries this out in a fuller and at the same time a more plausible manner, in the accessory villainy of Lady Macbeth, who is both extraordinarily efficient and extraordinarily bad. At the same time she is sufficiently human to share, in the end, in the tragic pity as well as the tragic doom.

Some critics, we should perhaps recall, have interpreted *Macbeth* in ways which may be thought to go even further in the direction of a sympathetic mitigation of villainy. The hero has been viewed as driven inexorably by evil forces outside himself, like Orestes, whom the Furies pursued with madness for doing that which a god had commanded, or like any poor human creature who, in a world interpreted according to the sterner side of Calvinism, is under a divine decree both to do evil and to be damned for it. Such views appear to be due to the exaggeration of the supernatural element in the tragedy. They should be corrected, in the first place, by returning to the source, and observing what the chronicler made of the three weird sisters. Their place in Macbeth's story was due simply to the fact that they knew the future, and hence gave him a strange glimpse of a destiny which he was tempted, instead of awaiting as the gift of Fortune, to hasten with his own hand. Shakespeare uses them in precisely the same way, and all interpretations of them as, on the one hand, created symbolically by murderous purposes already within his breast, or, on the other, as driving him into crime at the behest of powers whom he could not escape, are very modern and wholly gratuitous. Certainly there is not a line in the play to intimate that Macbeth could not have refused to do evil if he would, and (as we saw in the first chapter) the Elizabethans were not troubled by suspicions of this deterministic character. They believed in powers of evil, and the play of *Macbeth* is overhung with awful suggestions of the horror of that region of darkness which begins to impinge upon humanity when humans ally themselves with its forces; but nothing in that region touched a personality, like Banquo's or Macduff's, which moved steadily on the level of common duty in the normal human world.

It is clear, then, why this drama, though less intense, less irresistible in its emotional power, than *Othello* or *King Lear*, and less fascinating and profoundly reflective than *Hamlet*, is Shakespeare's chief tragic gift to the world at large. It has much of the imaginative gloom and grandeur of *Lear*, but is more plausible and human, like *Othello*. It satisfies both the sympathies and the moral judgment; it presents both the mystery of destiny and the responsibility of the individual will. It depicts the corruption of a soul so much greater than our own that we thrill at its crag-like eminence, and at the same time sufficiently like our own in motive and passion to cause us to seem to share the awful possibilities of its capacity for self-destruction.

In this series of studies of tragic evil, Shakespeare next turned back to Plutarch. He had apparently been fascinated by Plutarch's picture of the Roman empire, and by his portrait of Antony in particular, at the time of writing *Julius Cæsar*, and perhaps at that time had meditated a second play which should represent, as a kind of

Roman chronicle-history, the era of the breaking-up of the triumvirate whose rise to power the death of Cæsar made possible. Returning to this material, then, he composed a drama which is at the same time chronicle-history and personal tragedy. In structure it reverts, in an extraordinary degree, to the old loose chronicle method, with a total of forty-two scenes, set in every part of the Roman empire, and the primitive moving-picture method of representing battles on land and sea. Nor can it be said that the interest in this larger drama of the decaying empire is slight or mean. But in the midst of it we are led to concentrate on the tragedy of Antony, as one might, in watching the struggles of a mass of drowning men after a great shipwreck, find the attention centered on a single heroic figure.

It is sometimes asked whether the Antony of this play is the Antony of *Julius Cæsar* at all. He has his old fascinating eloquence, but his effective career is over, and his place in the drama is changed accordingly. Shakespeare, as many readers have remarked, was not only interested, in a very special way, in men who failed, but was in the habit of setting over against them men who succeeded, but whom we love less in their success than the others in their defeat. In *Julius Cæsar* Antony was the efficient and the fortunate, while Brutus failed; but here his part is changed,—his sun is declining, and that of a new Cæsar is in the ascendant. It is characteristic, then, that Shakespeare makes us admire and love him more, despite his weakness, than when he was plotting with Octavius to divide the world between them, and that we feel nothing but coldness for Octavius Cæsar at the same moment that we perceive the just and inevitable course of his imperial progress to the throne.

But Antony's tragedy is not chiefly political. It is that of a destructive passion; love—no mere "fancy" now—appears as a force of tyrannic power, which, instead of building up the inner nature into ideal unity, as in Othello's case, is essentially disintegrating, and debasing to the will. This theme Shakespeare also found in his source. "Antonius," wrote Plutarch, "being thus inclined, the last and extremest mischief of all other, to wit, the love of Cleopatra, lighted on him, who did awaken and stir up many vices yet hidden in him, and were never seen to any; and if any spark of goodness or hope or rising were left him, Cleopatra quenched it straight, and made it worse than before."[15] And again: "Antonius was so ravished with the love of Cleopatra that, though his wife Fulvia had great wars, and much ado with Cæsar for his affairs, and that the army of the Parthians ... was now assembled in Mesopotamia ready to invade Syria, yet, as though all this had nothing touched him, he yielded himself to go with Cleopatra into Alexandria, where he spent and lost in childish sports (as a man might say) and idle pastimes the most precious thing a man can spend, as Antiphon saith, and that is, time......And in the end, the horse of the mind, as Plato termeth it, that is so hard of rein (I mean the unreined lust of concupiscence), did put out of Antonius' head all honest and commendable thoughts."[16] Now this is a world-old tragic theme, and in itself demands for detailed fulfilment only the con-

[15] *Shakespeare's Plutarch,* pp. 36-37.
[16] *Ibid.,* pp. 41, 5.

ventional seductive siren of a thousand tales. But when Antony was to be destroyed, the Fates knew that they must choose a queen for bait, and no common queen at that. Even Plutarch, stern moralist as he is, admits that Cleopatra was possessed of extraordinary attractions. "She furnished herself with a world of gifts, store of gold and silver, and of riches and other sumptuous ornaments;..... but she carried nothing with her wherein she trusted more than in her self, and in the charms and enchantment of her passing beauty and grace."[17] He indicates, too, that much of her power over Antony was not physical, but temperamental, displayed in unparalleled skill in the art of coquetry. "She subtly seemed to languish for the love of Antonius, pining her body for lack of meat. Furthermore, she every way so framed her countenance, that when Antonius came to see her she cast her eyes upon him like a woman ravished for joy. Straight again, when he went away from her, she fell a weeping and blubbering, looked ruefully of the matter, and still found the means that Antony should oftentimes find her weeping; and then, when he came suddenly upon her, she made as though she dried her eyes."[18]

Now it is one thing to describe queenly beauty and charm, or to sketch in this outline fashion what North (in the margin of his translation) calls "the flickering enticements of Cleopatra unto Antonius," and quite another thing to present them directly in the action and dialogue of drama. Shakespeare's achievement, in this regard, is his supreme piece of art in realizing concretely

[17] *Ibid.*, p. 38.
[18] *Ibid.*, p. 84.

a general concept of character,—one of the supreme pieces of such art in all literature. If any should doubt it, let him study the third scene of the play, which is Shakespeare's rendering of the passage just quoted from Plutarch, and ask himself whether the caustic Enobarbus went too far in admitting that

> Age cannot wither her, nor custom stale
> Her infinite variety. Other women cloy
> The appetites they feed; but she makes hungry
> Where most she satisfies; for vilest things
> Become themselves in her.
> (II, ii, 240—44.)

In these last words there is a suggestive likeness to certain lines in one of the sonnets on the dark woman who was called the poet's "worser spirit":

> Whence hast thou this becoming of things ill
> That in the very refuse of thy deeds
> There is such strength and warrantise of skill
> That, in my mind, thy worst all best exceeds?
> (Sonnet 150.)

The resemblance has led some to suspect that Shakespeare went back to his acquaintance with the half-fascinating, half-repellent enchantress for aid in drawing his portrait of Cleopatra. One would like to know. One wonders, too, whether any boy-actor of the King's company can have begun to satisfy Shakespeare's conception of the part. That he had dark suspicions on this point we may infer from that marvelous bit of insight which led him to represent Cleopatra as fearing that, if taken captive to Rome, she would be made into a popular play (the idea, of course, is Elizabethan rather than Roman), and might herself see "some squeaking Cleopatra *boy*" her greatness. Shakespeare had already seen Desdemona, Cordelia, and Lady Macbeth *boyed* with varying success; and here was a task far more difficult than any of them had set.

This is Antony's tragedy, however, not Cleopatra's. So its nature as historical drama would imply; so Plutarch's version made it. It ought to have ended, then, with Antony's death, which does all that could be asked by way of stirring our pity for "the noble ruin" of his greatness, and at the same time satisfies our stern judgment of his folly. Since Cleopatra is to die also, her end should be a mere accompaniment or accessory of his; conventionally, she should die first. But a strange thing happened. Her end is not only drawn out beyond Antony's, as history dictated, but it is made the theme of an entire final act, giving the play a very singular structure, with two approximately equal catastrophes at the close of the fourth and fifth acts. And that is not the most puzzling feature of this conclusion. Cleopatra grows so rapidly in apparent seriousness of character, in a certain beauty of spirit, from the moment of Antony's death till her own, that the last act becomes her tragedy in more than a technical sense. She has had charm at all times, but hitherto it has been presented coldly and objectively; Plutarch would have been content with Shakespeare's presentation of it as mere coquetry raised to its highest power, and we have been angry and ashamed over Antony's yielding to it. Now we are swiftly caught up into that kind of self-identification which we have noticed before, in the case of characters with whom sympathy was to be developed, and Cleopatra's death comes upon us as the real catastrophe of the play. For the moment we care nothing about Antony, save that he was so cruel as to die and leave for the queen "nothing remarkable beneath the visiting moon." When she cries,

> Give me my robe, put on my crown; I have
> Immortal longings in me,

she seems to be a tragic heroine of towering nobility, despite the fact that she never did an admirable deed in her whole life. This even reacts, if we are not careful, upon the interpretation of the earlier acts, and has beguiled one very distinguished Shakespearean into saying that Cleopatra's love for Antony had from the first moment "burned with the unflickering flame of wifely devotion"![19] The judgment is dazzled; or, if it retains its discerning power, it conflicts squarely with the sympathies which the dramatist awakens,—perhaps the only case in Shakespeare, save that of the comic Falstaff, where this is true. Just what happened it is difficult to say. Perhaps the inconsistency was carefully planned; perhaps Cleopatra, greatest enchantress that the world had known, was so marvelously re-created that she caught not only Cæsar and Antony, but Shakespeare, "in her strong toil of grace."

It seemed in *Othello* that Shakespeare's dramatic style had reached its highest point, in its capacity to convey at once the impression of reality of utterance and supreme poetic beauty. Yet in *Macbeth,* and again in *Lear,* there were moments when it seemed to go even further in the

[19] Furness, *A. and C.,* New Variorum ed., Preface, p. xii.

same direction. In *Antony and Cleopatra* it is somewhat less firm and clear; there are signs of that over-compactness, and that loss of perfect rhythmic balance, which in some of the later plays become unmistakable; but for essential power and beauty of phrasing we feel ourselves once more to have come close to the limits of human speech. Antony is even more eloquent than in the days when he held the mob in the hollow of his hand, but Cleopatra's language is something beyond eloquence. It is as wonderful as everything else about her: she can make it soothe, or stab, or dazzle, or snarl, or sing; and when she dies, saying,

> Dost thou not see my baby at my breast,
> That sucks the nurse asleep?

it is as if the last divine miracle of words were being silenced.

Timon of Athens was called a tragedy, but for our purposes it is preferable to reserve it for consideration with another group of plays; we may pass, then, to *Coriolanus*, Shakespeare's final tragic work. This drama is strangely wanting in the poetic intensity which has just been discussed; if we did not know that *The Tempest* was still to come, we might mourn lest the poet's power had gone from him. Scarcely a line is remembered for its intrinsic charm, as distinguished from content and dramatic effectiveness. But all this is appropriate enough to the spirit of the tragedy, which implies a return to the ironic sternness of Plutarch and *Julius Cæsar,* with no such intrusion of sympathy with passion as Plutarch would have viewed with suspicion in *Antony and Cleopatra*. In the story of Coriolanus Shakespeare again found an ideal tragic theme,—

the conflict of a noble personality with a society with which it was incapable of coping. There is something more, however, in the way of inner personal tragedy; the nature of Coriolanus is not only at odds with its environment, but, far more than that of Brutus, at odds with itself. Hence the climax of the action is a great dilemma scene, presenting a situation in which the hero's loyalties clash and struggle with one another, with the certainty that, no matter which wins his allegiance, he will be brought to ruin.

Plutarch had depicted Coriolanus as a kind of untaught or self-made warrior and publicist, whose mind brought forth "many good and evil things together, like as a fat soil" that has had no proper care. The Roman people admired him for "his constancy, that he was never overcome with pleasure, nor money," and "would endure easily all manner of pains and travails." But "his behavior was so unpleasant to them by reason of a certain insolent and stern manner he had," that they never felt actually "acquainted with him."[20] Indeed "he was so choleric and impatient that he would yield to no living creature"; yet on the other hand so devoted to his mother that he married his wife to please her, and still remained as son in her house. In these passages is the germ of the whole tragedy. And Shakespeare presents the character so impartially that one can never predict how its totality will affect reader or critic. Thus one writer calls Coriolanus "at heart the basest of human creatures," another an "uncompromising idealist"; to one his conduct seems that of a proud and selfish braggart, to another only "the passionate excess of inherently noble traits." Often such differences would be

[20] *Shakespeare's Plutarch,* ii, 138.

thought to evidence fumbling characterization on the part of the dramatist, but in this case it is quite possible that Shakespeare intended to produce such a result. At times he seems to make his hero more worthy of condemnation than Plutarch had represented him; and on the other hand he treats the Roman populace with astonishing severity, for which there was no warrant in his source, as if to emphasize the baseness of that which drove Coriolanus to scorn and anger. The outcome, then, is singularly true to both personal and political experience; no one is to blame, no one has the right to call himself admirable, and the tragic fall is clearly due to a coalition between the evil forces in personality and those in environment. As if to avoid obscurity here, since the character of Coriolanus is so open to misapprehension, Shakespeare makes Aufidius sum up the chief points in an unusually explicit passage. "First," he says, Coriolanus "was a noble servant" to his people; but "he could not carry his honors even." "Whether 'twas pride," or "defect of judgment," or an incapacity of his nature "to be other than one thing,"—that is, to adapt itself to changing circumstances,—one of these, or traces of them all, "made him feared, so hated, and so banished." "So," he comments, *"our virtues lie in the interpretation of the time."*[21] A great soul out of its place, or born out of due time, destroying itself the more surely, the more fully it expresses its own nature,—this is a tragic theme which we have seen Shakespeare repeatedly approximating, and which is now fitly adopted for his final tragedy. How far we have gone from the

[21] IV, vii, 35-50.

old type, based on the story of a bad man scattering crime and bloodshed as he goes!

But the thoughtfulness of *Coriolanus* is out of all proportion to its concrete sensational interest, and its appeal to the judgment similarly out of proportion to its play upon the sympathies. Hence, though by no means wanting in effective scenes, it was doomed to be comparatively forgotten. There is no evidence of any popularity in its own time, and our time feels little affection for it either as drama or social philosophy. No doubt we should count it a very great play if it were not for the so much greater ones that went before. In the presence of the majestic strength and sadness of the five tragedies from *Hamlet* to *Antony,* the other tragic works of Shakespeare, as of the whole modern world, pale their ineffectual fires.

CHAPTER VII

THE TRAGI-COMEDIES

FROM about 1603 to the end of Shakespeare's career there are commonly dated a number of plays which refuse satisfactory classification under any of the three types which we have been engaged in considering. The editors of the First Folio found it possible to put each of these dramas among either the comedies or the tragedies, and they have been followed (with some variations in the grouping) by many of their successors; but no careful reader can have failed to note the difficulties to which such a classification gives rise. In some instances, and especially in the plays of the earlier part of the period in question, the difficulty is simply a matter of mood or emotional effect, and is often met by describing the plays as comedies of a dark, severe, bitter, or ironic character. In others, and conspicuously in those associated with the final period of Shakespeare's work, the structure and whole dramatic method seem to change, and the difference is expressed by the use of type-names admittedly vague or ambiguous, such as "tragi-comedy" or "dramatic romance."

By tragi-comedy one may mean any one of a number of things. John Fletcher, following an Italian source, said that such a play "is not so called in respect to mirth and killing,''—that is, because of the mixture of comic matter with a tragic plot, to which the term came often to be applied,—"but in respect it *wants* [i.e. lacks] *deaths . . . yet brings some near it.*"[1] In other words, it develops a situation of mortal peril, from which the characters eventually escape. This we have already found approximated by Shakespeare in such comedies as *The Merchant of Venice* and *Much Ado,* where we paused to ask ourselves whether they could be called examples of true comedy, in view of the serious situations and emotions involved; and one may frankly admit that the line between these plays and certain of those reserved for this chapter is rather insubstantial. At this point, then, tragi-comedy is very close to romance. For it is of the nature of romance to represent perilous adventure and deliverance, to thrill with uncertainty and surprise by fortunate escape, and in general to interest us much more in what *happens* to its characters than in what they are in themselves or accomplish because of what they are. If the story is in dramatic form, the difference between romance and comedy is only relative, a matter of emphasis rather than of material. Plays of this more romantic and less dramatic kind became increasingly popular during the closing years of Shakespeare's activity, and he experimented with them as he had done with almost every other fashion of the stage.

But there is another blend of tragic and comic which is not concerned with happenings; it is primarily a matter of mood. The sterner or more ironic side of the comic spirit may treat of the follies of human life—its blunders, illusions, and hypocrisies—with a seriousness which stifles

[1] Preface to *The Faithful Shepherdess.*

the very laughter to which it gives birth. The story is absurd, but it cuts too deep to be disposed of by Puck's merry philosophy of "What fools these mortals be!" If the dramatist keeps it technically outside the field of tragedy by refusing to carry through the sinister course of the action to a logical catastrophe, we nevertheless feel that the "happy ending" is lacking in happiness, and that a mixed type of art and of appreciation has resulted. One sees all this much more clearly in certain modern dramas, such as *An Enemy of the People* or *Pillars of Society*, than in anything which the Elizabethans produced. But Shakespeare, consciously or unconsciously, sometimes approached similar effects. We have seen them in the caustic wit and mocking humor of Hamlet, though in that case subordinated to the "high seriousness" and the tragic matter of the greater part of the play, and they reappear in some of the minor pieces of the same period and a little later, with no truly tragic seriousness or nobility to obscure them. Either kind of tragi-comedy will be likely to fail of the finest effects of the purer types: the romantic kind diminishes the emphasis on character, and on the major laws of cause and effect, of which drama is the supreme exponent in art; and the other sort is likely to produce much of the painfulness of tragedy without the nobility of its passions or the satisfying inevitableness of its catastrophes. The strength of unromantic tragi-comedy lies—as with the plays of Ibsen mentioned above—in the elements of intense veracity and acute social criticism, and in these the Elizabethans were not interested. The strength of romantic tragi-comedy lies in its free return to the happy irrationality of childhood, which Shakespeare

THE TRAGI-COMEDIES

perfectly accomplished in his one masterpiece in the mixed type, *The Tempest.*

Troilus and Cressida, apparently the earliest of the tragi-comedies, is the most difficult of all the Shakespearean plays to classify, as it is the most difficult to explain. Everything about its history conspires to add to its puzzling character. The quarto title-page called it a "history"; the writer of the publisher's preface spoke of it as a comedy; the folio editors classified it as a tragedy. There is evidence of its having been performed by Shakespeare's company, yet the preface just referred to claimed that it "was never staled with the stage." Incidentally there was trouble with the copyright; and when the folio was being printed it appears that this play was temporarily omitted, being eventually restored in a different place in the volume from that originally assigned to it, with a resulting disturbance of pagination and other details. Dark suspicions that it figured in the quarrels of the theatrical companies, and that the character of Ajax was intended to parody Ben Jonson, have added to the difficulties of discussing it. Regarding this latter point it may be said at once that the more it is investigated the less foundation for the suspicion appears. For present purposes all these accessory problems can be dismissed; but the play itself still leaves quite enough to perplex us.

To its contemporaries *Troilus and Cressida* was what the quarto called it, a history-play, dealing with the familiar story of the Trojan War. Probably not long before its appearance, the versatile Heywood had produced a popular success on the same subject, *The Iron Age,* and the theme had been abundantly used in other literature, both dramatic and non-dramatic, of the period. Instead of following Heywood in attempting to treat the whole story of the conflict between Greeks and Trojans, the writer of the present version (perhaps not Shakespeare himself, in the first instance) confined the "historical" action to the time of the final duel between Hector and Achilles; thus the Prologue takes pains to point out that the play "leaps o'er" the early incidents of the struggle,

> Beginning in the middle, starting thence away
> To what may be digested in a play.

With this matter of Achilles and Hector, and associated persons, the dramatist combined the equally familiar story of the love of Troilus for the faithless Cressida, as it had been told by Chaucer and further developed by many of Chaucer's successors. The two plots were well adapted for union in the manner of Elizabethan multiplicity, and are dexterously interwined in the exposition of the play. So far all is promising; but disappointment soon sets in. The dramatist turns out to have no real interest in Cressida, either as the sympathetically interpreted coquette of the Chaucerian version or the utterly abandoned woman that she had become in the lore of the fifteenth and sixteenth centuries. He accepts the latter point of view, in general, but makes nothing of it; the love story, having started as ribald comedy, and being apparently on the way to some degraded sort of tragedy, disappears altogether as if lost in the mire, and plays no part in the concluding action. The story of Hector and Achilles appealed to the author more strongly, and is made the opportunity for a few effective and noble scenes. But this also fails to be worked out according to the plot which seems to have been newly designed for it (the plan to arouse Achilles by a sense of rivalry with Ajax), and the close of the principal story is handled in the manner of mere chronicle-history. Indeed it is difficult to exaggerate the dramatic futility of the whole effect. The final scenes cannot represent Shakespeare's intention; and, since their style and verse also give evidence of another hand, it is agreed that for some reason he did not write the conclusion of the play. Perhaps he was, throughout, rewriting a play now lost, and, failing to complete the task, left the original scenes to survive at the close. Perhaps he left an unfinished and unsatisfying sketch of his own, which was botchily completed by another. No evidence enables us to decide.

But the trouble is deeper than this. The mood or spirit of the play is more baffling than the abortive plotting. We have seen that it has never been clearly distinguished as either comedy or tragedy, and this is by no means wholly due to the ambiguous ending. The end of Hector's story was certainly tragic, and that of Troilus and Cressida was bound to be so too,—if it had been wrought out to an end at all. But in the play as a whole the comedy element is actually far more prominent. Both the supposedly serious plots are interpreted with an almost brutal flippancy which makes impossible any definite attachment of the sympathies, and produces the effect of a moral and emotional hodge-podge. The matter of the irreverent treatment of Homeric tradition has been much over-emphasized by modern readers, and need not in itself disturb us; for recent historical study has made it clear that in this respect the Shakespearean play is only carrying on traditions which the Troy story had accumulated in the generations preceding Shakespeare's time. The unromantic and even repulsive Cressida, the farcically unheroic Ajax, had already become conventional, and surprised no Elizabethan audience. We cannot then explain the play as deliberately satiric, as if it were written in conscious despite of the classical tradition, or with a cynical desire to make light of both love and valor. In fact it no more maintains a satiric tone than any other. In a few sincere and serious scenes the nobler Greeks, and more especially the nobler Trojans, are presented with all the dignity which we could desire; and these scenes make the loose-tongued and loose-knit comedy of the rest of the play the more conspicuous. We have, then, when we look below the surface, not a drama at all, in the usual sense of a dramatic whole, but a series of scenes whose relation to one another and to the purposes of their writers remains unexplained.

Beauty, then, we should hardly hope to find in *Troilus and Cressida*. Yet there is some astonishing poetry, of a more prevailingly intellectual sort than Shakespeare found place for in any other drama. Whether from hints given by the writer whose work it is supposed he was remodeling, or from his own interest in classic lore, he seems at times to have deliberately adapted his style to the venerable material of the play, in a certain learned weightiness both of form and substance. Especially in representing Ulysses, famed for his mentality among other warriors distinguished for physical prowess, the verse takes on this curiously academic tone:

> How could communities,
> Degrees in schools, and brotherhoods in cities,
> Peaceful commerce from dividable shores,
> The primogenitive and due of birth,
> Prerogative of age, crowns, sceptres, laurels,
> But by degree, stand in authentic place? . . .
>
> The still and mental parts,
> That do contrive how many hands shall strike
> When fitness calls them on, and know by measure
> Of their observant toil the enemies' weight,—
> Why, this hath not a finger's dignity.
> (I, iii, 103—08, 200—04.)

How little here of the melody for which Shakespeare has taught us to listen in his more finely wrought utterances! We shall hardly find those melodies anywhere in the present play; but in certain other passages Ulysses rises to imaginative as well as intellectual impressiveness:

> Time hath, my lord, a wallet at his back,
> Wherein he puts alms for oblivion,
> A great-sized monster of ingratitudes.
> Those scraps are good deeds past, which are devour'd
> As fast as they are made. . . .
>
> One touch of nature makes the whole world kin,
> That all, with one consent, praise new-born gauds,
> Though they are made and molded of things past,
> And give to dust that is a little gilt
> More laud than gilt o'erdusted.
> (III, iii, 145—49, 175—79.)

One perceives that the great Ithacan could have conversed on fairly equal terms with Hamlet or Horatio, had he included Denmark in his travels. Yet such lines only renew our wondering query as to what possible audience could have enjoyed reflective scenes like this and also the negligent ribaldry of a great part of the play.

In *Measure for Measure,* which may have followed *Troilus and Cressida* at no great interval, we have no such problem as in the earlier play. This is a strong and firmly wrought story; nor has there commonly been any hesitation in placing it among the comedies. Originally the plot came from the same source as that of *Othello,* Giraldi Cinthio's collection of tales, but Shakespeare found it in a comedy written by George Whetstone some twenty-five years before. In the older versions the story was highly conventional,—one of many tales of unjust judges who took advantage of their position to seduce the honor of petitioning ladies, and restored that honor by marrying them in the end. Such a tale, however, could not be used by Shakespeare without undergoing a change in moral quality, and the present one he clearly took some pains to transform. The heroine he made wholly pure, and her personality alone almost ennobles the sadly sordid mass out of which it blooms. Angelo the judge he undertook to make a real man, falling from honest purposes into evil, and shocked at his own moral collapse, instead of the conventional seducer of other versions. Yet something in Shakespeare's material, or in his attitude toward it, impaired the powers of characterization which we have found so highly developed in the other plays of this period, so that we can call the result no more than a partial success. Angelo is demoralized with a suddenness, and discusses his desires with a bald effect of meeting the dramatic emergency, which remind us of the less honorable devices of Beaumont and Fletcher in their many plots of sensual passion some few years later. Again, since the design demanded at the same time a seduction plot and a happy ending, Shakespeare found a solution of the moral difficulty by introducing the sub-plot of Mariana, and making Angelo only the seducer of his deserted fiancée in disguise. A solution it is, in a certain real sense, and, merely as a story, a highly interesting addition; yet it is obvious that it does not go very far toward making true comedy out of situations which imply either tragedy or particularly ignoble farce.

From this it may be partly evident why the play produces a tragi-comic effect. Not chiefly because it brings some of its characters near death (according to Fletcher's formula) yet saves them alive, though it does this with sensational effectiveness, but because from first to last it seems sombre, despite the abundant low-comedy detail, and at the close has accumulated the materials for a tragedy, from which it is saved by only half legitimate means. This is partly, no doubt, a matter of altered taste; perhaps very few of Shakespeare's original audience had any such scruples. But, whether he realized it or not, it was impossible for him to enter into the spirit of the story, viewed as comedy, as Boccaccio could have done in an earlier day, or Fletcher in a later. He shows that sense of the mingled folly and vileness of human nature which his tragedies of the same period were exhibiting beyond any other works in the world.

> Our natures do pursue,
> Like rats that ravin down their proper bane,
> A thirsty evil; and when we drink we die;—
>
> (I, ii, 132—34.)

a paraphrase, one might say, of the sonnet on lust. Man,

> like an angry ape,
> Plays such fantastic tricks before high heaven
> As makes the angels weep.
>
> (II, ii, 120—22.)

Shakespeare does not boggle, then, with truth of character or conduct, striving to force us to admire the unadmirable. We know precisely what to think of Angelo,—Angelo does himself. The boggling is only with the outcome. There is no true "measure for measure" in it, and Shakespeare might himself have agreed with Coleridge, who called the whole "a hateful work."[2]

But again we find poetry of a mature and noble kind. The lines just quoted are memorable examples; and there is also Isabella's plea for mercy, wherein Portia's is rewritten and made both deeper and more dramatic:

> Why, all the souls that were were forfeit once,
> And He that might the vantage best have took
> Found out the remedy. How would you be,
> If He which is the top of judgment should
> But judge you as you are? Oh, think on that,
> And mercy then will breathe within your lips.
>
> (II, ii, 73—78.)

[2] *Table Talk,* June 24, 1827.

On the other hand, the Duke's great speech on being "absolute for death," though rhetorically magnificent, is a rare survival of the undramatic interlude or monologue,— not now lyrical, as in earlier plays, but profoundly reflective.

The third of the sombre comedies, *All's Well that Ends Well*, is peculiarly difficult to date. It gives evidence of representing Shakespeare's style in periods both earlier and later than that when it is generally thought to have been produced; perhaps it is safest to believe the play to be a late re-working of a composition which he had begun some years before. In any case it forms a kind of link between the tragi-comedies of the *Measure for Measure* type and those which are more of the nature of romance; it resembles the former in certain disagreeable qualities of theme and mood, and the latter in its adventurous richness of plot. The story is from Boccaccio (found in the Third Day of the *Decameron*), and in its Italian form was destitute of either moral or psychological significance. The principal device in its plotting is much the same as that which Shakespeare had used in the story of Mariana; now he not only makes it again a solution of the knot of the play, but puts it into the action of the principal heroine,— a daring experiment from the standpoint of the sympathies. Boccaccio's story, in other words, requires the dramatist to interest us in a heroine who chooses and marries a husband against his will, and eventually wins him by substituting herself, in a disguise plot, for his mistress. Shakespeare knew but one way to solve the difficulty,— by creating a heroine of precisely the character to make this conduct plausible, dignified, and consistent with true womanliness. The result is Helena. That he succeeded wholly in so all but impossible a task, one may not care to affirm; but that many readers have thought he succeeded is in itself a notable tribute to his powers.

The hero, on the other hand, is an unmitigated rascal, not quite bad enough to be worth while as a study in villainy, and certainly far too bad (like a number of Shakespeare's minor heroes) to be a mate for the woman whose union with him we are asked to consider a happy ending. Shakespeare did not interest himself greatly in Bertram's personality. If he had, tragedy would have loomed up even more certainly than in *Measure for Measure*. Indeed, though the atmosphere of the present play is less gloomy,—less touched with an intimate sense of moral vileness,—it is once more true that the essential characters and situations imply a tragic outcome as the only satisfaction for the judgment; and once more we have a hasty whitewashing of the villain and a patched-up resolution as of a comic plot. Boccaccio's cynical cheerfulness has been lost, as it was bound to be in Shakespeare, and the result is again morally honest, but without either dramatic logic or intelligible unity of sympathetic appeal.

Shakespeare's want of sympathy with his own material in *All's Well* is also evidenced by the comic under-plot of Parolles. This personage, a braggart coward soldier (or *miles gloriosus*), is of a type very familiar on the later Elizabethan stage,—notably represented, for example, by Jonson's Bobadil in *Every Man in his Humour*. Falstaff himself is sometimes referred to the same type, but if he belonged to it in origin, he speedily broke through his mold; whereas Parolles is characterized in an essentially conventional manner. Neither can he be said greatly to promote our cheerfulness. No one, to be sure, would refuse him a laugh, and the termination of his career in the brilliant discomfiture scene in the fourth act is a dramatic triumph in its kind. But Shakespeare treats Parolles satirically rather than sympathetically; he ministers less to a sense of good humor than to the conviction that the world is made up chiefly of rascals. On this conviction Jonson's comedy was largely based, and he appropriately used a succession of rascally character-types to carry it out; but the mood clashes oddly with Shakespeare's romantic plots and his prevailingly romantic modes of interpretation.

Since our chronology is uncertain, and we have no evidence to show just why Shakespeare undertook experiments like *Measure for Measure* and *All's Well*, apparently as a minor task in the period of his great tragedies, we cannot trace out with much assurance what happened in the development of his tragi-comic art. The natural first impression, safe enough in itself, is that his interest at this time was so concentrated in the tragic field that any demands for plays of other types received only the dregs of his imaginative energy. Works thus written could not wholly escape his masterly technical powers, nor fail of stirring him to occasional ascents on the wings of poetry; but they did not stimulate any such unifying creative mood as he had formerly found in stories of fortunate love and was now finding in stories of passionate failure. It was the more base and sinister side of love which now revealed itself, even in the matter which he chose for comic interpretation, and he did not try to hide it, but let it have its evil way, until some stroke of Fortune or the dramatist thrust it aside. The result of this was unhappy plays with "happy endings." Another natural result was a decline in dramatic characterization; for plots not logically dependent upon the motives involved in them do not demand the same vital realization of personality as those treated in a finer fashion. Nevertheless, while he was doubtless aware of these defects, Shakespeare may have found himself becoming interested in the technique of tragi-comic drama,—in the problem of admitting the evil in human life and at the same time opening ways of escape from it. He came back to this problem, at any rate, at the close of his tragic period, and studied anew the possibilities of tragi-comic romance.

Meantime we must give passing notice to the exceedingly unromantic play of *Timon of Athens,* which Shakespeare may be thought to have undertaken as a by-product of his reading in Plutarch, and to have left unfinished. It was included by his editors in the folio, but is universally admitted to be in part the work of another writer; and the more it is studied, the more likely it appears that the unknown collaborator completed what Shakespeare had begun.[3] In the Life of Antony, Plutarch had given an account of a famous Athenian misanthrope, and Lucian the satirist had also a dialogue on the subject, which Shakespeare evidently made use of directly or indirectly. The story, which concerns a man who came to hate his fellows because he discovered that they had loved him only for his wealth, is clearly matter for comedy, as

---

[3] The scenes most commonly ascribed to Shakespeare are I, 1; II, 1; III, i and ii; IV, 1; V, i, ii, and iv; and considerable portions of II, ii; III, vi; IV, ii and iii.

Lucian had treated it; and the Shakespearean drama is satiric comedy almost throughout. But Timon's grave and epitaph were an important feature of the legend (they are introduced into the play almost in the literal words of North's version of Plutarch); hence the action must end with his death, and merge into ostensible tragedy. So far, however, from there being a tragic catastrophe in the usual sense, Timon dies off stage (we do not even know why), and the spectator sees only his tomb, discovered on "the beached verge of the salt flood." The question whether the play should be classified with the tragedies or the comedies is of no importance in itself, save to an occasional editor, but the point is that it reverses, in an interesting way, the case of *Measure for Measure* and *All's Well*. In them the story was treated with much seriousness, but brought to a professedly cheerful conclusion; here the plot is made to work out as tragedy, but is treated for the most part in a comic spirit. Take for example the scene in which the guests at Timon's banquet are served only warm water in their dishes:[4] farce and irony are its essence, as they are of a good part of the play. The same scene also brings out the undramatic character of *Timon*. Though effective enough for narrative, the incident is of slight value for theatrical representation; and the same is true of the story as a whole. It is fitted only to play an under-part to some more truly dramatic plot. Very possibly it was Shakespeare's growing realization of the fact that led him to abandon the undertaking. At any rate, our interest in his work upon it is limited largely to two matters: the ironic mixed mood which is so oddly allied

[4] III, vi.

to both the tragic and the comic incidents, and the brilliant rhetorical violence of Timon's outbursts, which sometimes rise into really noble poetry. In the scenes where these occur, the misanthrope becomes a kind of glorified Thersites, or scurrilous Jeremiah.

Of the same period, apparently, is another play of perplexing composite authorship, *Pericles, Prince of Tyre*. In quarto it was published with Shakespeare's name, but his editors did not include it in the folio,—it is difficult to conjecture why. That he did not write the whole drama is admitted: recent opinion is pretty well agreed that the first two acts are the work of another, while most of the remainder may be called Shakespeare's. Presumably he either consented to complete an unfinished play which had come into the possession of his company, or undertook to rewrite a complete one, but for some reason left the opening acts much as he found them. The moment we enter the third act, and pass the doggerel prologue, his verse unmistakably breaks upon us in the storm scene:

> Thou god of this great vast, rebuke these surges,
> Which wash both heaven and hell; and thou that hast
> Upon the winds command, bind them in brass,
> Having call'd them from the deep!

The story was a very old one, being familiar in the Middle Age under the name of "Apollonius of Tyre"; it was known to English readers especially through its retelling in the *Confessio Amantis* of John Gower, whom the designer of the play of *Pericles* appropriately makes the speaker of the explanatory prologues.

The folio editors, no doubt, would have put this drama

among the comedies, if they had included it at all, yet it represents a type so distinct from that of any earlier Shakespearean play as to call for some new dramatic category. The title of the quarto gives us more than a clue to its nature in adding the words, "With the true relation of the whole history, adventures, and fortunes of the said Prince; as also the no less strange and worthy accidents in the birth and life of his daughter." That is to say, the play is a pageant of adventure rather than a true drama,—the dramatizing of an elaborate romance rather than of a concentrated story of one or two single actions. Momentarily it recalls *Henry the Fifth,* especially since the same device of partly narrative prologue-choruses is once more called in to supplement the dramatic scenes. But in *Henry the Fifth* there was an expository purpose which provided a peculiar kind of unity of theme; moreover, the greater part of the action was devoted to a single military campaign. In the *Pericles* type of play the only unity, as in a romance, is that of the person or persons who experience the long succession of adventures that pass before our eyes. It is as if the artistic progress of a whole generation had been lost, and we had returned to the crude undertakings of the early dramatizers of biblical and historical material. Shakespeare, of course, was quite conscious of this, and doubtless found the experiment amusing in both senses of the word.

Now such a tale requires no characterization to make it effective; indeed it would be a positive hindrance to seek to derive any considerable portion of the action from the inner nature of the persons. The very essence of the old story is that Pericles was tossed about on the sea of mysterious fortune, the flotsam of the winds of destiny, and brought to port at last only by a final favorable breeze. No chance, here, for either comedy or tragedy of character; and the prevailing mood is one neither of sadness nor merriment, but of expectant childlike wonder. Yet Shakespeare did not stop with this aspect of the story. In Pericles' daughter Marina he saw opportunity not merely for the creation of another charming feminine personality, but for making that personality count in its own dramatic fortunes. Thus the fourth act, which tells of Marina's being sold to the pirates, imprisoned in a brothel, and delivering herself by her mere purity and courage, is a true condensed drama set in the midst of the romantic pageant. Repulsive scenes like those in the brothel at Mytilene seem to have been a decadently popular feature of the Elizabethan stage in this era, and we have seen Shakespeare approximating to them in some of the earlier plays. (Perhaps it is needful to recall the disagreeable fact that a brothel, for the Elizabethans of London, was as familiar a circumstance as the liquor saloon in the life and literature of America in the nineteenth century.) He caters frankly to the low taste that revels in their foul details, and himself revels in presenting the contrast of a purity which they could not smirch. Marina's character, then, gives us another example of the indispensable connection of characterization with truly dramatic structure. We might note, finally, that the scene of her reunion with her father, in the last act,[5] is one of the most beautiful examples, for these later plays, of Shakespeare's blending of poetry with dramatic speech.

[5] V, 1, 85-215.

Cymbeline must have followed not long after *Pericles,* but it represents a decided development in experimentation with similar material. The folio editors called it *The Tragedy of Cymbeline,* but perhaps for no better reason than that it purported to deal with the fortunes of a king; modern editors place it among the comedies because of its happy ending. In fact it is a romantic tragi-comedy curiously set in a framework of chronicle-history,—a story of Italian intrigue, drawn from Boccaccio, and transferred with great boldness to a setting taken from Holinshed's chronicle of Britain. Time and place, of course, are nothing: the atmosphere is that of neither Renaissance Italy nor primitive Britain, but of the wonder-world of romance. With technical skill almost unprecedented even in his own work, Shakespeare crowded into the limits of the two interwoven plots sufficient adventure to satisfy the hungriest story-loving soul; the final act alone has been alleged to contain a score of "situations" any one of which might make the fortune of a play. Some of these devices were recalled to life from the romantic comedies of from ten to twenty years before,—strange poisonous drugs, apparent death, forest wanderings, a maiden disguised as a boy, —while others were added from the still unused treasures of fiction. In the wealth of plot detail one finds, if he consider too curiously, a number of inconsistencies or minor flaws, which have led some to think that the play contains the work of an inferior hand; but on that there is no sound basis for agreement. The dramatic unity is certainly greater than in *Pericles,* yet the author followed the same general method, taking the action from one point to another, both of space and time, as an effective scene suggested itself, with small effort to select and concentrate his material. Hence the outcome is a brilliant many-sided story, but not what either the conscience of Shakespeare or of anyone else would admit to be a good play.

Yet in one important respect *Cymbeline* seems much more a drama than *Pericles;* the action is less a matter of fortune, and more a matter of the clash of human wills. Most of the characters, to be sure, are but slightly individualized; Posthumus and Iachimo, when compared with Othello and Iago, whose relations were so similar, fade into insignificance; nevertheless they act and react in the manner of real *dramatis personæ,* if not of the real persons of human life. But the personality of Imogen is the chief point. It pervades the whole play, not animating one act only, as with Marina in *Pericles,* and seems to make other persons and their actions exist for her sake. Again Shakespeare had conceived a heroine who retained both purity and strength of will in a world swept by evil passions,—

> a mark of everlasting light
> Above the howling senses' ebb and flow;

and again he asks us to rejoice over her final union with a hero unworthy to lick the dust at her feet. How far Imogen is individualized with creative vividness is a matter that has proved debatable; thus one distinguished critic goes so far as to call her the "woman above all Shakespeare's women," while another views her as primarily a type,—the idyllic heroine of the whole period of the dramatic romances.[6] Both exaggerate: Imogen has a charm all

---

[6] See the extracts from Swinburne and A. H. Thorndike in the New Variorum edition of *Cymbeline,* pp. 511, 514.

her own, quite beyond the reach, in its mingled delicacy and intensity, of any other dramatist of the period; yet one feels, as with all the other characters of these later plays, that her personality is determined specifically by her circumstances, by her story, rather than that her story arises from herself. For whatever reason, Shakespeare's supreme power of individualization of character had either greatly weakened, or, during this whole last period, was deliberately laid aside.

The style of *Cymbeline* is exceedingly uneven,—often pregnant and vivid, frequently cumbrous and difficult, like the structure. Here we meet for the first time in its full effect that characteristic verse and manner of Shakespeare's final period, which we have been approaching in the later tragedies and the earlier tragi-comedies. The element of melody has grown pretty steadily less; the weight of thought has tended to obscure rhythm, and to approximate the movement of prose. In the plays of the early period one is frequently tempted to read the verse with something of lyric movement and tone, and to neglect the *nuances* of dramatic dialogue, just as pure speech emphasis always disappears in song. In the middle period, generally speaking, one can emphasize both verse and meaning at once,—either will take care of the other, so perfect is the equipoise of poetry and speech. In this last period, the verse is in danger of losing out in the interest of the meaning, and the single iambic line often disappears altogether as a unit of rhythmic structure. Obscurity of rhythm thus tends to go hand in hand with obscurity of close-packed thought. Compare, for example, this bit of military narrative with any one of similar purport in the days of *Henry the Fourth* or *Henry the Fifth:*

> These three,
> Three thousand confident, in act as many—
> For three performers are the file when all
> The rest do nothing—with this word "Stand, stand,"
> Accommodated by the place, more charming
> With their own nobleness, which could have turned
> A distaff to a lance, gilded pale looks,
> Part shame, part spirit renewed; that some, turned coward
> But by example—Oh, a sin in war,
> Damn'd in the first beginners!—gan to look
> The way that they did, and to grin like lions
> Upon the pikes o' the hunters.
>   (V, iii, 28—39.)

One sees the analogy between the evolution of this sort of style and that of the later prose of Henry James, or of the musical style of Beethoven in his later sonatas. A marked intellectual development, with greatly increased proportionate interest in ideas, has impaired the simpler sense of form and the function of direct communication with the average hearer. But a taste to the manner trained may find a special kind of pleasure in this subtler structure of both thought and form.

The next dramatic romance, *The Winter's Tale*, tells a story more closely akin to that of *Pericles* than to that of *Cymbeline*. It was made from the contents of a prose romance of Greene's, and deals with a plot which demands the o'er-leaping of many years; that is, the infant of the opening scenes is to be, like Marina, the heroine of the closing ones. But how different from that of *Pericles* is

THE TRAGI-COMEDIES

the method which Shakespeare now devises! He divides the matter of the story into two parts, each fairly unified in both action and time, each presented with utter clearness and—what is more important still—with an intensity of sympathy which has not appeared to at all the same extent in the other tragi-comic plays. The first part is to all appearance a tragedy, built on the same theme that had been studied in *Othello* and *Cymbeline,* the groundless questioning of a wife's fidelity (a conventional Renaissance theme); only now it is not due to villainy, as in the other cases, but to an ignoble gust of jealous passion, which we are to accept as the very datum of the story. The second part is a pastoral comedy of the younger generation, united with the happy solution of the seeming tragedy of their elders. To serve as link between the two actions, Shakespeare creates a highly significant character, Paulina; and further, at the single point of division, the opening of the fourth act, he introduces a prologue chorus in the old manner, announcing the leap over sixteen years. Thus all the charm of the long-drawn adventurous romance is preserved, with most of its dramatic drawbacks done away.

The stage sensationalism which was now insistently demanded in the London theatre is still ministered to abundantly in *The Winter's Tale,* as it had been in *Pericles* and *Cymbeline.* There is a wild bear, a shipwreck, the discovery of a foundling, a pastoral dance or two (one of shepherds, one of satyrs), and, to crown all, the great statue scene—the finest legitimate piece of theatrical sensation in English drama. All this marks the fact that we are still among the romances. So does the fact that we are intended to be wholly surprised by the dénouement.

When the third act is over we believe—if we are reading or seeing the play for the first time—that Hermione is dead: the trick is not merely on Leontes, it is on the audience. Such a method marks an essentially inferior type of drama, beautifully effective as it is in this instance. But while we find all these signs of what may be called a decadent type still with us, we also find, more here than in *Cymbeline,* as we found more in *Cymbeline* than in *Pericles,* that the elements of human character and motive are made essential to the action; the outcome does not depend on the caprices of fortune alone. The person of Paulina, though in our sympathies less important than Hermione or Perdita, exemplifies this most clearly: she is individualized rather more than any other serious person in the whole group of romances, and this is because she is so largely a motive-force in the drama. We are quite prepared to find Shakespeare throwing all his emphasis in the way of sympathetic characterization into the three women who have just been named. The parts of Hermione and Perdita are largely passive, so that we are still disposed to be more interested in what happens to them than in what they are; but either of them, if occasion required, could easily become a heroine of the old-time effective sort. When Perdita, thinking that her love affair with Florizel is forever ended, beautifully brings the incident to a close in saying,

> Will 't please you, sir, be gone?
> I told you what would come of this. Beseech you,
> Of your own state take care. This dream of mine,
> Being now awake, I'll queen it no inch farther,—
>
> (IV, iv, 456—59.)

we seem for the moment to be back in the days of Shakespeare's chief feminine creations. But presently Perdita retires into her place as a lovely passive figure in the romance, in the last act being hardly allowed a word. Yet how grateful we are for this autumn blooming of young love, near the close of Shakespeare's work, and for his exquisite linking of it to the richly mature affections of Perdita's mother!

For the male characters of the play, we can only pause to notice that there is again a reminder of Shakespeare's earlier period in the special zest which he throws into the characterization of the humbler persons. Autolycus and the shepherd-clown both introduce a touch of spicy English realism which has not appeared in such full measure since the days of *As You Like It;* and in general, as has already been hinted, Shakespeare embedded in the second part of this tragi-comedy a revival of pure comic mirth such as we could scarcely have hoped—after what we have passed through in his later career—to meet again.

The Tempest must have been first composed very close to the time of *The Winter's Tale.* We know that it was produced at court in the autumn of 1611, and next hear of it as one of the plays performed at the festivities in honor of the marriage of the Princess Elizabeth, in the spring of 1613. Like the *Midsummer Night's Dream,* it gives every reader the impression of having been written expressly for a wedding festivity, an impression strengthened by the fact that it is much shorter than the usual stage-play and by the further fact that it was apparently designed for extraordinarily elaborate scenic presentation. All these circumstances are best explained by the theory that it was first written in 1611, as a tragi-comedy of the usual length, and was revised and shortened in 1613 for the occasion of the court marriage,—perhaps now introducing, as some suppose, certain touches designed to suggest a parallel between Prospero and King James, and between Miranda and the Princess Elizabeth. Just what alterations were made, if this view is the true one, it is not needful to inquire; but there is much plausibility in the conjecture, lately made by a clever Shakespearean, that the marriage masque in the fourth act was substituted for a more serious—perhaps even semi-tragic—story of a conflict between Prospero and the evil forces led by Caliban, of which we have incomplete hints in the play as it stands. In other words, if this were true we should recognize that *The Tempest* was originally a romantic tragi-comedy, in much the same sense as *Cymbeline* and *The Winter's Tale*, whereas it has become a simpler and more beautiful, but rather less dramatic composition,—a masque-like dramatic romance.

Two comparisons are inevitable in the consideration of this play, that with the plays immediately preceding it, and that with the *Midsummer Night's Dream,* which it seems to resemble in being a festival *pièce d'occasion*. From the first point of view, resemblances and contrasts are equally striking. There is the same type of story,—events whose scope covers two generations, full of adventure of the most brilliantly sensational character; great wrong, followed by reconciliation; idyllic pastoral simplicity in contrast with grotesqueness and violence. Yet the dramatic method is wholly regenerated. The change, to be sure, had been anticipated in the bettering of the method of *Pericles* in *Cymbeline,* and the still greater improvement in *The Winter's Tale.* This evolution toward sound artistic form is now carried to its last possibility. The life-time story is concentrated into a single day; there has been no such unity of time since the *Comedy of Errors,* no such unity of place anywhere in Shakespeare. It is as if he had resolved to hold fast to all the riches and variety of the new romantic drama, and to show the possibility of combining with them the technique of the classical school,—"infinite riches in a little room." In any case the outcome is one of the world's supreme pieces of dramatic composition. The principal plot has not been traced with definiteness to any source; but it is clear that for the setting of his drama Shakespeare drew upon recent accounts of voyaging and exploration in the western hemisphere. Caliban the monster, too, must have been composed in part from tales of "cannibal" savages of the new world, in whom interest had lately been stimulated by the importation of certain specimens into England. Recent investigation also makes it probable that many of the principal incidents of *The Tempest* were suggested by performances of Italian players in the *commedia dell' arte,* such as we know were frequent in London at this period. Thus a single manuscript record of the scenarios of some of these comedies includes the representation of a magician on an island, the raising of a tempest, the summoning of outlandish satyrs through the arts of a magic book, together with the adventures of strangers who lose and find one another in the same land of supernatural mystery. All this carries us far from the more conventional plots of *Cymbeline* and *The Winter's Tale,* and teases the fancy strangely, as one pictures Shakespeare for the last time drawing upon the old treasure-house of Italian story, and blending with its wonders others from the latest lore of British seamen.

When we turn to the comparison with the *Midsummer Night's Dream,* every reader first observes a difference between the effects of the supernatural elements in that early composition and those in *The Tempest.* The fairies of the former play were creatures of a more or less conventional type, and might be thought of as familiar residents of Europe; Ariel and the other strange beings of the island are new creations, dwellers on this one enchanted spot. More important is the fact that the supernatural persons and powers of the late play seem somehow to be of more serious import than those of the earlier. They impress one not as mere toys of the fancy, designed to make sport of the more fantastic aspects of human fortune, but as significant of deeper experiences. No doubt this has been much exaggerated in modern criticism: one who goes back and reads the play as if he had never seen a commentary on it will be likely to throw overboard much of the baggage of interpretation with which it has been weighted; and if he sees it well performed, he will discover how large the element of jovial, even farcical, comedy must have loomed before its early audiences. Yet one cannot get away from the other element, and the fact that the play tempts sane commentators to symbolic interpretations. The names of Ariel and Caliban are not merely fanciful, but suggestive; and their natures may also be thought to savor of symbolism. The same is true of both the name and the nature of Prospero. Hence we have an atmosphere unlike anything else in Shakespeare, and somewhat akin to that of the *Faery Queene,*—one which leads men to try to show that Prospero stands for King James, for Providence, or for Shakespeare himself. Certainly nothing of the kind is worked out in full allegory, and one should hesitate long before making affirmations which imply a type of art so foreign to the known method of the author of the play. It is safe only to say that the gravely mature use of the supernatural made by Shakespeare in *The Tempest* hints at an experiment of a new kind, in which he touches the mystery of human fortune with a certain vague symbolism, half personifying the forces of good and evil which wait upon men's motives, and the ultimate order or cosmos which brings peace and unity out of their strife.

The most tempting of the symbolic interpretations, according to which the poet is representing the end of his own career in Prospero's abandonment of his "so potent art," every reader wishes to be true. The only serious objection to it is the want of a scintilla of evidence that it *is* true. Yes, it is even to be feared that we have some evidence pointing the other way,—such as Shakespeare's inveterate suppression of himself in his writings, and the questionable boldness of intruding such a matter as his retirement upon the great presence for which *The Tempest* was probably composed. Yet there may be no harm in fancying that he saw how far certain of his lines were susceptible of a more personal meaning than the scene required; or, that some of those who saw the play performed at Whitehall, on the most brilliant occasion that the palace had ever known, were aware that its author would contribute nothing more to the glories of such festal nights, and, so informed, smiled sadly at one another when Prospero promised to break his staff.

To whatever extent we read anything of symbolism into the drama, a vaguer and more typical kind of characterization is clearly appropriate to such a manner than that fitted to dramatic action of the normal and rational human kind; and this is just what appears. Miranda, as her name demands, has been greatly—and cannot be too greatly—admired, yet surely every reader feels that she is a lovely type of maiden innocence,—of Eden nature, before the eating of the tree of knowledge,—rather than a strongly individual creation. Nothing could be more appropriate to the story. In like manner the peculiar conditions of *The Tempest* justify the romantic practice, which in other cases may be called decadent, of making the element of action superior to that of character. With Prospero and his wand in control of events, how could we ask that they should arise chiefly from the personalities of those concerned? Drama would disappear altogether if we could clearly see the threads of the pattern woven by the Destinies; and this play puts us, for the nonce, in a similar position. Hence it might be said to move in a plane above, instead of below, that of ordinary dramatic art.

The element of reconciliation, so beautifully characteristic of *The Tempest,* we have seen growing steadily into the fibre of Shakespeare's tragi-comedy. In one sense it is a natural feature of the technique of such plots: when wrong has been done, if everything is to end happily, a good way out is to pardon the wrong. In *Measure for Measure* and *All's Well* we saw that the easy pardoning of offences produced a disagreeable impression of illogicality,—of a hurried makeshift ending of the story; and the same might be said of *Cymbeline.* ''Pardon's the word to all,'' says the king; but one wonders just what Imogen thinks about it. In *The Winter's Tale* the case is very different: there the spirit of reconciliation is embodied in Hermione. There is nothing tawdry about it, nothing of makeshift; the charracters of both the king and the queen have been developed by suffering to the point where forgiveness is a spiritual fact. In *The Tempest*, for reasons just noted, the conclusion is not so fully expressed in terms of character development, yet Prospero again may be said to sum up in himself the attainment, through years of spiritual experience, of both peace and pardon. Translated into the religious terms of Milton's generation, his story might well end with the great words that close the *Samson Agonistes:*

> His servants He, with new acquist
> Of true experience from this great event,
> With peace and consolation hath dismissed,
> And calm of mind, all passion spent.

Why did Shakespeare pass from the more stable and artistically serious types of drama on which he had spent the better part of his life, to this looser and experimental kind which marks his later period, whether we call it tragicomedy, romance, or drama of reconciliation? Two widely different answers have been made, representing different schools of criticism. One of these emphasizes the dramatist's personality. Assuming that Shakespeare wrote at least in part to please himself, and was inevitably tied to his own moods, we may suppose (it is said) that in his middle period he was profoundly affected by the problem of evil and its relation to human fortunes, so that even his comedy could not escape the influence of this tone of mind. Later, however, he rose above the darker mood, emerged into one in which evil was still frankly admitted, but might be both overcome and forgiven. To some also it seems significant that there is a simple and joyous outdoor atmosphere in these late romantic plays, written at just the time when their author may have been planning to return permanently to his boyhood's country home.

The other answer emphasizes the dramatist's relation to his profession and his public. Since it is evident that there was a growing demand, in the period opening about 1608-10, for melodramatic plays marked by abundant sensational incident, loosely composed adventurous action, and surprisingly happy endings, we may assume (it is said) that Shakespeare, as he had always done, yielded to popular taste, at the same time showing that, whatever the form desired, he could master it triumphantly and raise it to a new level of beauty. In particular, the young dramatists Beaumont and Fletcher were beginning their brilliant joint career at this time, in plays of precisely the type indicated, and were suggesting to Shakespeare new tricks of technique in tragi-comic art. It is of special interest to find that their romance of *Philaster* was written for Shakespeare's own company, and probably was produced in the same year as *Cymbeline,* namely 1610. Unfortunately we cannot say which play appeared first, and are unlikely ever to know whether *Philaster* gave hints to *Cymbeline* or *Cymbeline* to *Philaster.* Certainly, if the older dramatist borrowed something from Beaumont (for it seems to be Beaumont who was responsible for the characteristic features of the new type of play), Beaumont had for a long time been learning from him; in general he was distinctively Shakespeare's dramatic disciple. There need therefore be no jealousy on Shakespeare's behalf. Friends, companions in both poetry and wit, and now co-laborers for the same company of players, they worked, one may suppose, in close conjunction, in developing the new type of dramatic romance, whichever of them happened first to bring it to marked success upon the stage. Beaumont was not only the inferior poet—that would go without saying—but was utterly incapable of informing the new type with the moral dignity and purity which the heroines of the Shakespearean romances characteristically incarnate. There is therefore the less regret that he did not outlive his master, to influence the further development of the form.

These two explanations of Shakespeare's interest in tragi-comedy, though as different as possible, will be seen not to be contradictory. Both could be true at once, provided Shakespeare's mood and taste chanced to coincide with the mood and taste of the public. Of no great popular writer is it possible to say whether he follows his public more or less than it follows him. We may therefore, if we choose (being, as usual, without positive evidence either way), conceive of the forms of Shakespeare's later dramatic work as determined in some degree by theatrical fashion, but may also suppose that the spirit of tragi-comedy was increasingly congenial to his mind. Having sounded the depths of human evil and suffering, he could hardly do other than choose between a relapse into sombre silence and a growing consciousness of the forces of reconciliation. These forces did not make for increased dramatic effectiveness; a tragi-comedy, no matter how fine, is rarely so good a play as a good tragedy. Drama is conflict, and tends, as we have seen, to decay when conflict is avoided or solved. But the brighter forces did make for that serene wisdom which is the finest achievement of a long and sympathetic life. For youth, tragic pain is likely to seem beautiful but unreal; for full manhood, it grows very real, and either stirs the soul to heroic adventure or drives it into bitterness; a still riper age, if the spiritual adventure has been accomplished, is likely to find some resolution of the tragic chord. Sophocles, most like Shakespeare of his predecessors, and Goethe, Wagner, and Ibsen, three great imaginative students of evil in later times, all ended their tragic studies in this mood of reconciliation. To some, this tendency of later life seems a mere weakening of intellectual fibre, a senile unwillingness to "face the facts"; to others it implies an insight into that region where tragedy disappears because the whole course of the passions has done its perfect work, and the human spirit has come into its inheritance.

CHAPTER VIII

SHAKESPEARE

THE man who wrote the poems and plays which we have had under review was first of all a child of his age, a son of Elizabethan England and the Renaissance. In breadth of intellectual curiosity and richness of emotional experience, in strength of national feeling and at the same time in world-wide humanism, he expresses the values of the time in the field of the imagination, as it was given to other men to express them in politics, exploration, and war. And those values were so great in themselves, besides being capable of transmission with relatively little loss through the lapsing centuries, that if Shakespeare had done nothing save to represent them adequately, making no distinctive contribution of his own, he would have been certain to occupy an important place among the poets. To discriminate what he did contribute from the representative elements in his work has been one aim of the whole preceding study, and is the theme of the final attempt to interpret what we have found.

As dramatist, Shakespeare was an Elizabethan to an extent which modern scholarship has tended to make increasingly impressive. At every point his work attaches itself to that which preceded it, without notable break or contrast, so far as the main outlines of his method are concerned. Like his fellows, he undertook primarily to tell vivid and appealing stories in dramatic form, and availed himself of the materials already provided in classical, medieval, and Renaissance fiction, rarely troubling himself to invent, and never exhibiting any specific taste for plotting as an art in itself. A surprisingly large number of his plays appear to be the mere rewriting of novels or plays by other hands, and there is faint evidence that this is true in a number of instances where our information is imperfect. Neither did he contribute anything of a positive character to the technique of his art. He early mastered its essentials, adapted them with growing skill to the conditions of the various periods and types of his work, and was never at a loss to find the right dramatic method for the story in hand. But he was content to use, on the whole, the conventional processes of the playwrights of his time, and set no distinctive stamp upon his dramaturgy which is forever associated with his name, as Molière did, and Ibsen. It seems clear that he was neither greatly interested in the theory of his art nor very conscientious in its practice. Ben Jonson always finds a way to tell us what he thinks of the aim and method of his composition, and we know that he will work it out according to the deep-laid principles of his critical theory. Shakespeare never explains his intentions, and we cannot be sure whether he will carry his structure to a beautifully finished conclusion, or dismiss it hurriedly with only such attention as to ensure a reasonably effective final scene upon the stage. He wrote no play, it seems, to fit a chosen type or to satisfy a pet theory, without reference to his audience, and he gives no sign of being fascinated by the problem of dramatic technique as an end in itself. On the other hand, he cheerfully experimented with, and triumphantly mastered, almost every theatrical mode which, throughout the twenty years of his play-writing, gave pleasure to the Elizabethan public.

In comedy, we have found him first trying out various types which were suggested to him by recent drama of the court, the schools, or the popular stage, and soon settling upon the romantic type, which was concerned chiefly with the interpretation of love and adventure in the comic spirit. That is, he gave up the possibilities of comedy as a means for the satiric "taxation" (as the Elizabethans had it) of the fashions and follies of his fellow-mortals, choosing instead the joy of satisfying their love of story and of idealizing the emotions to which romance gave birth; he sacrificed criticism to poetry, social anatomy to beauty. This means that the proportion of the purely comic is diminished in his product,—for comedy *is* by nature critical, and will only visit the land of romance, not actually dwell there,—and that he is shut out from the company of the chief masters of that realm, Aristophanes, Cervantes, and Molière. Yet he devised, in compensation, a characteristic harmonious concord of the comic and romantic spirits, which only Ariosto and Scott can be said to have approximated; and in that blended art he stands unapproachably first.

In tragedy he adopted the prevailing modes more definitely than in comedy, accepting their extravagances of both action and emotion, but gave the impression of transforming them by the very intensity with which he conceived those deeds and passions. Hence the outline of one of his tragedies will seem both conventional and crude, while the work itself may catch one up with the force of a new-born tornado. Although a thorough Elizabethan in his tragic form, he was so much akin to Sophocles in his perception of the bitter ironies of the human lot and in the sympathy with which he identified himself with those who suffer from them, that in world tragedy he stands by the side of the Athenian master, and no third has arisen to be named beside them. One of the special conventions of the drama of his age, its grotesque mingling of comic with tragic material for sensational variety, Shakespeare transfigured in an extraordinary way, causing the two moods to interpenetrate one another, and the clown to be less an intruder than a minister to the principal theme. This element of the serious-grotesque was originally medieval, and it allies Shakespeare's tragic spirit, in certain aspects, more closely to Dante than to Sophocles. In his tendency to bring the tragic spirit through catastrophe to a point of reconciliation, he was like them both, though in the art of this son of the Renaissance the method of reconciliation was much less spiritual, more earthly, than theirs.

Whether in tragic or comic drama, Shakespeare's chief interest seems to have been in personality. In this he was by no means unique, for it was a characteristic of the humanism of his age. Marlowe, for instance, his immediate predecessor and—in some sense—teacher, we have seen centering his dramas in extraordinary personalities marked by wills doomed to clash with the forces that opposed them. But it was in Shakespeare that Renaissance individualism found its highest expression. We have found him, for the most part, forming his characters from the stories in which they were to play a part,—not making the story to fit a determined character,—and asking himself, apparently, of just what sort of person could these things be true? The answer (especially in his early period) might be largely conventional or typical, the incarnation of an idea appropriate to the conditions. But more and more often it came to be a new creation, so rich and full-blooded as to take the place of a living acquaintance in our minds, and to tempt critics to discuss the character as if it were that of a person who had lived before the play was written, or who continued to exist when the play was done. Thus we have essays written on "the girlhood of Shakespeare's heroines," and others imagining the future careers of lovers whom he shows us only in their youth. All this is likely to prove fallacious: the character, after all, was made for the play, and we can usually make a sound answer to any question raised concerning it only by inquiring what Shakespeare was engaged in doing as a dramatic artist. With the more rudimentary or conventional characters this is absolutely true; to discuss them apart from their immediate place in the action is to fall into hopeless fatuity. Yet the fact that we notice an indefinable gradation in the author's art, from such characters up to those which are supremely individualized, gives interpreters some warrant for viewing the latter sort somewhat after the manner of actual human beings. It is well known that creative artists often find their characters taking on such an aspect in their own minds, and seeming to refuse to follow passively the intentions of their creator. That this was so with Shakespeare is what we should have every reason to expect, in view of the extraordinary vitality of his processes of characterization; and in the study of the plays some evidence of it has appeared. In such different characters as Shylock, Falstaff, Hamlet, and Cleopatra—all of them among the astonishingly vivid, the three-dimensional figures (so to say) of the plays—we found reason to believe that they had taken on such vitality under the dramatist's hand that they filled a different part in the action from that designed for them at the outset, and teased his own purpose by their independent strength. Whether that be so or not, they have taken some such place in the consciousness of the whole world. The artistic process, in instances of this kind, is no doubt essentially the same as with the humblest artist who brings forth a creation that proves to be alive apart from the environment for which it was made; but in degree of effectiveness, and breadth and richness of product, Shakespeare's powers in this realm were unparalleled. His psychology, in general, was that of his time; he availed himself of its familiar conceptions of villainy, virtue, and the relations of desire and thought and will. It would be idle to suppose that he could have used on the popular stage any different system for the interpretation of human conduct from that possessed by his audience, and to read into his creations the metaphysical subtleties of the age of Coleridge and Hegel is as vain and misleading as to show that he knew all that modern science has learned of diseases of the mind. On the other hand, every real dramatist knows more of essential psychology than he has been taught or could formulate; and of this Shakespeare is again the supreme example. For the "sullen and assumed humors" of Edgar's pretended madness he could draw deliberately upon the details of a contemporary tract, but for the processes of the mad Lear's mind (such as, "What! have his daughters brought him to this pass?"[1]) he had only to identify himself with the king through one of his many miracles of imaginative sympathy. So everywhere in his finer work: there are no strange or inspired theories of mental habit, but there are countless instances of the processes of personality outgoing any theory which Shakespeare could have undertaken to explain.

The case is similar when we raise the question of his ideas,—of the intellectual and moral content of the dramas, apart from that which is wrapped up in the action. The age was not an age of new ideas, but of a new zest for the best old ones; and Shakespeare himself contributed practically nothing to the common store. As there is no mode of dramaturgy associated with his name as pioneer, so there is no doctrine of which he was herald or prophet. In the region of ideas his creative energy was wholly unremarkable; practically all our favorites among his sayings are commonplaces in substance, and were when he said them. Why is it, then, that they impress us often as the fresh revelation of truth? Mere perfection of phrasing of course contributes to the impression, but that is not the whole story. It is again largely a matter of the intensity and vitality with which the ideas come to us. They do not arise from a stock of abstract conceptions, but from the experimental process of dramatic life. That is, Shakespeare was an inductive, not a deductive, moralist, as he was an inductive maker of character. Jonson, a deductive artist, built every character on a moral idea, and took pains that the general concept should appear in his text.

[1] *King Lear,* III, iv, 65.

Shakespeare made perhaps only one character by the deductive process, that of Henry the Fifth, and we have seen that the result was not satisfactory in the usual way. He was a moralist, as truly as Jonson, in the sense that his conception of the process of living was animated by moral ideas, and that he warmed to the admiration and expression of them. Sometimes he formulated them in the way of deliberate generalization, as in the noble but conventional farewell speeches of parent to child,—Polonius to Laertes, or the Countess of Rousillon to Bertram.[2] But more commonly, as has been said, he came upon them only as the natural product of an experience, warm with its life-blood. Two typical instances are the great speeches on Mercy, Portia's and Isabella's, spoken from the heart of the dramatic moment.[3] Dr. Johnson said that from the precepts in Shakespeare's plays a whole "system of social duty may be selected," not because the poet was undertaking to set one forth, but because "he that thinks reasonably must think morally." A critic of the romantic age would be more likely to find the reason in the doctrine that he that thinks *sympathetically* must think morally. In fact, neither statement is strictly true; but Shakespeare's ideas, being the outcome of dramatic thinking which is both reasonable and sympathetic, have many chances of being morally sound.

The bad man, as we have seen repeatedly, was a very real and familiar figure to the Elizabethans, and in general they were good Calvinists in assuming the existence

[2] *Hamlet*, I, iii, 58-81; *All's Well*, I, 1, 70-79.
[3] This statement is in no wise nullified by the fact that at least the first of the speeches in question, Portia's on "the quality of mercy," was probably derived from Seneca's essay *De Clementia*.

of a certain number of persons who were born with utterly depraved natures and at the same time were to be held morally responsible for their sins. All this Shakespeare accepted and used. In his early period he presented the more obvious but less plausible villainies of Aaron the Moor and Richard the Third, at the height of his power the more terrible and more lifelike Iago, Goneril, and Regan, followed by the only partly depraved Macbeth and Antony, and at length by Coriolanus, of whom it is still debated whether he was depraved or good. One sees the tendency toward psychologic and moral realism, and toward an increase of sympathy with the evil-doer yet with no disposition to condone his sins. Many of these evil-doers impress us as so ill born, in the sense of being endowed by Fortune with the seeds of their misconduct, that they could not do otherwise than sin: the extreme instance is Richard of Gloucester, who is declared to have been

> sealed in [his] nativity
> The slave of nature and the son of hell.
> (*Richard III*, I, iii, 229—30.)

One also remembers Hamlet commenting sombrely on men who suffer

> for some vicious mole of nature in them
> As in their birth, wherein they are not guilty,
> Since nature cannot choose his origin;
> (*Hamlet*, I, iv, 24—26.)

and Timon telling Apemantus that he had better curse his father for compounding him a "rogue hereditary."[4]

[4] *Timon*, IV, iii, 274.

These sayings, however, cannot be thought to represent Shakespeare's characteristic emphasis when touching the mystery of inherited nature as related to personal will. When the question of individual responsibility is raised, the more clear-sighted thinkers in the plays reject all effort to foist one's sins on Fortune or Destiny. Cassius's familiar saying,

> The fault, dear Brutus, is not in our stars,
> But in ourselves, that we are underlings,
> *(Julius Caesar, I, ii, 140—41.)*

is repeated in substance again and again. When the amiable but sapless Lepidus undertakes to excuse Antony's misconduct as hereditary

> Rather than purchas'd; what he cannot change,
> Than what he chooses,

Cæsar answers sternly that Antony is to be rebuked like ill-behaved boys

> who, being mature in knowledge,
> Pawn their experience to their present pleasure.
> *(Antony & Cleopatra, I, iv, 13—32.)*

Still more striking is the case of Edmund, who, as a bastard, was traditionally eligible to the defence that he was among the misborn. When his father weakly suggests that, since the (supposed) treachery of Edgar cannot be explained by heredity, it must be due to "these late eclipses in the sun and moon," the vigorous-minded young rascal soliloquizes thus:

"This is the excellent foppery of the world, that, when we are sick in fortune,—often the surfeits of our own behavior,—we make guilty of our disasters the sun, the moon, and the stars, as if we were villains on necessity, fools by heavenly compulsion, knaves, thieves, and treachers by spherical predominance, drunkards, liars, and adulterers by an enforc'd obedience of planetary influence, and all that we are evil in, by a divine thrusting on."

(*King Lear*, I, ii, 127—37.)

At the same time, such is the twofold nature of the problem that when the play is over one has also a certain impression—precisely as one often derives it from experience in real life—that the villain is what he is because of the circumstances of his birth, and that the sins of the father are strangely visited upon both himself and his children. Thus Edgar:

The gods are just, and of our pleasant vices
Make instruments to plague us.

(V, iii, 170—71.)

As to the punishment of wrong-doing, we do not now believe, as it used often to be held, that the moral attitude of the dramatist should be discernible in the nice adjustment of reward and punishment to conduct. Dr. Johnson, while admitting the essentially moral quality of Shakespeare's thoughts about life, was offended by his disposition to carry "his persons indifferently through right and wrong," and to dismiss them at the close "without further care." In this respect, of course, the poet was a realist. Perceiving the fact that both wickedness and ill fortune may ruin happiness, without reference to the deserts of the sufferer, he presented relentlessly the resulting tragic actions. On the other hand, since he was interested above all in relating action to personality, he commonly made it clear that the sufferer had opened the way for his tragedy by his own conduct; hence those readers who seek earnestly for some kind of "tragic fault" are usually able to find a semblance of it, even in the plays which are most remote from poetic justice. Othello and Desdemona are certainly not to blame, in any usual sense of the words, but if they had not done and said precisely what they did,—if they had not been precisely what they were,—Iago could not have enmeshed them in his plot. As has often been observed, Hamlet would have been able to save himself in Othello's place, and Othello to have succeeded where Hamlet failed. In all this, to be sure, there is no moral, unless it be that many persons should be other than what they are. The moralist, however, finds the tone and significance of the whole work to be sound: evil is evil, and good is good. Even in those plays whose moral effect is most open to suspicion, the late comedies in which the action seems to have been wrenched to an unnaturally happy ending, we have seen that there was no boggling with the matter of the sympathies as related to the moral judgment. The reader is not made to admire the unadmirable, or to despise the good;—wherein, as Macaulay once pointed out in a pregnant essay, Shakespeare's comedies (and, for that matter, those of his contemporaries generally) differed strikingly from those of the next age. It may also be noted that in most of the plays—the only exceptions being those in which there is a tragi-comic "reconciliation"—evil is awarded its just deserts, even if good is not. The tragedies never attain that intolerable bitterness where villainy not merely succeeds in its immediate aims, but survives triumphant. Some find this a source of distinctively moral satisfaction, but in fact it is largely a mere matter of dramatic art, which Shakespeare shared with his contemporaries. Indeed one might say that the only respect in which he notably surpassed the more serious work of his fellow-dramatists, in this ethical realm, was in his exquisite adaptation of the moral judgment to a sympathetic realism. No one else dared so to violate the easy theory of good and bad meeting appropriate rewards, and yet to hold the balance true.

But a dramatist's treatment of evil is a less important test, after all, than the matter of his emphasis on the admirable. Here it is not altogether easy to analyze Shakespeare's attitude,—to say what he chiefly called good. In the comedies he rarely deals with moral ideas except of the familiar and accepted kind, and in the tragedies, as the world knows, he was not concerned with ideal heroes, but usually with those who in one way or another proved failures. Henry the Fifth, of course, is an ideal king, but we have seen that he was built up on conventional lines. Hamlet, no doubt, comes nearest to representing Shakespeare's conception of an ideal *mind;* but Hamlet was certainly dissatisfied with his own character. In his thinking he was a brilliant innovator, but in ethics conventional. We have a much clearer view, it may be supposed, of Shakespeare's ideal woman than of his ideal man: Portia and Rosalind would go far to fill in its outlines, with a touch of Beatrice for more of spice, and of Viola, Cordelia, Hermione, and Imogen, for more serious elements after their kind. Yet here also there is nothing highly characteristic in the moral ideal. Shakespeare's only distinctive contribution, apart from the power of heightening and vitalizing the familiar elements of womanly charm, was in a peculiar combination of sympathy, wit, and effectiveness, which he never vouchsafed in the same way to any man. Our impression, then, of his notion of what is good must be a general one, induced from a thousand fugitive impressions of detail. Courage, fidelity in friendship, serenity in hardship, readiness in action,— these are the qualities which Shakespeare causes us chiefly to admire. Of course they are not original with him, even in form or emphasis; he found them in Plutarch, in Holinshed, in the ideals of his own time; but to each of them he evidently warmed with some eagerness, as opportunity presented itself, and joyfully incarnated them in the persons of his lovable men. There are two moments, in two of the most serious-minded plays, which elicit significant utterances, of a certain finality of tone, from characters whom we feel especially sure that we are intended to admire; we have therefore sound reason for giving them special heed. Hamlet, in his last moment alone with Horatio, with a premonition of the fatal end of the duel in which he is about to engage, nevertheless declines the invitation to forestall it, saying:

"Not a whit; we defy augury. There's a special providence in the fall of a sparrow. If it be now, 'tis not to come; if it be not to come, it will be now; if it be not now, yet it will come; *the readiness is all.*"

(V, ii, 230—33.)

And Edgar, in his final interview with his father, finding

the old man utterly broken in hope and in care for life, almost echoes Hamlet's word:

> Men must endure
> Their going hence, even as their coming hither;
> *Ripeness is all.*
>
> (*King Lear*, V, ii, 9—11.)

All this may be said to be truly Shakespearean, yet it is also highly representative. It touched familiar strings in every contemporary bosom. There is another element in his ideal of character which, though by no means startlingly new, is yet more peculiarly his own: the element of kindness. Surveying his dramatic action, characterization, and incidental comment as a whole, one cannot hesitate to say that for Shakespeare kindness was the cardinal, the regal virtue, and unkindness the one unpardonable sin. And his emphasis here is not representative; it goes distinctly beyond the norm of his age. Humanism is by no means necessarily humanitarian, as the Renaissance in certain of its aspects amply proved. Shakespeare, too, like his contemporaries, fell short of any notion of socializing the sympathies according to ideas developed only in the nineteenth century. Yet we recognize a notable and a characteristic spirit in the famous passage where King Lear, spiritually redeemed by his sufferings, identifies himself with the poor of his England:

> Poor naked wretches, wheresoe'er you are,
> That bide the pelting of this pitiless storm,
> How shall your houseless heads and unfed sides,
> Your loop'd and window'd raggedness, defend you
> From seasons such as these? Oh, I have ta'en
> Too little care of this!
>
> (III, iv, 28—33.)

The origin of the lines is purely dramatic: they arise from no problem of poverty, but from self-identification with a particular suffering personality. Yet we find them harmonizing with the prevalent Shakespearean stress on the art of living. This is why Shakespeare's ethical thought is so generally, and so justly, viewed as essentially Christian, though he was representative of the Renaissance in making small use of distinctively Christian material. For him, as for Christianity, love was the fulfilling of the law, and charity "the greatest of these."

The problem of Shakespeare's view of society is perhaps more warmly debated than any other aspect of his thought. He is held to be positively aristocratic, and as positively republican; and the very same passages or plays are brought in evidence on either side. The main reason for this is clear. His interests were individualized, as those of a poet or dramatist normally are, and he followed out the particular human problem on which he might be working to its proper conclusion, without reference to any obvious theory of society or the state. Thus the tragedy of *Coriolanus,* the special battle-ground of this question, is in fact a tragedy of personality, not of politics, and cannot be used as propaganda for or against the aristocracy. The mob or populace was for Shakespeare a kind of personality, which he represented sometimes as the clown of the drama, sometimes as a strange, brute, tragic force; in so doing he was following accepted social theory, the common tradition of both the chroniclers and the dramatists. It is clear that he neither liked nor honored the populace; but he did not think of it as in any sense the corporate people of England. On the other hand, he had no more liking than his countrymen had for an arrogant or tyrannical aristocrat. His tyrant kings are presented with unrelenting sternness; his ideal king, Henry the Fifth, is portrayed as mingling in friendly converse with his soldiers, calling them "brothers, friends, and countrymen," and laying before them the liberal doctrine that "every subject's duty is the king's, but every subject's soul is his own."[5] All this, to be sure, is absolutely representative; it was the English ideal; as a sound historian of the drama puts it, "almost every English king was expected to display on occasion a willingness to hob-nob with the first comer."[6] We can therefore say no more than that Shakespeare had no reason to dissent from the tradition. Another famous passage, much used in the study of his political thinking, occurs in the same play, *Henry the Fifth,* in the dialogue between Exeter and the Archbishop of Canterbury on the nature of government.

> For government, though high and low and lower,
> Put into parts, doth keep in one consent,
> Congreeing in a full and natural close,
> Like music.
>
> Therefore doth heaven divide
> The state of man in divers functions,
> Setting endeavor in continual motion,
> To which is fixed, as an aim or butt,
> Obedience.
>
> (I, ii, 180—87.)

And in the lines that follow there is the familiar simile of the ordered functions of a hive of honey-bees. Beside

[5] *Henry V,* IV, i, 185-86.
[6] W. D. Briggs: Marlowe's *Edward II,* p. lxxii.

this discussion should be set the equally famous speech of Ulysses, in *Troilus and Cressida,* on "degree," where the word is lifted, for the moment, from its natural meaning of rank or distinction in office, to something like the fundamental notion of a political order or cosmos,—much as Wordsworth, in celebrating the nobility of duty, represents it as keeping "the stars from wrong."

> The heavens themselves, the planets, and this centre
> Observe degree, priority, and place,
> Insisture, course, proportion, season, form,
> Office and custom, in all line or order; . . .
> Take but degree away, untune that string,
> And hark, what discord follows! each thing meets
> In mere oppugnancy.[7]
>
> (I, iii, 85—111.)

With not a little more, depicting the chaos of anarchy. All this matter was familiar Renaissance doctrine, going back ultimately to Homer and Plato, with a line of descent through St. Augustine, Boëthius, and perhaps Montaigne; in Shakespeare's elaboration the form is closely parallel, whether by coincidence or direct relationship, with Hooker's defence of the polity of England in his great contemporary treatise. Finally, we may recall the scene in *The Tempest* where the garrulous Gonzalo proposes to establish a happy commonwealth with neither magistrate, property, nor work.[8] "No sovereignty"—he says. "Yet he would be king on 't," innocently comments Sebastian. The description of the impossible commonwealth Shakespeare took from Montaigne, but the fine irony seems to be his

---
[7] See also the lines quoted on p. 297.
[8] II, i, 143-64.

own; whether it had any pat application at the time of the drama's performance, one cannot say.

The upshot of all such passages is that Shakespeare represented accurately the normal political thought of his generation. He was loyal to the throne, and to the constituted civil order; he distrusted the populace, and enjoyed no foregleams of the democracy of centuries to come. But he was also thoroughly English in thinking of sovereignty and office as resting ultimately neither on divine right nor on force, but on the corporate will of the lords and commons, and as hedged in by obligations which rested even more heavily upon a king than upon his subjects. In this sound and tonic strain of self-respect his historical plays, and all others that touch the matter, make for the democratic ideal, though with little or nothing of democratic theory behind them. So also does the essential humaneness of Shakespeare's interest in individuals; in this sense every true dramatist is a herald of democracy, whether he knows it or not. Perdita, in *The Winter's Tale*, supposing herself to be only a shepherd's daughter, tells Prince Florizel:

> I was about to speak, and tell him plainly
> The selfsame sun that shines upon his court
> Hides not his visage from our cottage, but
> Looks on alike.
>
> (IV, iv, 453—56.)

Here it turns out, to be sure, as commonly in the old romances, that she is in fact a princess: there was no real danger of marrying the prince to a lowly maiden. On the other hand, in *All's Well* Helena is in good sooth of lower birth than Bertram, and the king's defence of their union includes some of Shakespeare's most forward-looking lines:

> Strange is it that our bloods
> Of color, weight, and heat, pour'd all together,
> Would quite confound distinction, yet stand off
> In differences so mighty. . . .
> From lowest place when virtuous things proceed,
> The place is dignified by the doer's deed. . . .
> Honors thrive
> When rather from our acts we them derive
> Than our foregoers.
>
> (II, iii, 125—44.)

Yet, while we call these sentiments forward-looking, we remember that they also look back to a sound English tradition, at least as far as Chaucer's "He is gentil that doth gentil dedes," and harmonize, too, with the standard classical and Renaissance theory respecting the origin of aristocracy.

A poet's doctrine of love is always of prime importance among his ideas, and if Shakespeare had aught to say on that theme which in any way differentiates him from his age, we are sure to be eager to discern it. For the most part, of course, he speaks for the Renaissance, touching lightly on its more mystical and symbolical theories, humanizing its ideals of passion with full tints of flesh and blood, and at the same time accepting much of that portion of its doctrine which rose above the level of the senses. There is no evidence of any characteristic individual philosophy of the subject. In the comedies we have found Shakespeare treating love in the comic spirit, chiefly as a fine madness of the fancy, "engender'd in the eye," yet touched, in a Portia, a Rosalind, or a Viola, with a high seriousness allied not only to poetry but to the things of the mind. In tragedy he did not make love a principal theme, but in two of the tragic plays he exhibited it as an ennobling force, which wrought out heroines from shy maidens, and transfigured the ardent spirits of youth (in Romeo) and full manhood (in Othello); later (in Antony) he studied its debasing splendors in the lawless passion of manhood's decline. The Elizabethans were much more plain-spoken than we in matters of sex, and even in thought they put more emphasis on the physical aspects of marriage than is common, on corresponding levels of decency, after the social evolution of the past three centuries. Nor was Shakespeare squeamish in speech; on the contrary he often "spake full broad," as his audience was pleased to hear him. It is therefore the more significant that his presentation of love and marriage is so marked, in the immense majority of instances, by purity and idealism; for we know it is not a matter of timidity of phrasing. In both *Romeo and Juliet* and *Othello,* the two great serious studies of marital love, the element of sensuous passion is frankly admitted and expressed, in language plainer than we expect to-day. But it is also very plainly made the mere base of something finer and more essential; it is the half-concealed sub-structure which exists for that which is built upon it. This is typical of the whole process which civilization has worked out through slow centuries of toil of sense and spirit,—a process wrapped up in the multiple and gradually transfigured meanings of the old word *love*. Othello gives more than a hint of it in discussing with the senators the question of taking his bride to Cyprus:

> I therefore beg it not
> To please the palate of my appetite, . . .
> But to be free and bounteous to her mind.
> (I, iii, 262—66.)

While in the same scene Iago's viewpoint gives us the opposite doctrine, that of the reflective sensualist: "That you call love," he tells Roderigo, is a scion of "our carnal stings"; it is "merely a lust of the blood and a permission of the will."[9] For that matter, of Roderigo's love this was doubtless quite true.

The permanence of true love—and here there is no distinction of that between man and man and between man and woman—was no invention of Shakespeare's; it is an age-old doctrine of romance. Yet he seems to have held it seriously, setting it forth both in the more personal form of sonnet lyric and objectively in the plays. And not only is love said to be lasting when both lovers are true; he takes the harder side of the never settled controversy whether either lover by himself can destroy the product of the two.

> Love is not love
> Which alters when it alteration finds,
> Or bends with the remover to remove,—
> (Sonnet 116.)

he had written in one of the most impressive of the sonnets. And Desdemona, Cordelia, and Hermione prove it

---
[9] Lines 336-40.

SHAKESPEARE 347

in their several ways. Of this view the doctrine of forgiveness is but a corollary, which again we have seen Shakespeare setting forth repeatedly in both sonnets and dramas. "I do forgive thy robbery," said the sonneteer whose love had been stolen by his friend.

> The power that I have on you is to spare you,
> The malice towards you to forgive you,
> *(Cymbeline,* V, v, 418—19.)

said Posthumus to Iachimo, who had all but ruined his life.

Do all these things go so far as to constitute, or imply, a philosophy underlying the works of Shakespeare? Had he a system of thought, a *Weltanschauung,* which one may attempt to summarize as a whole? It is more than doubtful. We have seen how evidently he represents, for the most part, the normal thinking of his time, commonly close to its highest level, and how the things which he especially emphasizes are those that arise from an interest in individuals rather than in classes or theories. His thinking allies itself readily, now with the brooding rationalism of Montaigne, now with the sturdy liberalism of Hooker, now with the cold epicureanism of the Renaissance Italians, now with the warmer ethics of Christianity,—all with no concern for inconsistencies, or search for a unifying system. Curiously enough, the only character whom Shakespeare represents as specifically troubled by a problem of theology is the desultory Richard the Second, when he is in prison and has nothing else to do.[10] Hamlet is often spoken of as skeptical, and so, of course, he is, in the mood where the tragedy finds him; but his doubts are far more concerned

[10] V, i, 12-17.

with humanity than with the order of the universe. And neither he nor any other Shakespearean personage is to be clearly identified with any specific problem of philosophic thought.

In this connection the question of chief significance is not whether individual characters are skeptics, optimists, pessimists, or what not, but what total impression is left by the plays as a whole, and especially by the greater tragedies. Viewed in the large, do they (for example) present a pessimist's view of human life and the world order? Experience shows that there is not likely to be agreement on the answer; for Shakespeare invites readers to interpret the facts of his plays according to their individual beliefs, and they have accepted the invitation with eagerness. But we can recall the chief facts summarily. Shakespeare combined, in the tragedies, a keen sense of the evil in human nature with an equally clear consciousness of the mystery of fate or fortune. He represented evil as a poison infecting the human will, perhaps incurably, and spreading its malignant effects not only through the lives of those who had tasted it voluntarily but through the wholly innocent lives around them. He also represented certain natures as destined for evil-doing through heredity, and others destined to suffer not because of moral wrong but because of strange accidents of fortune; while in still other instances accident and wickedness combine in a dreadful alliance to crush the innocent. The emphasis, as has already been said, is more on defect of will than on taint of blood or stroke of destiny; so that there is a certain excuse for the familiar and exaggerated saying that the tragedy of the Greeks was based on fate while Shakespeare's was based on character. The truth is that the main basis of Shakespeare's tragedy was the facts of life, —heightened, of course, by the colors of romance,—and not any doctrine either of humanity or the superhuman. But this is not the whole story. There must be a point of view whence the facts are observed, and it makes much difference whether evil is presented as normal or abnormal, —whether the nature of the world, or of man, seems to be indifferent to goodness, hostile to it, or on its side. Here there can be no doubt respecting Shakespeare's tragedies: they are clearly made from the point of view that evil is abnormal (which is not at all the same thing as implying that it is either unreal or unusual), and that the universe is on the side of good. In each of the four chief tragedies goodness is defeated, in some very real sense, yet each of the four loses its meaning if goodness be not the norm from which the whole measure of life is taken. Moreover, in each of them goodness appears rather the better than the worse for the test of its quality; it even appears, in another real sense, to be actually triumphant in defeat. Love, purity, courage, honor,—the tragic forces assail them with heart-breaking violence, but in vain. By the dead body of Hamlet, or Othello, or Cordelia, our final word is likely to be, "What know we greater than the soul?" Of this Shakespeare may have been quite unconscious; it has already been admitted that he was not writing the plays to illustrate a spiritual philosophy. But one sees, noting the spiritual implications even of his most sombre works, why optimism as well as pessimism finds itself reflected therein.

If we inquire whether this idealism or optimism was rooted in anything of the nature of religious faith, the answer is not easy. Just as Shakespeare has been proved to be aristocrat and democrat, optimist and pessimist, so he has been proved to be both atheist and Christian. For reasons that must already have become clear, it is exceedingly hazardous to emphasize, as has frequently been done, the particular passages which chance to favor one or another religious implication,—most of them being representative either of the dramatic need of the moment or of conventional attitudes of the age. Two things are equally true: that Shakespeare repeatedly refers to the subject-matter of Christianity with an air of reverent acceptance, especially where it is associated with the national tradition, as in the utterances of Henry the Fourth and Henry the Fifth; and that in the majority of the dramas religious motives and ideas play little or no part. In the former respect the poet was a normal Englishman; in the latter he was a normal artist of the Renaissance. The Renaissance, as we know, had reacted from the domination of the religious element in the thought and art of the Middle Age, and substituted for it— sometimes deliberately, sometimes unconsciously—a more than pagan spirit of secularity, concerned frankly with this present world. The spirit might be definitely anti-religious, or, again, entirely compatible with a reserved minimum of fairly orthodox belief. In this want of other-worldliness, then, Shakespeare is a true child of his age, making no effort to spiritualize (in the religious meaning of the term) the secular materials of which he availed himself, and devoting his art to problems for the most part merely human and earthly in their scope. The most notable instances of this are found in the numerous death-scenes in the plays, depicting moments when, if ever, men turn from their human existence to thoughts of persons and realms beyond mortality; very few of them, with Shakespeare, bring such thoughts to light. Again, one remembers the extraordinary fact (or one which would be extraordinary outside the atmosphere of the Italian Renaissance) that at the opening of the third act of *Measure for Measure,* when the Duke, in the guise of a friar, is consoling the condemned Claudio in the impending presence of death, there is no syllable respecting the hereafter, or of any more spiritual consideration than the vanity of living. To the same end there have often been cited the exquisite lines of Prospero,

> We are such stuff
> As dreams are made of, and our little life
> Is rounded with a sleep.
> *(Tempest,* IV, i, 156—58.)

Clearly, however, there is a sense in which all men of imagination must agree that this saying is true, and there is nothing in the scene or the spirit of the play (despite the gratuitous solemnity which in our time is often read into it) requiring us to take it in other than its more superficial or fanciful meaning. And on the other side of the account we may set the great sonnet on the soul and its ultimate triumph over death, and the circumstance that Hamlet, commonly thought to be closer to Shakespeare's self than any other of his creations, is more religious than most of them. We have seen how in one of his most soul-disclosing moments he alludes to Christ's teaching of Him who numbers the sparrows, and remember how, in bidding Horatio live instead of following his friend, he phrases it, "Absent thee from felicity awhile." But the sum of such attempted proofs remains quite insufficient to enable the candid reader to find either positive faith or unfaith in Shakespeare's writings as a whole.

All the foregoing matters combine to give us some concept of the personality of William Shakespeare himself; yet how faint and unsatisfying is the portrait which the world continues to attempt to draw! When every line that he wrote has been scrutinized for evidence, the sum of our intimate knowledge is a beggarly account. Some trifles, and some few matters not so trifling, may be agreed on: Shakespeare disliked dogs, cosmetics and artificial hair, drunkenness, crowds of dirty and ill-smelling citizens, pedantry, affectation, and self-conceit; he was fond of horses, flowers, music, puns, downrightness, loyalty, and his country. When, in one of his sonnets, he summed up the things that made life hardly worth living, he threw the stress on distorted social judgments which invert the true honors of life, such as

> Art made tongue-tied by Authority,
> And Folly, doctor-like, controlling skill,
> And simple Truth miscalled Simplicity,
> And captive Good attending captain Ill;
> (Sonnet 66.)

and Hamlet, brooding on the same theme, once more emphasized

> The insolence of office, and the spurns
> That patient merit of the unworthy takes.
> (III, i, 73—74.)

From which one may infer that, although so little of his writing was devoted to social criticism, Shakespeare was keenly sensitive to those contemporary wrongs which specially appealed to his penetrating concern for human values. We know that he was interested in all kinds of people, was peculiarly conscious of the charm and the mental and spiritual prowess of women, and was profoundly moved by both the joyous and the tragic possibilities of friendship and love. Despite this intense humanism, he appears to have been but slightly concerned with systems of thought respecting human character and conduct in the large, and, in like manner, while seemingly possessed of reverence and a certain ultimate attitude of faith, to have been relatively little interested in theology or religion. Even his own art he viewed, so far as we can judge, almost wholly in the concrete, as a practitioner and not a theorist. When he spoke of poets and poetry, it was commonly with the unprofessional lightness of tone of a man of the world; one may be certain that he was never afflicted with the special types of pedantry and self-consciousness which the artist class is heir to. In this respect he must have resembled most closely, among the English poets, Chaucer, Scott, and Browning.

There are certain other things about Shakespeare's personality which are more important than any of these. One of them is his extraordinary combination of wit and poetry, of high seriousness with the comic spirit. Most men of letters, like most of our acquaintances, are in possession of one of these points of view, one of these aspects of life, in disproportion to the other: we are not quite sure that they understand our lighter moods—or else our deeper ones. Rarely some spirit appears who can enter into both with equal ease. Shakespeare is the supreme example of this double capacity. It is for this reason that Rosalind and Hamlet may be thought to speak most directly for him of all his characters, the one on the lighter, the other on the more sombre side; for each of them, life does not cease to be a serious matter because it is comic, nor to be ridiculous because it is both beautiful and tragic. Of all later poets, Browning alone is Shakespeare's equal in this regard, although, for reasons which cannot be entered upon here, he did not accomplish equal results in the twofold interpretation of human experience. Another significant matter is the unique combination, in Shakespeare's personality, of the epical and the lyrical—or, to fumble with more pedantic terms, the objective and the subjective—points of view. Therein lie both the mystery and the charm of his attitude. He must have watched the pageant of life go by with a strangely dispassionate face, observing and interpreting all sorts and conditions of men, often without taking sides or letting himself be carried from that serenely impassive station; yet he must also have so lived within himself the life of the passions, have so felt the joys and sorrows that spring up within every child of mortality, that one can fancy those who knew him longing to cling upon his bosom because it was vibrant with every human chord. It is this twofold endowment, indeed, which makes any true dramatist; for it is of the essence of dramatic composition to combine the external and the internal points of view: every drama is a pageant passing before the eye, and also a series of personal or lyrical utterances coming from the hearts of the characters to the ear. But no one has so accomplished the double end as did Shakespeare.

In thus attempting to review our inferences regarding his personality, we have inevitably returned to Shakespeare's work as a dramatic poet, and have also come upon some of the chief reasons for the unique place which has been accorded him in the modern world. It has been necessary to admit limitations or defects which one might have supposed would shut out any one of whom they could be predicated from the title of Master Spirit. That is, Shakespeare lacked, on the one hand, a taste or a conscience for perfection of form, and on the other, a deeply philosophic or spiritually interpretive mind. He gives us no such examples of finished poetic or dramatic technique as Virgil and Molière, no such spiritual profundities as Dante, no such penetrating studies of philosophic and ethical problems as Goethe or Tolstoy. There is none of his dramas which does not contain matter that can be understood only when corrected according to the parallax of his age,—by an understanding of its thought, which he commonly represented so faithfully, and of its dramatic fashions, which he also followed in both their merits and their faults. Yet we know that, notwithstanding these limitations, his works have proved to have larger elements of lasting vitality than any others in human speech outside the Holy Scriptures. In Dr. Johnson's noble words, "The stream of time, which is continually washing the dissoluble fabrics of other poets, passes without injury by the adamant of Shakespeare."

Two final reasons may be suggested why this is so. The first is, that Shakespeare, though not an original thinker in abstract terms, is the writer who has thought most inclusively and effectively in terms of concrete human feeling and conduct. Thoughtful men cannot but lament, now and again, that he who did so much should not have done more,—that there could not have been combined with our greatest poet the maker of a system of thought for his race. Yet we may suppose that if he had written to illustrate a philosophy of abstract validity, unspoiled by the particular persons and deeds which interested his age, the very fact would have doomed it to be temporary, as every human system is doomed to have its day and cease to be. Thus Dante, despite the greatness of both his soul and his art, is much further from us than his distance in time alone would make necessary; and Goethe is already more distant than Shakespeare. For Shakespeare, doing his thinking in concrete detail of personality, took only the common stuff of the passions for his essential material; hence the temporary fashions in which he clothed it drop aside, and since the passions are unchanged the process is valid still. Of course this is also true of Homer, and in varying degrees of every master spirit of poetry. But it is a commonplace that the materials of Shakespeare's dramatic thinking are richer and more representative, therefore more widely and lastingly valid, than those of any other in the realm of fiction. As Dryden has it, "he was the man who of all modern, and perhaps ancient poets, had the largest and most comprehensive soul."[11]

Again, Shakespeare attained supremacy, as compared with any other writer since the days of Sophocles, in the specifically *poetic* interpretation of human experience.

[11] *Essay of Dramatic Poesy.*

It has been reiterated again and again, in the foregoing chapters, how he gradually perfected a style which united the reality of direct dramatic utterance with the transfiguring powers of poetry. But this achievement of form is only a symbol of something deeper. What is it to think in a truly poetic manner? or to interpret conduct in such a manner? This is not the place to answer systematically questions of so wide a scope. Yet to ask them is to remind ourselves what our impoverishment would be if the poetic interpretation of thought and action, as well as feeling, were blotted from among our possessions. There is little danger that the poetic interpretation of thought can be so blotted out; for lyric poetry, the characteristic form for the modern world, is so intertwined with all the reflective processes of the race that, wherever they go, its interpretations are certain to follow. But *dramatic* poetry, the poetic interpretation of action, is in peril, for those who speak the English tongue,—or would be were it not for the vitality of Shakespeare. He still shows us what it means to lift the level of word and feeling and deed—not as "recollected in tranquillity" but as coming swiftly from the moment of dramatic stress—to the high places of a poet's insight and a poet's expression. We hesitate over this type of art, because of our overdone training in the representation of life in terms of the "natural" or the "real." To show men in action, as drama is written to do, is so essentially an imitative thing,—must we not also imitate their humdrum speech? Some lines of Shakespeare's suggest an answer. He was not in the habit of talking—unless merely among friends—of such theoretic matters as nature and art; but he amused himself by putting into the most charming scene of *The Winter's Tale* a comment on those who tried to distinguish the two.

> Nature is made better by no mean
> But Nature makes that mean; so, over that art
> Which you say adds to Nature, is an art
> That Nature makes.
> (IV, iv, 89—92.)

In other words, the art of transfiguring the natural is Nature's own gift—perhaps her best. And the poet's power of thus transfiguring the common passion and the common utterance of mankind is the supreme instance of that gift.

Wordsworth, who was not at all gifted with this power in the dramatic realm, but was a faithful and far-seeing student of it in the lyrical and reflective fields, once defined the nature of poetic thinking in these lines:

> If thou partake the animating faith
> That poets, even as prophets, each with each
> Connected in a mighty scheme of truth,
> Have each his own peculiar faculty,
> Heaven's gift, a sense that fits him to perceive
> Objects unseen before, thou wilt not blame
> The humblest of this band who dares to hope
> That unto him hath also been vouchsafed
> An insight that in some sort he possesses,
> A privilege whereby a work of his,
> Proceeding from a source of untaught things,
> Creative and enduring, may become
> A power like one of Nature's.
> (*Prelude*, xiii, 300—312.)

One sees how doubly true this is, when the dramatic process is added; one sees, too, how accurately the lines apply to Shakespeare's achievement. Strange it is, and all irrational, that we insist on talking of his persons, their deeds and their passions, as if they had actually lived, and were still living, in the real world with ourselves, though we are able to trace their origin to this earlier play, this old romance, this need or fashion of the dramatist's time. But nothing can stop us. When all the truth of historical interpretation is learned, the truth of absolute poetic humanism remains. And this is because Shakespeare enjoyed not only the sources which we dutifully set down in our books, but the "source of untaught things," so that his work became "a power like one of Nature's," and abides, "creative and enduring," among mankind.

BIBLIOGRAPHICAL NOTES

(The books chiefly recommended to the general reader are listed topically, according to the subjects of the preceding chapters. There follow, for each chapter, references of a more special character, pertaining to matters discussed on the pages cited; these indicate either the sources of statements made in the text or writings where recent discussion of disputed matters may be found.)

CHAPTER I (The Age).

On the general aspects of Shakespeare's age:

ONIONS, C. T. (editor): *Shakespeare's England*. Oxford, 1916.
STEPHENSON, H. T.: *Shakespeare's London*. New York, 1905.
EINSTEIN, L.: *The Italian Renaissance in England*. New York, 1902.
LEE, VERNON (pseud. for Violet Paget): *Euphorion* (essay on "The Italy of the Elizabethan Dramatists"). London, 1885.
LEE, SIDNEY: *The French Renaissance in England*. New York, 1910.
TAYLOR, H. O.: *Thought and Expression in the Sixteenth Century*. New York, 1920. (This appeared too late to be used by the present writer.)
CRANE, T. F.: *Italian Social Customs of the Sixteenth Century*. New Haven, 1920. (This appeared too late to be used by the present writer.)

On the Elizabethan theatre and drama:

ADAMS, J. Q.; *Shakespearean Playhouses*. Boston, 1917.
THORNDIKE, A. H.: *Shakespeare's Theatre*. New York, 1916.
LAWRENCE, W. J.: *The Elizabethan Playhouse and Other Studies*. Stratford-on-Avon, 1912. Second Series, 1913.
SCHELLING, F. E.: *Elizabethan Drama, 1558-1642*. Boston, 1908.
CREIZENACH, W. M. A.: *The English Drama in the Age of Shakespeare*. Philadelphia, 1916.

(Page 8.) On Shakespeare's use of classical material, see ROOT, R. K.: *Classical Mythology in Shakespeare*. New York, 1903.
(Page 9.) On Italian literature in Elizabethan England, see SCOTT, MARY A.: *Elizabethan Translations from the Italian*. Boston, 1916.
(Page 10.) On the Renaissance lyric in England, see the introduction of PADELFORD, F. M.: *Early Sixteenth Century Lyrics*. Boston, 1907. Also BERDAN, J. M.: *Early Tudor Poetry*. New York, 1920.
(Page 14.) On the neo-platonic doctrine of love, see CASTIGLIONE: *The Book of the Courtier*, translated by L. E. Opdycke (especially pp. 288-308). New York, 1903. Also the introduction of WINSTANLEY, L.: *Spenser's Four Hymns*. Cambridge, 1907.

(Page 16.) On villainy and Machiavellianism in Elizabethan literature, see STOLL, E. E.: "Criminals in Shakespeare and in Science," *Modern Philology*, x, 55 (1912); and BOYER, C. V.: *The Villain as Hero in Elizabethan Tragedy*, London, 1914.
(Page 22.) On Elizabethan personality, see LEE, SIDNEY: *Great Englishmen of the Sixteenth Century*. London, 1904.
(Page 33.) On Hooker's liberalism, see GAYLEY, C. M.: *Shakespeare and the Founders of Liberty in America* (chapter 5). New York, 1917.
(Page 35.) On Elizabethan superstitions, see STOLL, E. E.: "The Objectivity of the Ghosts in Shakespeare," *Publ. of the Modern Language Association*, xxii, 201 (1907).
(Page 37.) On Elizabethan psychology, see DOWDEN, E.: "Elizabethan Psychology," in *Essays, Modern and Elizabethan*. London, 1910.

CHAPTER II (Life and Works).

On the life of Shakespeare:

HALLIWELL-PHILLIPPS, J. O.: *Outlines of the Life of Shakespeare*. London, 11th edition, 1907.

LEE, SIDNEY: *A Life of William Shakespeare*. Revised edition, New York, 1916.

NEILSON, W. A., and THORNDIKE, A. H.: *The Facts about Shakespeare*. New York, 1913.

On his works, studied in connection with the development of his personality:

DOWDEN, E.: *Shakspere: a Critical Study of his Mind and Art*. London, 1875.

WENDELL, B.: *William Shakspere*. New York, 1894.

BRANDES, G.: *William Shakespeare, a Critical Study;* translated by William Archer, London, 1898.

BAKER, G. P.: *The Development of Shakespeare as a Dramatist*. New York, 1907.

RALEIGH, W.: *Shakespeare* (Men of Letters Series). New York, 1907.

(Page 58.) On Shakespeare's boyhood, imaginatively reconstructed, see MADDEN, D. H.: *The Diary of Master William Silence: a Study of Shakespeare and Elizabethan Sport*. London, 2nd edition, 1907.

(Page 59.) On the marriage, see GRAY, J. W.: *Shakespeare's Marriage, his Departure from Stratford, and Other Incidents in his Life*. London, 1905. This work is of special importance for the correction of Lee's one-sided account of the problems connected with the marriage.

(Page 62.) On Shakespeare's reading, see ANDERS, H. R. D.. *Shakespeare's Books*. Berlin, 1904.

(Page 68.) The interpretation of Greene's remarks here followed is substantially that of TUCKER BROOKE, in "The Authorship of

BIBLIOGRAPHY

the Second and Third Parts of King Henry VI,'' *Transactions of the Connecticut Academy of Arts and Sciences,* xvii, 190 ff. (1912).

(Page 72.) In a still unpublished paper on ''The Date and Composite Authorship of 1 *Henry VI,*'' DR. A. GAW presents various evidence against the usual view that Shakespeare was already writing for Lord Strange's men in 1591-94, and in behalf of the hypothesis that he was connected with another company, such as Lord Pembroke's.

(Page 73.) On the question of the coat-of-arms, S. A. TANNENBAUM presents cogent arguments for the issue of the patent in 1596, in his privately printed monograph, *Was Shakspere a Gentleman?* New York, 1909.

(Page 76.) On Shakespeare's professional associations and income, see WALLACE, C. W.: ''Shakespeare and his London Associates as Revealed in Recently Discovered Documents,'' *University of Nebraska Studies,* x, 261 (1910); also, by the same author, ''Shakespeare's Money Interest in the Globe Theatre,'' *Century Magazine,* lxxx, 500 (1910). Respecting the matter of income, Lee's exaggerated estimates are corrected in an article by A. THALER, ''Shakespeare's Income,'' *Studies in Philology,* xv, 82 (1918).

(Page 80.) On the theatrical quarrels see PENNIMAN, J. H.: *The War of the Theatres,* University of Pennsylvania, 1897; and SMALL, R. A.; *The Stage Quarrel between Ben Jonson and the So-Called Poetasters.* Breslau, 1899.

(Page 85.) On Shakespeare's residence with the Mountjoys, see WALLACE, C. W.: ''New Shakespeare Discoveries,'' *Harper's Magazine,* cxx, 489 (1910), and the same author's monograph on ''Shakespeare and his London Associates,'' cited above.

(Page 89.) For arguments favoring some controversy between Shakespeare and Chapman, see ROBERTSON, J. M.: *Shakespeare and Chapman.* London, 1917. The identification of Chapman as the rival poet of the Sonnets was first made by MINTO in his volume called *Characteristics of English Poets,* chapter 5. London, 2nd edition, 1885.

(Page 90.) On Shakespeare's possible friendships with Selden, Greville, etc., see GAYLEY: *Shakespeare and the Founders of Liberty,* cited under Chapter I.

(Page 94.) For the extant allusions to Shakespeare in contemporary writings, see *Shakespeare's Centurie of Prayse,* Publ. of the New Shakespeare Society, 1879; or, Munro, J.: *The Shakespeare Allusion-Book,* London, 1909.

(Page 98.) On the contemporary editions of the plays, see POLLARD, A. W.: *Shakespeare Folios and Quartos.* London, 1909. Pollard's view of the relatively great authenticity of the old texts, as here followed, is further elaborated in his lectures on *Shakespeare's Fight with the Pirates and the Problems of the Transmission of his Text,* 1917. See also WILSON, J. D.: *The Copy for ''Hamlet''* 1603 *and the Hamlet Transcript,* 1918.

(Page 100.) For the plays doubtfully attributed, in whole or in part, to Shakespeare, see BROOKE, T.: *The Shakespeare Apocrypha*, Oxford, 1908.

NOTE:—No appropriate place has been found, in a volume of the present character, to discuss the various heresies which have troubled not a few amateur students—but no scholar trained in Elizabethan letters—respecting the authorship of the Shakespeare plays and poems. They all depend on the assumption that there is insufficient reason for connecting these works with the name of William Shakespeare of Stratford, and on that matter the facts and traditions collected in Chapter II perhaps form a sufficient commentary. Readers desiring a detailed consideration of the subject are referred to ROBERTSON, J. M.: *The Baconian Heresy*, 1913.

CHAPTER III (The Poems).

The best one-volume edition of Shakespeare's complete works is that of W. A. NEILSON, Boston, 1906 (Cambridge Poets). The best editions in separate volumes are *The Tudor Shakespeare*, edited by NEILSON and THORNDIKE, New York, 39 volumes; and *The Arden Shakespeare* (also issued in America as *The Dowden Shakespeare*), London, still in progress. In both these editions each volume is edited by a separate scholar; in the former series the introductions and notes are brief, in the latter they are elaborate. For serious purpose of reference, the standard edition is the *New Variorum Shakespeare*, edited by H. H. FURNESS, Philadelphia, still in progress.

The best separate edition of the poems is that of G. WYNDHAM: *Poems of Shakespeare*, London, 1898. An admirable edition of the Sonnets, in addition to those mentioned above, is that of H. C. BEECHING, Boston, 1904. The edition of C. M. WALSH, London, 1908, is characterized by an interesting attempt to rearrange the sonnets topically and chronologically. For serious purposes of reference, see the variorum edition of the Sonnets, by R. M. ALDEN, Boston, 1916.

On *Venus and Adonis, The Rape of Lucrece*, and *The Passionate Pilgrim*, see the introductions by SIDNEY LEE in the facsimile editions issued by the Oxford Press, 1905.

(Page 117.) For Chapman's alleged authorship of "A Lover's Complaint," see ROBERTSON, *Shakespeare and Chapman*, cited above under Chapter II.

(Page 119.) On the sonnet fashion of the age, see LEE, *The French Renaissance in England*, cited under Chapter I, and the same writer's introduction to *Elizabethan Sonnets*, New English Garner series, London, 1904.

(Page 120). On the conceits of the sonnet-writers, see ALDEN, R. M.: "The Lyrical Conceit of the Elizabethans," *Studies in Philology*, xiv, 130 (1917).

(Page 121.) On the conventions of the Italian lyrists there is a valuable article by WOLFF, in German, in *Englische Studien*, xlix, 161 (1916), which is partly paraphrased in English in Alden's variorum edition of the Sonnets, pp. 459-461.

CHAPTER IV (The Chronicle-Histories).

The best general accounts of the English chronicle-drama are found in SCHELLING, F. E.: *The English Chronicle Play*, New York, 1902; and BRIGGS, W. D., introduction to his edition of Marlowe's *Edward the Second*, London, 1914. For the sources, in the chronicle, of Shakespeare's plays on English history, see BOSWELL-STONE, W. G.: *Shakespeare's Holinshed*, London, 1896.

(Page 149.) On the authorship of *Edward the Third*, see the introduction to *The Shakespeare Apocrypha*, cited under Chapter II. On that of the old plays which are viewed as the originals of the Second and Third Parts of *Henry the Sixth*, see BROOKE'S monograph on "The Authorship of the Second and Third Parts of *King Henry VI*," already cited under Chapter II.

(Page 154.) On the First Part of *Henry the Sixth*, see HENNEMAN, J. B.: "The Episodes in Shakespeare's 1 *Henry VI*," *Publ. of the Modern Language Association*, xv, 290 (1900); GRAY, H. D.: "The Purport of Shakespeare's Contribution to 1 *Henry VI*," *ibid.*, xxxii, 367 (1917); and BROOKE, T.: introduction to his edition of the play in the *Yale Shakespeare*, 1918. The account given in the text is indebted to all these discussions. A more exhaustive discussion of the play will be found in the still unpublished paper of A. GAW, cited under page 72 above.

(Page 160.) On the traditional character of Richard the Third, in chronicle and earlier drama, see CHURCHILL, G. B.: *Richard III up to Shakespeare, Palaestra*, x (1900).

The theory that *Richard the Third* is merely a revision by Shakespeare of a lost play, originally written in continuation of *The True Tragedy*, is supported by A. W. POLLARD, in the second of two articles on "The York and Lancaster Plays," London Times Literary Supplement, Sept. 20 and 27, 1918 (pp. 438, 452).

(Page 177.) On the history of Falstaff criticism, see STOLL, E. E.: "Falstaff," *Modern Philology*, xii, 197 (1914). On the relation of Falstaff to the *Famous Victories*, see MONAGHAN, J.: "Falstaff and his Forebears," *Studies in Philology*, xviii, 353 (1921). On the treatment of Falstaff in the coronation scene, and its relation to the characterization of Henry the Fifth, see BRADLEY, A. C.: "The Rejection of Falstaff," in *Oxford Lectures on Poetry*, London, 1909.

(Page 186.) On the origins of the legends of the dissolute youth of Henry the Fifth, and the tendency in recent criticism to depreciate his character as presented by Shakespeare, see CUNLIFFE, J. W.: "The Character of Henry V as Prince and King," in *Columbia University Shaksperian Studies*, New York, 1916.

CHAPTER V (The Comedies).

There is no standard work on Shakespearean comedy. For an excellent brief survey, see E. DOWDEN'S essay, "Shakespeare as a Comic Dramatist," in the first volume of *Representative English Comedies*, edited by C. M. GAYLEY, New York, 1903.

(Page 191.) On the problem of the revision of *Love's Labor's Lost*, see GRAY, H. D.: *The Original Version of "Love's Labour's Lost,"* Stanford University, 1918.

(Page 201.) On Greene's romantic plays in relation to Shakespeare, see TYNAN, J. L.: "The Influence of Greene on Shakespeare's Early Romance," *Publ. of the Modern Language Association*, xxvii, 246 (1912), where his influence on Shakespearean comedy is exaggerated; and WOODBERRY, G. E.: "Greene's Place in Comedy," in Gayley's *Representative English Comedies*, cited above, where the influence is minimized.

(Page 211.) On the Shylock problem, and its history in Shakespeare criticism, see STOLL, E. E.: "Shylock," *Journal of English and Germanic Philology*, x, 236 (1911).

(Page 222.) On the pastoral element in *As You Like It*, see THORNDIKE, A. H.: "The Pastoral Element in the English Drama before 1605," *Modern Language Notes*, xiv, 114 (1899), and "The Relation of *As You Like It* to the Robin Hood Plays," *Journal of Germanic Philology*, iv, 59 (1902); also GREENLAW, E.: "Shakespeare's Pastorals," *Studies in Philology*, xiii, 122 (1916).

(Page 231.) On the problem of "Love's Labour's Won " see TOLMAN, A. H.: "What has become of Shakespeare's Play, 'Love's Labour's Won'?", in *Views about "Hamlet" and Other Essays*, Boston, 1904. The weight of modern opinion tends to identify the missing play with *All's Well that Ends Well*. For a conjecture that it may have been an early version of *Twelfth Night*, see an essay appended to H. D. GRAY'S monograph on *Love's Labour's Lost*, cited above.

CHAPTER VI (The Tragedies).

The best general accounts of Shakespearean tragedy are found in BRADLEY, A. C.: *Shakespearean Tragedy*, London, 2nd edition, 1905, and THORNDIKE, A. H.: *Tragedy*, Boston, 1908. The former work deals in detail only with the four principal tragedies.

See also FANSLER, H.: *The Evolution of Technic in Elizabethan Tragedy*, Chicago, 1914; and BOYER, C. V.: *The Villain as Hero in Elizabethan Tragedy*, cited under Chapter I.

(Page 237.) For the arguments against Shakespeare's authorship of *Titus Andronicus*, see ROBERTSON, J. M.: *Did Shakespeare Write "Titus Andronicus"?* London, 1905. On the other side see PARROTT, T. M.: "Shakespeare's Revision of *Titus Andronicus*," *Modern Language Review*, xiv, 16 (1919). The tendency of recent criticism is to the affirmative view, but with the assumption that Shakespeare was rewriting the work of an earlier dramatist. On the other hand, for the view that the play as we have it represents his work revised by others, see GRAY, H. D.: "The Authorship of *Titus Andronicus*," *Flügel Memorial Volume*, Stanford University, 1916.

(Page 239.) On the use of madness in Elizabethan tragedy there is a valuable brief discussion in CORBIN, J.: *The Elizabethan*

BIBLIOGRAPHY

Hamlet, London, 1895,—unfortunately now out of print; also in WENDELL's *William Shakespere*, cited under Chapter II.

(Page 243.) For the earlier history of the Romeo and Juliet story, see Brooke's *Romeus and Juliet*, edited by J. J. MUNRO, London, 1908; for Shakespeare's alleged use of an earlier play, FULLER, H. D. W.: "Romeo and Julietta," *Modern Philology*, iv, 75 (1906).

(Page 249.) On the tragedies of Roman history, see MACCALLUM, M. W.: *Shakespeare's Roman Plays and their Background*, London, 1910; and, for the sources in Plutarch, *Shakespeare's Plutarch*, edited by TUCKER BROOKE, London, 1909. On the dramatic history of the Cæsar theme in the Renaissance, see AYRES, H. M.: "Shakespeare's *Julius Caesar* in the Light of some Other Versions," *Publ. of the Modern Language Association*, xxv, 183 (1910). MacCallum, in the work just cited, gives evidence favoring Shakespeare's acquaintance with Garnier's tragedy of *Cornélie*. Again, for evidence on behalf of an Italian source, see BOECKER, A.: *A Probable Italian Source of Shakespeare's "Julius Caesar,"* New York, 1913.

(Page 253.) On the history of *Hamlet* criticism, see TOLMAN, "A View of the Views about *Hamlet*," *Publ. of the Modern Language Association*," xiii, 155 (1898), also reprinted in the volume cited above under Chapter V; and STOLL, E. E.: *Hamlet: an Historical and Comparative Study*, University of Minnesota, 1919. The play was first studied with relation to its sources in CORBIN's essay, *The Elizabethan Hamlet*, cited above; similarly, and more fully, by LEWIS, C. M.: *The Genesis of Hamlet*, New York, 1907, which is followed, substantially, by the present writer. See also, for the typical character of the play in Elizabethan drama, THORNDIKE: "The Relations of *Hamlet* to Contemporary Revenge Plays," *Publ. of the Modern Language Association*, xvii, 125 (1902).

(Page 256.) Recent discussions of the differences between the first and second quartos of Hamlet are found in an article by H. D. GRAY in the *Modern Language Review*, x, 171 (1915), and in the monograph by J. D. WILSON, cited under Chapter II. The weight of opinion favors the theory that the first quarto (admittedly piratical) was based on an early version of Shakespeare's play, which he altered later; but Gray argues for only a single authentic version. The first quarto text has recently been reprinted, with introduction and notes by F. G. HUBBARD, Univ. of Wisconsin *Studies*, 1920.

(Page 258.) Of the two explanations of the discrepancies in the structure and characterization of *Hamlet*, the first (speaking generally) is that of STOLL, in the monograph cited above; the second is effectively developed in the book by C. M. LEWIS.

(Page 260.) On the comic matter in the tragedies, see ALDEN, R. M.: "The Use of Comic Material in the Tragedy of Shakespeare and his Contemporaries," *Journal of English and Germanic Philology*, xiii, 281 (1914).

(Page 262.) On the history of *Othello* criticism, with special reference to the relation of structure and characterization in the play, see STOLL, E. E.: *Othello, an Historical and Comparative Study*, University of Minnesota, 1915. Stoll's somewhat destructive analysis should be corrected by a comparison with Bradley's more sympathetic account in *Shakespearean Tragedy*.

(Page 268.) For the history of the Lear story, see SIDNEY LEE'S edition of the old *Chronicle History of King Leir*, London, 1909.

(Page 269.) Of the two reasons for the double-plotting of *King Lear*, the first is expounded by PRICE, T. R.: "*King Lear:* a Study of Shakespeare's Dramatic Method," *Publ. of the Modern Language Association*, ix, 165 (1894); the second is suggested by BRADLEY.

(Page 271.) The unexpected catastrophe in *King Lear* is discussed in detail by BRADLEY, whose view is substantially followed by the present writer.

(Page 275.) On the sympathetic treatment of the character of Macbeth, see especially the discussion by BOYER, in the work on *The Villain Hero* cited above.

(Page 278.) For the view of *Macbeth* as akin to the Orestes story of supernatural tragic forces driving to evil, see the introduction by M. H. LIDDELL, in his edition of the play (The Elizabethan Shakespeare). For the view that Macbeth's fate is presented in a manner akin to Calvinism, see WENDELL'S account of the tragedy in *William Shakspere*.

(Page 280.) The best critical account of *Antony and Cleopatra* is found in BRADLEY'S lecture on the play, *Oxford Lectures on Poetry*, London, 1909.

(Page 287.) For the favorable interpretation of the character of Coriolanus, see the introduction of S. P. SHERMAN in his edition of the play in the *Tudor Shakespeare;* for the opposite view, BAKER'S discussion in *The Development of Shakespeare as a Dramatist*, cited under Chapter II.

CHAPTER VII (The Tragi-Comedies).

The best accounts of the mixed dramatic types are found in THORNDIKE, A. H.: Introduction to *Beaumont and Fletcher's Maid's Tragedy and Philaster*, Boston, 1906 (Belles Lettres Series); and RISTINE, F. H.: *English Tragi-Comedy*, New York, 1910.

(Page 293.) On the Troilus and Cressida story as it was inherited and used by the Elizabethans, see ROLLINS, H. E.: "The Troilus-Cressida Story from Chaucer to Shakespeare," *Publ. of Modern Language Association*, xxxii, 383 (1917); and TATLOCK, J. S. P.: "The Siege of Troy in Elizabethan Literature," *ibid.*, xxx, 673 (1915).

It has often been supposed that the irregularities in the folio printing of *Troilus and Cressida* were due to hesitation in classifying it as

BIBLIOGRAPHY

either tragedy or comedy; but that the whole problem is one of the publisher and the printer has been pretty well established. See especially, on this matter, ADAMS, J. Q.: *"Timon of Athens and the Irregularities in the First Folio," Journal of English and Germanic Philology*, vii, 53 (1908).

(Page 304.) On the problem of the authorship of *Timon of Athens*, see WRIGHT, E. H.: *The Authorship of "Timon of Athens,"* New York, 1910.

(Page 306.) There is some evidence for the view that the non-Shakespearean portion of *Pericles* was the work of George Wilkins, who published a novel with the same plot in 1608; see BAKER, H. T.: "The Relation of Shakespeare's *Pericles* to George Wilkins's Novel," *Publ. of the Modern Language Association*, xxiii, 100 (1908). For the earlier history of the story, see SMYTH, A. H.: *Shakespeare's Pericles and Apollonius of Tyre*, Philadelphia, 1898.

(Page 309.) For evidence of mixed authorship of *Cymbeline*, drawn from inconsistencies and imperfections in the text, see FURNESS, H. H., in his introduction to the play in the *New Variorum Shakespeare*.

(Page 316.) For a discussion of the hypothetical original version of *The Tempest*, see GRAY, H. D.: "Some Indications that *The Tempest* was Revised," *Studies in Philology*, xviii, 129 (1921).

(Page 317.) The suspected sources of *The Tempest* in narratives of Virginia colonists are discussed with special thoroughness in GAYLEY'S book on *Shakespeare and the Founders of Liberty*, cited under Chapter I. A different theory, to the effect that the storm scene was based on passages in a dialogue of Erasmus's, the *Naufragium* (translated by Burton, 1606), has been lately proposed by REA, J. D.: "A Source for the Storm in *The Tempest*," *Modern Philolgy*, xvii, 279 (1919). On the supposed connection of Caliban with the importation of savages into England, see LEE: "The American Indian in Elizabethan England," *Scribner's Magazine*, xlii, 313 (1907), and "Caliban's Visits to England," *Cornhill Magazine*, n. s. xxxiv, 333 (1913). The Italian scenarios which seem to furnish sources for the principal plot of *The Tempest* are found in NERI: *Scenari delle Maschere in Arcadia*, Città di Castello, 1913, and are described by GRAY, H. D.: "The Sources of *The Tempest*," *Modern Language Notes*, xxxv, 321 (1920).

(Page 321.) For the more subjective explanation of Shakespeare's interest in the dramatic romances, see DOWDEN: *Shakspere, His Mind and Art*, cited under Chapter II; for the more objective explanation, THORNDIKE: *The Influence of Beaumont and Fletcher on Shakespere*, Worcester, 1901. The theory of indebtedness to Beaumont and Fletcher is opposed by SCHELLING, in *Elizabethan Drama*, cited under Chapter 1, and by GAYLEY, in *Beaumont the Dramatist*, New York, 1914.

Chapter VIII (Shakespeare).

On the general subject of Shakespeare's work as a dramatist, viewed in the light of modern criticism, see (in addition to the works cited under Chapter II):

MATTHEWS, B.: *Shakespeare as a Playwright*. New York, 1913.
QUILLER-COUCH, A.: *Notes on Shakespeare's Workmanship*. New York, 1917.
THORNDIKE, A. H.: "Shakspere as a Debtor," in *Shaksperian Studies*, Columbia University, 1916.

On his personality:

BRADLEY, A. C.: "Shakespeare the Man," in *Oxford Lectures on Poetry*, London, 1909.
BREWSTER, W. T.: "The Restoration of Shakspere's Personality," *Shaksperian Studies*, Columbia University, 1916.

(Page 329.) On the questionable method of interpreting Shakespeare's characters independently of their place in his dramas, see STOLL, E. E.: "Anachronism in Shakespeare Criticism," *Modern Philology*, vii, 557 (1910), and other articles by the same writer cited under Chapters V and VI.

(Page 332.) On the moral ideas of Shakespeare's dramas, interesting but by no means wholly convincing discussions will be found in MOULTON, R. G.: *Shakespeare as a Dramatic Thinker*, New York, 1907 (published 1903 with the title *The Moral System of Shakespeare*); and SHARP, F. S.: *Shakespeare's Portrayal of the Moral Life*, New York, 1902.

(Page 340.) On Shakespeare's political and social attitude, see, for the view that he was anti-democratic, TOLSTOY: *On Shakespeare and the Drama*, 1906, and CROSBY, E.: *Shakspere's Attitude to the Working Classes*, London, 1907; for the view that he was a liberal, GAYLEY: *Shakespeare and the Founders of Liberty*, cited under Chapter I. The whole matter is reviewed by TOLMAN, A. H.: "Is Shakespeare Aristocratic?" *Publ. of the Modern Language Association*, xxix, 277 (1914). For evidence that Shakespeare's representation of the populace was largely traditional, see TUPPER, F.: "The Shaksperean Mob," *ibid.*, xxvii, 486 (1912).

(Page 342.) On the Platonic and other alleged sources of the political passages in *Henry the Fifth* and *Troilus and Cressida*, see the appendix to GAYLEY's work, just cited, and HANFORD, J. H.: "A Platonic Passage in Shakespeare's *Troilus and Cressida*," *Studies in Philology*, xiii, 100 (1916).

(Page 355.) For unfavorable criticism of Shakespeare's work as a whole, in dissent from the usual view of his supremacy in dramatic art, see TOLSTOY's essay on Shakespeare, cited above; BERNARD SHAW's *Dramatic Opinions and Essays*, New York, 1906; and PELLISSIER, G.: *Shakespeare et la Superstition Shakespearienne*, Paris, 1914.

INDEX

accident in tragedy, 245, 271.
actor, profession of, 84.
A King and No King, 45.
Alchemist, The, 95.
Alleyn, E., 66.
All's Well that Ends Well, 301-03, 305, 320, 332, 343-44.
Amoretti, 123, 137.
Anti-Machiavel, 16.
anti-Petrarchan sonnets, 133-34.
Antony and Cleopatra, 251, 279-86, 334.
Apollonius of Tyre, 306.
Apology for Actors, 148.
Apology for Poetry, 12-13, 47.
Arcadia, 13, 64, 222-23, 269.
Arden family, 73.
Arden of Feversham, 66, 100.
Ariosto, 9, 201, 327.
Aristophanes, 327.
Art of English Poesy, 11.
Arundel, Earl of, 24.
Ascham, R., 5, 27.
astrology, 36.
Astrophel, 107.
Astrophel and Stella, 64, 123, 126.
As You Like It, 13, 83, 222-26.
Aubrey, J., 61.
Augustine, St., 342.

Bandello, 9.
Barnfield, R., 94.
Basse, W., 96.
Beaumont, F., 88, 96.
Beaumont and Fletcher, 45-46, 322-23.
beauty, sonnets on, 131-37.
Bellott, S., 85.
Bensley, R., 229.
Bevis of Hampton, 62.
Bible: Authorized Version, 4; Bishops', 62; Geneva, 18, 62; Great, 62.

Blackfriars Theatre, 77.
Blount, E., 13, 100.
Blundevill, T., 113.
Boccaccio, 20, 301-02, 309.
Boëthius, 342.
Book of Martyrs, 18.
Bower of Delights, 64.
boy actors, 211, 283-84.
Briggs, W. D., 341.
Brooke, A., 243.
Brooke, C., 95.
brothel scenes, 308.
Browning, 353-54.
Bruno, Giordano, 27-28.
Burbage, J., 43, 72.
Burbage, R., 72-73, 79, 86, 94.

Cæsarism, 251.
Calvin, J., 18.
Calvinism, 278, 332-33.
canon of Shakespeare's plays, 100, 104.
Casa, della, 9.
Castiglione, 9, 40.
Caxton, 62.
Cervantes, 327.
Chapman, G., 45, 89-90, 117.
characterization: conventional, 172-73, 197-98, 220, 226; relation to plot, 152-53, 192, 206, 209, 220, 234, 304, 307-08, 310, 320.
Chaucer, 62, 109, 204, 294, 344, 353.
Cheke, J., 5.
Chester, R., 117.
Chettle, H., 68-69, 83, 98.
children's companies, 80.
chorus-prologue, 183-84, 307.
Christianity, Shakespeare's relation to, 340, 347, 350-52.
chronicle-histories, 52, 147-89.
chronology of the plays, 101-04.
Cinthio, G., 9, 262, 265, 298.

clowns, 202, 206, 210, 223, 228, 315.
coat-of-arms, Shakespeare's, 73-74.
Coleridge, 108, 300.
Colet, J., 5.
Colin Clout, 88.
Combe, J., 90.
comedy: Elizabethan idea of, 50-51; types of, 191-94; Shakespeare's, 190-231, 327; in tragedy, 260-61, 271-72, 292, 328.
Comedy of Errors, 73, 193, 198, 201, 317.
commedia dell'arte, 317.
Complaint of Rosamond, 109, 126.
conceits, lyrical, 120-21, 130-32.
Condell, H., 85-86, 99.
Confessio Amantis, 306.
Constable, H., 107.
Contention of York and Lancaster, 150, 156.
Coriolanus, 286-89, 340.
Cortegiano, Il, 9. (See *The Courtier*.)
Courtier, The, 9, 12, 14.
Coxe, L., 5.
criticism, Renaissance, 13.
Curtain Theatre, 43.
Cymbeline, 100, 309-12, 320, 322, 347.

Daniel, S., 64, 89, 109, 119, 125-26.
Dante, 328, 355-56.
dark lady, the, 78-79, 141, 283.
Davenant, Jane, 86.
Davenant, W., 61, 70, 86.
Davies, J., 39-40.
Davies, J., of Hereford, 83.
Davies, R., 61.
Decameron, 20, 301.
Defence of Poetry (see *Apology for Poetry*.)
Dekker, T., 45, 80.
democracy, Shakespeare's attitude toward, 343-44.
Derby, Earl of, 72, 203.

Desportes, 10.
Diana, 201.
Digges, D., 90.
Digges, L., 95.
Discovery of Witchcraft, 35.
Donne, J., 20, 39.
Drake, F., 3.
drama, Elizabethan, 41-55.
dramatic romance, 290-91, 306-23.
Drayton, M., 64, 89, 90, 126, 134, 145.
Dryden, 356.
Du Bellay, 10.
Duel of Love and Friendship, 202.

Ecclesiastical Polity, 33-34, 342.
Edward the First, 149.
Edward the Second, 153, 160, 167-68.
Edward the Third, 100, 149.
Elizabeth, Princess, 91-92, 315-16.
Elizabeth, Queen, 3-5, 24-25, 42, 204, 216.
Enemy of the People, 292.
epic elements in drama, 150, 182.
Essex, Earl of, 81-82, 101, 172, 184.
Euphuës, 12-13.
Every Man in his Humor, 74, 302.
Every Man Out of his Humor, 38.
evil, Shakespeare's idea of, 348-49.

Faery Queene, 64, 318.
fairies: belief in, 35-36; Shakespeare's, 206.
Falstaff, character of, 176-79, 216-17, 285.
Faithful Shepherdess, 291.
Famous Victories of Henry the Fifth, 45, 148, 176-77, 179, 183.
fancy, 230-31, 345.
farce, 191-94, 198-99, 203, 206, 215-16.

INDEX

Fasti, 109.
Fastolfe, Sir John, 177.
fate tragedy, 244-45.
Faustus, 171, 276.
feudalism, 23-24.
Field, R., 64, 69.
Fletcher, J., 92, 188-89, 290-91. (See also Beaumont and Fletcher.)
folio, the first, 4, 84, 96, 99-100, 290, 306, 309.
Ford, J., 46.
forgiveness, theme of, 202, 320-21, 347.
Fortune, 36-37, 43, 242, 245.
Fortune Theatre, 81.
Foxe, J., 18.
Friar Bacon and Friar Bungay, 190.
Fuller, T., 87-88.
Furness, H. H., 262, 285.

Galateo, 9.
Gascoigne, G., 42.
Gentillet, 16.
German *Hamlet*, 254.
Ghost of Richard the Third, 95.
ghosts, belief in, 35.
Ghosts, 48.
Giles, T., 43.
Globe Theatre, 43, 76, 81, 85, 92.
Goethe, 234, 324, 355-56.
Golden Epistles, 12.
Golding, A., 8, 63.
Gorboduc, 41.
Gothic elements in drama, 267-68, 271.
Gounod, 246.
Gower, J., 62, 109, 306.
Greene, R., 45, 64, 67, 68, 107, 148-49, 190, 200-01, 312.
Greville, F., 24, 27, 32-33, 90-91.
Guevara, 12.
Guy of Warwick, 62.

Hakluyt, R., 64.
Hall, J., 89.
Hallam, H., 144.
Hamlet (Kyd's), 66, 254-56.
Hamlet, 80, 82, 83, 253-62, 271, 292, 332-33, 336-38, 351-52, 354.
Harrison, W., 29.
Hathaway, Anne, 59-60.
Hecatommithi, 9, 262, 298.
Hemings, J., 85, 86, 99.
Henry the Fourth, 114, 174-79, 186-87, 217.
Henry the Fifth, 82, 101, 151, 180-88, 307, 332, 337, 341.
Henry the Sixth, 68, 72, 100, 149, 153-59.
Henry the Eighth, 92, 100, 188-89.
Henslowe, P., 43, 148.
heredity, 333-35.
Hero and Leander, 106-08.
Heywood, T., 45, 53, 109, 148, 293-94.
Hoby, T., 9, 14.
Holinshed, 63, 147, 163, 167, 181, 249-50, 273-74, 309, 338.
Homer, 342, 356.
Hooker, R., 33-34, 342, 347.
Hymns in Honor of Love and Beauty, 15.

Ibsen, H., 292, 324, 326.
insanity, dramatic treatment of, 238-39.
Iron Age, 293.
Italian fashions, 27.
Italian Renaissance, 9-17.

Jack Straw, Life and Death of, 148.
Jaggard, W., 77, 100.
James the First, 4, 35, 82, 316.
James the Fourth, 149.
Jew, Elizabethan attitude toward the, 211-13.
Jew of Malta, 16-17, 160, 214, 236, 240.
Johnson, S., 332, 335, 355.
Jonson, B., 38, 45, 47, 74-75, 80, 83, 86-90, 95-98, 194, 302, 303, 326, 331.
Julius Caesar, 249-53, 260, 279-80, 286, 334.

Kemp, W., 73, 94-95.
Kind-Heart's Dream, 68.
kindness, Shakespeare's emphasis on, 339.
king, English attitude toward the, 183, 341.
King John, 165-66.
King Lear, 188, 239, 267-73, 279, 331, 334-35, 338-39.
King Leir, Chronicle History of, 268.
Knight's Tale, 204.
Kyd, T., 45, 65-66, 236-38, 242, 254-55, 258.

Lamb, C., 229, 259, 270.
Lancaster, house of, 167, 172.
Latin, study of, 5.
Lee, S., 23.
Leicester, Earl of, 25, 43.
liberty, Elizabethan idea of, 32.
Lily, W., 58.
Livy, 109.
Locrine, 66.
Lodge, T., 13, 64, 106, 222.
London, Elizabethan, 22, 27-29.
Lord Chamberlain's Men, 72, 80-82, 98-99.
love, theme of, 131, 204-05, 224-25, 230-31, 242, 246, 281-82, 344-47.
Love's Labor's Lost, 90, 191, 193-98, 205, 221, 223, 230, 231.
Love's Labor's Won, 231.
Love's Martyr, 117.
Lover's Complaint, 117.
Lucian, 305-05.
Lucy, T., 61.
lust, sonnet on, 142.
Lyly, J., 12-13, 43, 45, 54, 63, 65, 190, 194, 222.
lyric elements in drama, 159, 163, 166, 174, 180, 207, 228, 247-48, 267, 286.

Macaulay, 262, 336.
Macbeth, 188, 273-79.
Machiaveli, 16-17.
madness, use of in tragedy, 238-39.

Malvolio plot, 228-29.
man, love of man for, 15, 130-31, 202.
Manningham, J., 79.
Mantuan, 9.
marriages, early, 31.
Marlowe, C., 16, 45, 54, 66-68, 106, 148-50, 153, 160-61, 167-68, 171, 214, 236, 239-40, 276, 328.
Marot, 10.
Marston, J., 45, 80.
masques, 46, 198, 226, 316.
Massinger, P., 46.
Measure for Measure, 63, 298-301, 305, 320, 351.
Menechmi, 198.
Menaphon, 64.
Merchant of Venice, 207-14, 230-31, 291.
Meredith, G., 192.
Meres, F., 75-76, 119, 231.
Mermaid Tavern, 88.
Merry Wives of Windsor, 11, 58, 216-17.
Metamorphoses, 105.
Metamorphosis of Scylla, 64, 106.
Middleton, T., 45.
Midsummer Night's Dream, 89, 203-07, 223, 230, 315-16, 318.
miles gloriosus, 302.
Milton, 321.
miracle-plays, 150. (See mystery-plays.)
Mirror for Magistrates, 63.
Molière, 326, 327, 355.
Montaigne, 33, 342, 347.
Montemayor, 201.
Montgomery, Earl of, 91.
moralist, Shakespeare as, 332-40.
morality, Elizabethan, 20, 30-31.
Mountjoy, C., 85.
Mr. W. H., 118.
Much Ado about Nothing, 13, 218-22, 263, 291.
Musica Transalpina, 10.
Mustapha, 33.
mystery-plays, 49. (See miracle-plays.)

INDEX

Nash, T., 45, 67, 147.
nationalism, Elizabethan, 24-26, 147.
neo-platonism, 14-15.
New Place, 74.
North, T., 8, 63, 282, 305.

Œdipus, 48.
Oldcastle, Sir John, 177.
Old Wive's Tale, 190.
Orestes story, 277-78.
Orlando, 201.
Othello, 85, 98, 247, 261-67, 269, 271, 273, 279, 285, 336, 345-46.
Ovid, 8, 63, 105-06, 109, 204, 276.

Painter, W., 10, 63, 109.
Palace of Pleasure, 10, 63, 109.
Palladis Tamia, 75-76.
Pandosto, 64.
Passionate Pilgrim, 77, 98, 116.
pastoral literature, 222-23.
patriotism, Elizabethan, 24-25, 147.
Peele, G., 45, 67, 68, 148-49, 190.
Pembroke, Earl of, 91.
penology, Elizabethan, 29.
Pericles, Prince of Tyre, 99-100, 306-08, 310.
Perimedes, 107.
personality, Elizabethan interest in, 232-33, 328-31.
Petrarch, 121.
Petrarchan lyrists, 10, 120-23, 126, 195.
Phoenix and the Turtle, 116-17.
Phoenix's Nest, 64.
Philaster, 322.
Pillars of Society, 292.
Plato, 342.
platonism, Renaissance, 14-15, 131, 137.
Plautus, 41, 190, 198.
plotting, multiple, 49-50, 175-76, 204, 208, 218-19, 269, 294.
Plutarch, 8, 63, 249-53, 279, 281-82, 284, 286-88, 304-05, 338.
poems, Shakespeare's, 105-46.
poetic justice, 335-36.
poetry; relation to drama, 53-55, 173-74, 248, 311, 357; sonnets on, 136-37.
political theory: Elizabethan, 31-34; Shakespeare's, 340-44.
Prayer, Book of Common, 62.
Prince, The, 16.
prologue, use of in *Henry the Fifth*, 183-84.
prose: Renaissance interest in, 12-13; in drama, 54, 224, 266-67.
psychology: Elizabethan, 37-40; Shakespeare's, 330-31.
Puritanism, 18-20, 229.
Puttenham, G., 11.

quartos, Shakespearean, 98-99, 174-75, 307.
Quiney, T., 92.

Rainsford, H., 89-90.
Rape of Lucrece, 69-70, 109-112, 135, 142, 241.
reconciliation, drama of, 320-24.
Reformation in England, 17-20.
religion, Shakespeare's, 350-52.
Renaissance, 5-17, 350.
Return from Parnassus, 80, 94-95.
Revels office, 43-44, 77.
revenge plays, 255.
Rich, B., 63.
Richard the Second, 81, 167-74, 249.
Richard the Third, 159-65, 248, 275, 333.
Robin Hood, literature of, 62, 222.
romantic comedy, 200-02, 210.
romantic tragedy, 242.
Roman history, drama of, 249-51, 279-80.
Romeo and Juliet, 237, 241-48, 260, 271, 345.
Romeus and Juliet, 243.
Ronsard, 10.
Rosalind, character of, 224-25, 354.
Rosalynde, 64, 222-23.

376 SHAKESPEARE

Rose Theatre, 43, 72.
Rowe, N., 74.
Royal King and the Loyal Subject, 53.

St. Bartholomew's day, 3, 16.
St. Paul's, boys of, 43, 80.
Samson Agonistes, 321.
Sannazaro, 9.
Schoolmaster, The, 27.
Scott, R., 35.
Scott, W., 327, 353.
Scottish history, dramatization of, 273-74.
Sejanus, 47, 83.
Selden, J., 90.
Seneca, 63, 332.
Senecan tragedy, 41, 235, 237-38.
sensationalism, theatrical, 313.
sensualism, poetic, 108.
sex, Elizabethan treatment of, 31, 345.
Shakespeare, Hamnet, 60, 93.
Shakespeare, John, 58-59, 73, 84.
Shakespeare, Judith, 60, 92.
Shakespeare, Susanna, 89, 93.
Shakespeare, William:
  baptism, 58.
  career as actor, 67-69, 72-73, 83-84.
  career as author, 69-71, 73, 83, 102-04.
  children, 59-60, 92-93.
  contemporary opinion of, 94-98.
  death and burial, 93.
  dramatic characteristics, 325-31.
  education, 58.
  financial success, 73-74, 76-77, 84-85.
  friendships, 78-79, 86-91.
  ideas, 331-52.
  marriage, 56-60.
  migration to London, 61.
  personality, 352-54.
  poetic characteristics, 115-16, 145.
  position in literature, 355-59.
  reading, 62-64.
  relations with Essex, 82.
  relations with Southampton, 70, 82.
  religion, 350-52.
  residence in London, 85.
  return to Stratford, 91.
  theatrical relations, 72, 76, 80-83.
  works (see under separate titles).
Shepherd's Calendar, 12, 222.
Shylock, problem of, 211-214.
Sidney, P., 11-14, 24, 47-48, 64, 119, 123, 125-26, 128, 145, 222, 269.
Sir Thomas More, 100.
society, Shakespeare's view of, 340-44.
soliloquy, dramatic, 160-62, 258-59, 277.
Soliman and Perseda, 242.
song, Elizabethan, 26.
sonnets: Elizabethan vogue of, 11-12; Shakespeare's, 70-72, 77-79, 98, 117-46, 283, 347, 352.
Sophocles, 324, 328.
soul, sonnet on the, 142-43.
Southampton, Earl of, 69-70, 81-82, 91.
Spanish Tragedy, 45, 65, 236, 238, 254-55.
Spenser, 12, 14-15, 19, 20, 64, 88-89, 96, 107, 123, 137, 222.
sport, Elizabethan, 26, 29.
Steevens, G., 144.
stichomythic dialogue, 163.
story, Elizabethan interest in, 52-53.
Stow, J., 63.
Strange's men, 72.
Stratford-on-Avon, 57-58, 84-86, 90-92.
style, Shakespeare's later, 311-312.
Swinburne, 310.
supernatural, Shakespeare's use of, 278-79, 318-19.
superstition, Elizabethan, 35-36.
Supposes, 42.

INDEX

Surrey, Earl of, 10-11, 126.
Swan Theatre, 43.
symbolism, 318-20.

Tamburlaine, 45, 54, 66, 160, 236.
Taming of a Shrew, 215.
Taming of the Shrew, 100, 214-16.
Tasso, 9.
Tears of Fancy, 123.
Tears of the Muses, 89.
Tempest, 91, 286, 293, 315-20, 342, 351.
Terence, 41.
Theatre, The, 43, 72, 76.
theatres, Elizabethan, 43-44.
Thorndike, A. H., 310.
Thorpe, T., 118.
Thyestes, 238.
Tilney, E., 43.
Timber, 87.
time, sonnets on, 134-39.
Timon of Athens, 100, 286, 304-06, 333.
Titus Andronicus, 100, 237-41, 254, 263.
Tolstoy, 355.
Tottel's Miscellany, 10-11, 63.
tragedy: nature and types of, 232-35; Elizabethan, 51; Senecan, 41; Shakespeare's, 232-89, 327-28, 335-37, 348-49.
tragi-comedy: 219, 290-324.
Tristan and Isolde, 246.
Troilus and Cressida, 80, 90, 100, 293-98, 342.
Troublesome Reign of King John, 148, 165.
Troy story, 293-96.

True Tragedy of Richard Duke of York, 67, 150, 156, 159-60.
True Tragedy of Richard the Third, 160.
Twelfth Night, 199, 226-31.
Two Gentlemen of Verona, 194, 200-03, 242.
Two Noble Kinsmen, 100.

unities, dramatic, 47-50, 317.

vaudeville spirit, 49.
Venus and Adonis, 69, 105-09, 116, 135.
versification, Shakespeare's later, 311.
villainy, theme of, 15-17, 233, 235, 240-41, 263-65, 275-79, 333-36.
Virgil, 111, 355.
vituperation, sonnets of, 134.
Volpone, 95.

Wagner, 324.
Watson, T., 123.
Webster, J., 45.
Whetstone, G., 63, 298.
White Devil, 45.
Wyatt, T., 10-11.
Whole Contention, 156.
Windsor, Lord, 24.
Winter's Tale, 91, 189, 219, 269, 312-15, 321, 343, 358.
women, Shakespeare's, 210-11, 222, 277-78, 314-15, 337.
Wordsworth, 144, 342, 358.
Wyndham, G., 144.

Yonge, N., 10.